SO-ABA-925

Training Theory and Practice

Training Theory and Practice

Edited by W. Brendan Reddy, Ph.D.
and Clenard C. "Chip" Henderson, Jr.

Copublished by
NTL Institute for Applied Behavioral Science
and University Associates, Inc.

© 1987 NTL Institute for Applied Behavioral Science.

Printed in the United States of America
ISBN: 0-9610392-4-8
Library of Congress Catalog Card Number: 87-062132

This book is copublished by NTL Institute for Applied Behavioral Science, P.O. Box 9155, Rosslyn Station, Arlington, Virginia 22209 and by University Associates, Inc. 8517 Production Avenue, San Diego, California 92121.

Some articles have been reprinted with permission from other sources. The first page of each article cites the holder of the copyright for that particular work. Some articles contain figures or tables reprinted with permission from other sources, which are cited below the reprinted material. To request permission to reprint material for which NTL Institute holds the copyright, write to the publications permissions desk of NTL Institute at the address provided above.

Managing Editor, NTL Institute: Catherine A. Messina
Production Manager, University Associates: Margaret Levene

*This book is dedicated to the memory of
our colleagues and friends:
Nancy Campbell, Bob Chasnoff, Bill Deutschmann,
Kaleel Jamison, Ron Lippitt, and Herb Shepard.*

Table of Contents

Introduction

The articles in this book represent the cutting edge, both of theory and practice, of laboratory training as provided by NTL Institute for Applied Behavioral Science. Articles on the topics covered were solicited to show diversity and range of experience and thought. Similarly, the authors are NTL Institute members and associates of these members, ranging from those of emeritus status to those new to the organization.

Consistent with NTL Institute's philosophy, this book is meant to inform, challenge, provoke, and engender thought, rebuttal, and questions—whether the reader is a trainer, a laboratory participant, or a manager interested in laboratory training.

All of the articles, except three, were written expressly for this book. These three, by Bernard Lubin and William Eddy, Eva Schindler-Rainman, and Peter Muniz and Robert Chasnoff, have been revised and updated. The book's articles, each providing a unique contribution, are arranged in five major sections.

The chapters in **Section I** are perspective pieces. That is, they help us look at where we have been with respect to small group training, where we are going, and what trainers will need to get us there. Bernard Lubin and William Eddy trace the history of small group work from its emergence with Kurt Lewin, through its many forms and variants, to its role and influence in organization development and management training. They explore professional and ethical issues as well as accreditation and certification. Eva Schindler-Rainman discusses six major changes and challenges that will affect the role of the trainer and consultant during the end of the 1980s. In addition, she articulates three threats that might override these changes.

The articles in **Section II**, Trainer Development, offer insights into the training and personal and professional growth of skilled practitioners. Chuck Phillips discusses the developmental processes that shape the effective laboratory educator and contends that the "trainer as person" is our most effective intervention. The dimensions of health and stress as they relate to the trainer are explored by John Adams, who states that trainer stress levels are much higher than those of the client groups they serve. Stress prevention and management strategies are examined. Philip Hanson and Bernard Lubin emphasize the value and importance of trainer awareness and present an instrument trainers can use to assess their skills by self, peers, and/or supervisors.

In **Section III**, authors explore theories and dynamics surrounding learning in small groups, of which the trainer must be cognizant so as to be effective. Birge Reichard focuses on specific elements of laboratory education that correlate with clinical "incidents," stressing the importance of trainers' explicitly making and meeting learning contracts with participants. Reichard points out that the major variable over which the trainer has control, and for which the trainer must assume complete responsibility, is one's own behavior. Lawrence Porter shows that the following three things are necessary for using "experience" legitimately as a learning vehicle: clear objectives (and commitment to them), time, and conscientious guidance for participants. He emphasizes a learning experience as an **entire** learning cycle.

According to Katharine Cole Esty, the life roles we assume are always related to others in the system, and thus played accordingly—most often without the recognition by role occupants that they have an option to leave the role set. Esty applies role theory to training and encourages trainers to become more aware of roles played, particularly so that they can manage subtle authority issues. Jane Moosbruker reviews and synthesizes models of group development, offering a generalized model in which at each stage attention is paid to probable member feelings, observable member behaviors, and group-level phenomena. The trainer is seen as the major agent for group transition.

Ronald Lippitt describes the teaching/learning process as a series of linkages of trainer interventions and learner tasks that are necessary for a complete training process to evolve. He articulates nine central linkages for creating a learning design or assessing the quality of a learning opportunity. Philip Hanson contributes a perspective for viewing group and/or life events, with the objective of increasing one's awareness of self and others. Hanson explores three realities— social, personal, and ultimate—and defines four steps in a method for developing awareness. Writing of the Tavistock Institute approach to training and development, Harold Bridger, in a personal account, compares and contrasts Tavistock's approach to NTL Institute's. He recounts designing (with Eric Trist and Hugh Coffey) the first "group relations training conference." Bridger ties contemporary events and developments into a conceptual basis for developing further the Tavistock approach with implications for organizations.

In **Section IV**, a wide range of training innovations are shared by nine NTL Institute members and associates. Tom Armor explores the impact of microcomputers on training and outlines current and potential applications from a new perspective. Realistic behavioral simulation is discussed as an alternative technology for laboratory education by Robert Kaplan and Wilfred Drath. They illustrate their view by describing the highly motivating Looking Glass, Inc. simulation developed at the Center for Creative Leadership, including its benefits, costs, and applications. Ronald Boyer also describes a simulation for developing consultation skills. Boyer asserts that this approach fits into a workshop "niche" between a cognitive emphasis and "hands-on" experience.

Exploring neurolinguistic programming (NLP) as a training innovation, Judith Katz and Cresencio Torres cite the implications for trainers. The authors show that NLP enables trainers to better understand how to create specific and "nonhaphazard" training results. Otto Kroeger contends that the Meyers-Briggs Type Indicator is the "revolutionary" training tool of the 1980s because it helps make sense of what are often seen as confusing behavioral patterns in ourselves and others. Kroeger outlines the history, development, theory, and use of the instrument.

William Barber describes and illustrates a procedure, the role analysis group, which—prior to the end of a training session—enables participants to begin applying and transferring training to the back-home situation and to personally integrate workshop learning. The dynamics of the role analysis group are discussed, and a case study presented.

SYMLOG (a term standing for the systematic multiple-level observation of groups), a theory and set of methods for understanding group dynamics, is addressed by Michael Ichiyama and Brendan Reddy. This article provides the reader with an introductory synopsis of the system from its development and theory to its application and current research. Kaleel Jamison examines the power of spoken communication by addressing a concept called "straight talk." She presents ways of altering the normative foundation of communications during the contracting phase, giving multiple examples for practice and activity. Barbara Benedict Bunker and her coauthors cull the literature on designing and conducting training events, offering three "rules-of-thumb" groupings organized according to a preworkshop, designing, and intervening framework.

Section V offers four articles on cultural awareness and training. NTL Institute has long been in the forefront of multicultural training, so we consider it appropriate that a separate section of the book addresses this area.

Peter Muniz and Robert Chasnoff present a conceptual model that outlines six levels they maintain are necessary for a complete understanding of another culture. The model is set in a pyramid symbolizing the cultural awareness hierarchy. Edwin Fernández Bauzó presents a multicultural, pluralistic approach to cross-cultural training that contrasts with traditional approaches. He offers a series of structured experiences (developed with Joan Bordman) designed to be used with multicultural populations and with groups including members from diverse cultures and with diverse ethnic origins. In focusing on laboratory training, Patricia Bidol's objective is to increase the capacity of trainers to facilitate multicultural training programs. She presents an overview of current theory, goals, and assumptions, a model for synergistic training, and research directions, all within the context of multicultural training. Dick and Marion Vittitow move the book's discussion to the international training scene as they personally relate how their world view of training has changed and expanded as a result of their developing and **doing** a specific workshop.

As editors of this book, we are impressed with the originality, quality, and creativity of our colleagues as demonstrated by their contributions. We trust that the reader will also find these articles of value.

W. Brendan Reddy, Ph.D.
Clenard C. "Chip" Henderson, Jr.

Section I.
Small Group Training: Perspective

The Development of Small Group Training and Small Group Trainers

Bernard Lubin
William B. Eddy

Historical trends

During the last three decades, the small group has become increasingly popular as a training device. In many firms, institutions, and social agencies, educational involvement in an intensive small group setting has become commonplace. This article traces the emergence of intensive small group training techniques and explores distinctions among group modalities, outcome research, issues related to ethics, and the training of small group facilitators/trainers.[1]

The research of Kurt Lewin, Muzafer Sherif, Theodore Newcomb, and William F. White (Cartwright and Zander, 1968) in the 1930s established the field of group dynamics and emphasized the role of groups in training. Lewin found that members of groups changed their attitudes when they became involved in making and implementing joint decisions. The practical relevance of small groups was demonstrated dramatically by studies on nutrition, worker productivity, and leadership, and such research established the validity of the group as a powerful setting for learning and change.

An increasing amount of the work in organizations—such as planning, decision making, and problem solving—is now taking place in small, face-to-face groups, and this has contributed to the interest in group training. Organizations and individuals now recognize the need for training methods that improve the functioning of these groups and have developed a growing regard for temporary structures such as committees, project teams, task forces, conferences, consulting relationships, and the like (Bennis & Slater, 1968; Miles, 1964). Because of this, individuals have come to need the ability to move rapidly into team relationships characterized by mutual trust, adequate team spirit, and creative stimulations among members.

©1987 NTL Institute. All rights reserved.

The growth of group training is directly related to another phenomenon, the emphasis on adult learning and continuing education. No longer can we assume that our formal training from high school and college will be adequate for the rest of our careers, for professionals who do not continue their training risk becoming outdated in five years or less. Technical personnel promoted into managerial roles find they need a new set of skills for dealing with individuals and groups. Because of this expanding need for knowledge, organizations struggling to survive in a fast-changing and competitive world insist that their key personnel stay actively engaged in formal learning experiences. Group training workshops, designed to fit the special learning needs of adults, thus are a hallmark of these times.

The small group movement has also been affected by the growing awareness of the need to allow the affective dimension into the formal learning process. Whereas the traditional classroom setting emphasizes the cognitive aspect of human functioning and deemphasizes feelings, small groups—much more than settings with individuals seated in rows—provide the opportunity to deal with such emotions as competition, frustration, and conflict as well as warmth and support when they arise in the group's life. Institutions and organizations that need to examine attitudes and practices regarding race, gender, age, and disability provide examples of situations in which the affective dimension is important and is being addressed by small group methodology.

The growing availability of experiential learning materials also indicates the development of this methodology. As the training aspect of human resource development has gained in popularity, trainers and consultants have sought to make the learning experience more "practical" by simulating real-life situations. To do this, these facilitators use a plethora of decision-making games, in-basket exercises, role plays, and other exercises that treat the small group as the simulated operational group.

Finally, we conclude our list of stimulants to small group training with mention of the self-help or support group, whose development signals a growing recognition and acceptance of the small group as a source of help, support, solace, and escape from loneliness. In virtually every sector, small groups of people who need each other have come together. Divorced persons' groups, women's support groups, men's support groups, single parents' groups, and Alcoholics Anonymous groups represent only a small fraction of the self-help units that have sprung up. Sometimes these groups use facilitators with both group training skills and knowledge about the specific problems. In general, two types of groups have emerged: those that facilitate change and provide information and/or support, and those whose primary purpose is political activity aimed at improving the situation of a group of people (Lieberman & Borman, 1979; Lubin, 1983).

When intensive small group training methods grew out the workshop method developed during the 1930s and 1940s, they did not initially focus on personality change or overcoming social and psychological isolation. Rather, they began as a wedding between social action and scientific inquiry (Bunker, 1965). The innovations of Kurt Lewin, Ronald Lippitt, Leland Bradford, Kenneth Benne, and others were responsible for the first training workshops held, beginning in 1947, in isolated New England communities such as Bethel, Maine, that acted as "cultural islands," free from some of the usual situations in people's daily lives that promote pressure against change (Marrow, 1969). The National Training Laboratories (now NTL Institute for Applied Behavioral Science), originally affiliated with the National Education Association, grew out of these efforts. Early research found that participants learned and changed in their ability to deal with human relations problems not only by listening to lectures and participating in role-playing, but also by analyzing the here-and-now characteristics of their own conference groups. The social scientists discovered, partly by accident, that participants were very much interested in behavioral data that researchers and observers collected about the group interaction. The analysis of this "process" data provided trainees with a "laboratory" in which to deal more dynamically and personally with some of the human relationship issues they were studying.

Although NTL has played a major role in the evolution of group training, other important influences contributed to this methodology. Group trainers with clinical and counseling backgrounds brought to NTL workshops and similar programs the skills and interests for dealing with personality variables within groups. In addition, individuals with skills as consultants and change agents— many of them members of the NTL consulting network—have applied their efforts to programs in which the goals are to effect change in the organization and the community.

In another direction, the existential-humanistic "human potential" approach moved beyond the methods of traditional social science by employing various expressive, intrapsychic, and somatopsychologic techniques. Esalen Institute at Big Sur, California, led in this development.

For a more comprehensive history of group training, see Bradford, Gibb and Benne (1964) and Bradford (1967).

Some definitions

One cannot treat small group training and the issues and problems surrounding it as a single, general phenomenon. Widely different experience-based training approaches are currently being used, and to lump them together confuses rather than simplifies understanding. Furthermore, to make decisions about the appropriateness of programs and qualfications of trainers, one must be able to differentiate among kinds of programs. It is even questionable as to whether the various types of small groups used for educational training or therapeutic purposes should be subsumed under one rubric, for doing so implies more commonality than actually exists. Unfortunately, no generally accepted meanings exist for many of the terms often used. We therefore provide the following definitions, even though they are somewhat arbitrary, because they seem to mesh with the historical progression.

Sensitivity training is one of the first and most generic terms in the field. It originally referred to the small group training conducted by NTL. During the 1960s and 1970s, people applied the term to all small group training approaches. Most practitioners, however, did not find sensitivity training a useful term because it was employed so broadly—for example, to include group therapy— that it lost its power to define. Moreover, training personnel whose methods were only peripherally related to the original sensitivity training approach picked up the term and applied it to their ventures.

We find the term **laboratory training** a more useful conceptualization, using it to refer to an educational method that emphasizes experience-based learning activities. Participants may undergo any of a variety of experiences, usually including small group interaction, and their behavior provides the data for learning. Thus, laboratory training involves learning by doing. The subject matter of such programs often deals with some aspect of human interaction, and the goal is to have participants become more aware of and responsive to what is going on.

A basic element of most laboratory training workshops is the T Group (the T stands for training). In the standard NTL T Group, participants find themselves in a relatively unstructured environment in which their responsibility is to build out of their interaction a group that can help them meet their needs for support, feedback, learning, and the like. The behaviors exhibited by members as they act out their roles provide the material for analysis and learning. Thus, T Group members have the opportunity to learn about the ways in which their behavior is seen by others in the group, the kinds of styles and roles they tend to take, their effectiveness in playing various kinds of roles, the ways they can become more sensitive to the feelings and behaviors of other group members, and methods for understanding the dynamics of group behavior.

Some trainers within and outside the NTL network have developed T Groups that provide a personal growth focus. Weschler, Massarik, and Tannenbaum (1962), who first described a laboratory with a "personal-interpersonal emphasis," provide the following explanation and rationale:

> Our version of sensitivity training increasingly concerns itself with strengthening of the individual in his desires to experience people and events more accurately, to a process of individual growth toward ever-increasing personal adequacy. (p.34)

Tavistock groups are a variation of the T Group model. The Conference on Group Relations was developed originally at the Tavistock Institute of Human Relations in England. This organization of psychoanalytically oriented behavioral scientists developed a training approach that focuses primarily on issues of authority rather than on peer relationships (Rice, 1965; Rioch, 1970).

The term **encounter groups** was often used in the 1960s to refer to intensive small group experiences emphasizing personal growth through expanding awareness, the exploration of both intrapsychic and interpersonal issues, and the release of dysfuctional inhibitions. Little attention was paid the group as a learning instrument, the trainer took a more active and directive role, and physical interaction took place. Other modes of expression and sensory exploration—such as dance, art, massage, and nudity—were also tried as a part of the encounter experience. Marathon groups were a form of time-extended encounter group and used the experience and accompanying fatigue to break through participants' defenses. Many organizations sprung up around the country during the 1960s and 1970s to offer encounter groups and related continuing education programs. They often called themselves growth centers and viewed their offerings as contributing to the human potential movement.

Encounter groups thrived during the counterculture movement, the period of student unrest, and the revolt against an overly rule-conscious existence. The conservative swing in the United States during the 1980s saw the virtual demise of encounter groups.

Comparisons with counseling and therapy groups

All of the types of groups named above, in one way or another, deal with emotional experience, the self-concept, and impressions of the behavior of others, and all of them stress honest communication. Because of this, people sometimes ask, "How do these groups differ from therapy groups?"

Frank (1964) summarizes the differences:

> Therapy group members are seen by themselves and others as having psychological problems and needing help, whereas T-group members are seen as relatively well-functioning individuals interested in improving old skills and learning new ones; attitudes which therapy attempts to modify are usually concerned with persons who are close to the patient and therefore more central and resistant to change, whereas the T-group attempts to modify more peripheral attitudes; the therapist is a much more central person than the trainer and dependency upon him continues to be strong throughout: and the T-group, focusing less upon the individual, evokes more moderate emotional responses. (p. 328)

Moreover, the group-focused T Group emphasizes the here-and-now of development and transactions among its members, whereas the therapy group encourages the search for factors associated with conflicts and problems in the patient's past life experiences.

Another conceptualization of current group psychotherapy practices is provided by Parloff (1970), who suggests that the diversity of objectives of group psychotherapists can be reduced by sorting them into two broad categories:

"headshrinking objectives," which are similar to those mentioned by Scheidlinger (1967)—that is, amelioration of suffering and restoration or repair of functioning—and "mind-expanding objectives," which include heightened positive affective states, self-actualization, and self-fulfillment.

Effectiveness of laboratory groups

Do laboratory groups work? Do participants actually come to change their real-life behavior? If so, in what ways and for how long?

Although no absolute answers exist for these questions, research on T Group outcomes has not been ignored. We feel safe in asserting that more research has been done on T Groups than on any other training approach. An American Psychiatric Association task force (1970), points out:

> T-groups, springing from the field of social psychology, have behind them a long tradition of research in group dynamics. No comparable body of knowledge has been generated by group therapy, a field notoriously deficient in any systematic research. Thus, what is presently known of the basic science of group psychotherapy stems almost entirely from social-psychological research with task groups and T-groups; psychotherapy owes to the T-group much of its systematic understanding of such factors as group development, group pressure, group cohesiveness, leadership, and group norms and values. Furthermore, T-group research has elaborated a wealth of sophisticated research techniques and tools of which the group therapy field is now slowly availing itself. (p. 19).

Bibliographies and analyses of research studies have been compiled by Massarick (1985), Stock (1964), House (1967), Campbell and Dunnette (1968), Durham, Gibb, and Knowles (1967), Buchanan (1965), and others. Undoubtedly, disagreement exists as to what the findings, taken together, mean. We offer the following generalizations. A majority of participants (about 60%) report having strong to fairly strong positive feelings about their T Group experiences and believe these experiences have helped them change and improve their behavior. A minority (20-30%) report having either mild positive or neutral responses, and a smaller group (10% or fewer) feel negative about the experience. The question of what happens behaviorally after a T Group experience is most difficult to answer. One factor that has baffled research designers is that one cannot specify the same "desired" behavior outcomes for all participants. Each person comes to a T Group with a unique set of needs and interests that are pursued in one's own way and that may change in the course of the program. In addition, comparable indices of changes in performance-related behavior in the work or family setting are extremely difficult to develop. Several studies indicate that such changes do take place with significant frequency, although not all the studies are sufficiently well designed or controlled to satisfy the rigorous researcher completely.

One point seems fairly clear, however: Laboratory learnings are more likely to persist and to contribute to improvements in performance when they are supported and reinforced in the participants' back-home situations. Employees of firms that support the general norms of laboratory training through organization development programs, or married couples who have both had successful T Group experiences, are among those most likely to find lasting benefits. In an earlier article, we somewhat tentatively predicted that

> future trends in laboratory training will probably proceed in the direction of greater linkages between training and application. Laboratories will be augmented by further training experiences which deal with the real people, processes, and problems back home. Skills, norms, and approaches to problem-solving learned in training laboratories will be put into practice through programs at organizational or community levels. (Eddy & Lubin, 1971, pp. 631-632)

Laboratory training and management

Corporations and agencies have been among the strongest supporters of laboratory training. Since the late 1940s, thousands of managers from North America and elsewhere have participated in laboratories designed to help them function more effectively in their roles. The benefits of laboratory training experiences for managers have included the following.

Many managers with technical backgrounds have had little or no formal education preparing them for dealing effectively with people. T Group laboratories are a useful beginning point for learning human relations skills.

Managers who have had courses in human behavior sometimes find that the pressure of their work schedules causes them to forget to apply what they know about dealing with people. The laboratory provides an opportunity for renewing one's competency in interpersonal relations.

Many managers operate for years without clear-cut information about how they affect others and how others see them. In a majority of organizations, the climate does not encourage subordinates, peers, or even superiors to tell the manager directly about those behaviors hindering the manager's work performance. The T Group provides a safe environment in which participants can exchange feedback about their impact on one another, thus providing clues about one's probable impact.

Many organizations have instituted ongoing programs to improve the use of human resources. Organization development (OD), quality of work life (QWL), team building, and quality circles are among the terms applied to such efforts. Laboratory experiences are often used as "basic training" for providing managers with the sensitivity, skills, and program knowledge necessary to support such programs adequately and ensure their success.

The manager has a central role in changing institutional and organizational personnel practices with respect to race, gender, age, and disability. To implement organizational policy, managers must have the opportunity to examine and develop their own attitudes and feelings regarding the issues relevant to the policies. Laboratory training's emphasis on open communication, the importance of feelings, and constructive interaction provides the context and the methodology for managers to engage in such personal learning.

Finding time to pause and take stock of one's career and priorities is difficult for those involved in important and demanding roles. The laboratory provides a stimulating and supportive atmosphere in which one can join others in seeking perspective on life's questions and problems.

Professional and ethical issues

During its first years in existence, the laboratory training field did not encounter many problems related to maintaining standards for trainer preparation and behavior. Summer internship programs, followed by cotraining assignments, provided an avenue of induction for the modest number of newcomers to the field, most of whom entered with doctoral degrees in applied psychology or education. This situation has changed dramatically.

No one knows how many laboratory groups are held each week in the United States. Certainly the figure runs into hundreds. Some are conducted by qualified scientists who have acquired group training skills in special programs provided by NTL, universities, or other comparable organizations. Others are conducted by behavioral scientists—including psychiatrists, clinical psychologists, counselors, and others—who lack special training for working with groups and who assume that their therapeutic skills are sufficient. And many are being conducted by individuals with backgrounds peripheral to or outside behavioral science. Many now feel laboratory training is no longer "owned" by professionals because it is offered by a wide variety of individuals. Undoubtedly, some of the "amateur" group trainers are competent and ethical and help provide participants in their groups with a worthwhile experience. Others may not be competent and, in conducting groups, may be satisfying primarily their own needs for control, recognition, affection, and the like rather than the learning needs of participants.

One problem is that techniques of group training, as do those of therapy, appear deceptively simple and easy to reproduce. The T Group trainer remains silent much of the time, injecting only an occasional observation or comment. Furthermore, superficial observation might suggest that the encounter group leader requires only an easily memorized catalogue of behavioral interventions. Cookbook-type manuals of exercises, tapes, and films have helped provide leaders, including the marginally qualified ones, with additional tools.

Negative effects of training

A common criticism of laboratory training, heard more frequently during the 1960s and 1970s, is that it can potentially cause psychological harm. Stories about persons who "cracked up" while attending a laboratory program are not uncommon, and the assumption is that the T Group experience caused the problem. A few large sample studies and several anecdotal reports are available that address this issue. NTL Institute's records indicate that of 14,200 individuals who participated in its summer human relations programs and industrial training programs between 1947 and 1968, the experience was stressful enough for 33 persons (.2%)

to require them to leave the program prior to its completion. Almost all of these individuals had a history of prior emotional disturbances (NTL Institute for Applied Behavioral Science, 1969). The YMCA located four individuals who had "negative experiences" out of approximately 1,200 participants in its laboratory programs (.3%) (Batchelder & Hardy, 1968). Three of the four, upon follow-up examinations, seem to have gained ultimately from the disruptive experience.

The majority of studies report that the incidence of difficulty falls between .02 and .05% of participants. Others, however, have reported higher proportions of negative results. Most of these latter studies deal with only one or two groups, and many with situations that differ from the traditional one- or two-week laboratory of "strangers" led by professionals—that is, they refer to weekend encounter marathons, training programs for psychiatric residents, classroom-type settings, leaderless groups, and the like.

The most extensive evaluation of the positive and negative effects of various types of laboratory education was conducted by Lieberman, Yalom, and Miles (1973). One of their findings was that 7.8% of the total of 206 persons initially participating in the groups studied (9.1% of those who completed at least half of the group sessions) experienced significant psychological injury. Schutz (1975), Rowan (1975), and Smith (1975) each challenged the conclusions of Lieberman et al. (1973) regarding negative consequences, and Lieberman (1975) provided a rejoinder.

Although long-term effects might be inconclusive, the level of dysphoric mood—an operational definition of the effects of stress—has been studied and found to be significantly lower than that experienced by college students just prior to a scheduled examination (Lubin & Lubin, 1971).

A fair summarization of the data to this point seems to indicate that laboratory training should not be viewed as an absolutely benign and foolproof method. In residential programs run by professionals and having purposes advertised as clearly educational rather than therapeutic, the incidence of difficulty seems relatively low. Situations in which doubts exist about the qualifications of the trainer, the conference is promoted inappropriately, a great discrepancy exists between the program design and the expectations of the clients, great variability exists in the intensity and duration of the program, unevaluated "innovations" are presented and other situational pressures arise, however, provide reason for caution.

The responsibility of ethical trainers seems clear: They should have the competence to recognize when participants are experiencing excessive levels of affect, demonstrating disorganized thinking and behavior, and experiencing stimulus overload from excessive feedback or the like. Trainers also should be capable of intervening appropriately at these times.

Pressures to conform

Both group development and individual development are important goals of laboratory education. Some participants discover that a certain level of group development needs to occur before conditions arise allowing them to pursue personal development issues and projects. Paradoxically, in addition to nurturing and supporting its members, the group can also exert strong coercive pressure on individuals. The ethical trainer needs to be sensitive to this issue and to help individuals identify group pressure, and occasionally to support an individual's unique style, values, needs, or the like despite majority or group pressure.

Trainer development

Beginning in 1960, NTL began to train individuals as trainer-consultants. At first the objective was to develop staff for NTL's programs and institutes. With funding from the National Institute for Mental Health, NTL inaugurated the internship program at Bethel, Maine, and continued to offer it each summer for many years. Once its own need for new trainers was satisfied, NTL began to respond to requests from individuals and organizations to provide professional training for their trainers. These programs have taken on various forms and have been provided for varying lengths of time. A few of the trainer development programs currently offered include the Training of Trainers Conferences, Programs for Specialists in Organization Development, Training/Consultation Skills for International Human Resource Development Specialists, Training Program for Laboratory Education, Leadership for Educational Change, and the Graduate Student Professional Development Program. Each of these, as the titles indicate, is targeted to a different occupational group.

The summer internship in applied behavioral science is no longer being offered. Instead, NTL has moved to combine academic education and professional trainer consultant development by joining American University in providing a master's degree program in human resource development. At least one additional joint master's degree-level program, following a similar model, is under discussion with the Unversity of Massachusetts at Amherst.

What are some of the areas of competence in laboratory education that these programs seek to develop? Lippitt, Benne, Bradford and Gibb (1975, pp. 475-477) list these as diagnostic competence; competence in entry and contract development; design competence; intervention competence; ethical decision-making competence; competence in continuity, follow-up support and termination; and peer team-building competence. Another area of competence, identified recently as socio-political competence, plays an important role in several aspects of training consultation. In this connection, the facilitator is expected to have the attitudes and skills necessary to assist groups and individuals in examining and developing personal stances regarding race, gender, age, and disability and recognizing the subtle ways in which inequity is institutionalized.

Accreditation and certification

The correlative professional issue is that of accreditation or certification. NTL Institute has never accredited or certified trainers. In granting member status to behavioral scientists, it has included them in its "network" of trainers and change agents staffing NTL labortories and other programs. As a partial measure to exert some control over training quality, NTL Institute has developed and ratified a policy manual defining standards for the use of the laboratory method in NTL Institute programs (NTL Institute for Applied Behavioral Science, 1969). This manual sets forth the organization's position on such matters as trainer qualifications, participant selection, goals of training, professional ethics and values, and applications of laboratory learnings. The thrust of the policy statement is in the direction of more rigorous standards. NTL endorses the American Psychological Association's ethical standards (American Psychological Association, 1953), sets forth a comprehensive list of requisite skills, experiences, and ethics for its trainer members, and specifically rejects the notion that participation in one or more "basic" laboratory experiences constitutes sufficient preparation to provide training.[2]

The International Association of Applied Social Scientists, now known as Certified Consultants International, was established in 1972 as a certifying agency for laboratory trainers and practitioners in related fields. Its program description indicates that CCI "was created to establish clear criteria of competence; to develop and publicize standards for applied science practitioners; to foster the sound development of the profession, including access by new practitioners; and to aid the client public in understanding, properly selecting and utilizing applied behavioral social scientists certified by CCI."

By pursuing these purposes, CCI seeks to protect the public and potential clients by assuring the identification and periodic review of competent and self-accredited practitioners. It also helps qualified practitioners to maintain and improve their professional practice and to develop along responsible lines in this new profession as a whole.

The Association is cross-disciplinary in its membership and concerns. It places primary focus on the responsible delivery of professional services to client groups and organizations.

Members of CCI are practitioners who work either with individuals and small groups to facilitate re-education and learning through the use of laboratory education methods or with large social systems to facilitate systems through the use of collaborative and scientific methods.

The certification process places primary importance on an individual's demonstrated competence, rather than on academic or other credentials. Evidence of ability to incorporate in one's professional practice the concerns for dehumanization in our culture and environmental milieu is considered an important criterion for certification. Membership in any division indicates certification of one's competence and achievement in that area of work. Periodic review of every member assures that CCI certification attests to the practitioner's continued high professional standards. (Certified Consultants International, 1985).

Areas in which individuals are certified by CCI include: personal/professional development consulting (Division 1), group development consulting (Division 2), internal organization development practice (Division 3), organization development consulting (Division 4), and societal change consulting (Division 5).[3]

Summary

The field of small group training has provided one of the major contributions of the social sciences to adult learning. In an era when formal education has tended to stress technical training and the physical sciences, laboratory training programs have provided managers with the opportunity to upgrade their human relations skills. Such programs have also helped establish a foundation for organizational improvement strategies such as organization development. Because of its emphasis on open communicaton and on the important role of feelings in attitude and behavior change, laboratory training seems ideally suited to prepare managers and people generally to deal more effectively with issues of race, gender, age, and disability. Originally regarded as a rather innovative and adventurous technique, the T Group and its many derivatives—such as team building—are now well-accepted management tools. The past two decades have seen the formation of organized programs to develop and certify trainers/ consultants. Ethical trainers should remain alert to two major issues that have become increasingly clear: stressful participant experiences and excessive group pressures toward conformity.

NOTES

1. Portions of this article are adapted from an earlier work by the authors (Eddy & Lubin, 1971).

2. To obtain information on NTL Institute's professional training programs, write to P.O. Box 9155, Rosslyn Station, Arlington, VA 22209, or telephone (703)527-1500.

3. To obtain information on Certified Consultants International, write to box 573, Brentwood, TN 37027.

REFERENCES

American Psychiatric Association. (1970). *Encounter groups and psychiatry* (Report of the Task Force on Recent Developments in the Use of Small Groups). Washington, DC: American Psychiatric Association.

American Psychological Association. (1953). *Ethical standards for psychologists.* Washington, DC: American Psychologial Association.

Batchelder, R.L. (1964). History of the t-group in the laboratory setting. In L.P. Bradford, J.R. Gibb, & K.D. Benne (Eds.), *T-group theory and laboratory method: Innovation in re-education.* New York: Wiley.

Batchelder, R.L., & Hardy, J.M. (1968). *Using sensitivity training and the laboratory method: An organizational case study in the development of human resources.* New York: Association Press.

Bennis, W.G., & Slater, P.E. (1968). *The temporary society.* New York: Harper and Row.

Bradford, L.P. (1967). Biography of an institution. *Journal of Applied Behavioral Science, 3,* 127-143.

Bradford, L.P., Gibb, J.R., & Benne, K.D. (Eds.) (1964). *T-group theory and laboratory method: Innovation in re-education.* New York: Wiley.

Buchanan, P.C. (1965). *Evaluating the effectiveness of laboratory training in industry. Vol. 1. Exploration in human relations training and research.* Washington, DC: National Education Association.

Bunker, D.R. (1965). Individual applications of laboratory training. *Journal of Applied Behavioral Science, 1,* 131-148.

Campbell, J.P., & Dunnette, M.D. (1968). Effectiveness of T-group experiences in managerial training and development. *Psychological Bulletin, 70*, 73-104.

Cartwright, D., & Zander, A. (Eds.) (1968). *Group dynamics: Research and theory* (3rd Ed.). New York: Harper and Row. (pp. 11-21).

Certified Consultants International (1985). *Directory of certified practitioners*. Brentwood, TN: Certified Consultants International.

Durham, L.E., Gibb, J.R., & Knowles, E.S. (1967). A bibliography of research: 1947-1967. *In explorations in applied behavioral science*. Washington, DC: NTL Institute for Applied Behavioral Science.

Eddy, W.B., & Lubin, B. (1971). Laboratory training and encounter groups. *Personnel and Guidance Journal, 49*, 425-435.

Frank, J.D. (1964). Training and therapy. In L.P. Bradford, J.R. Gibb, & K.D. Benne (Eds.), *T-group theory and laboratory method*. New York: Wiley.

House, R.J. (1967). T-group education and leadership effectiveness: A review of the empirical literature and a critical evaluation. *Personnel Psychology, 20*, 1-32.

Lieberman, M.A. (1975). Joy less facts? A response to Schutz, Smith, and Rowan. *Journal of Humanistic Psychology, 15*, 49-58.

Lieberman, M.A., & Borman, L.D. (1979). *Self-help groups for coping with crisis*. San Francisco, CA: Jossey-Bass.

M.S., Yalom, I.D., & Miles, M.B. (1973). *Encounter groups: First facts*. New York: Basic Books.

Lippitt, R.O., Benne, K.D., Bradford, L.P., & Gibb, J.R. (1975). The professionalization of laboratory practice. In K.D. Benne, L.P. Bradford, J.R. Gibb, & R.O. Lippitt (Eds.), *The laboratory method of changing and learning: Theory and application*. Palo Alto, CA: Science and Behavior Books

Lubin, B. (1983). Group therapy. In I.B. Weiner (Ed.), *Clinical methods in psychology* (pp. 389-449). New York: Wiley.

Lubin, B., & Eddy, W.B. (1970). The laboratory training model: Rationale, method and some thoughts for the future. *International Journal of Group Psychotherapy, 20(3)*, 305-399.

Lubin, B., & Lubin, A.W. (1971). T-group stress compared with college exam stress. *Journal of Applied Behavioral Science, 7*, 502-507.

Marrow, A. (1969). *The practical theorist: The life and times of Kurt Lewin*. New York: Basic Books.

Massarick, F. (1985). *Bibliography on human relations training and related subjects*. Arlington, VA: NTL Institute for Applied Behavioral Science.

Miles, M.B. (1964). On temporary systems. In M.B. Miles (Ed.), *Innovation in education*. New York: Teachers College, Columbia University.

NTL Institute for Applied Behavioral Science. (1969). *Standards for the use of the laboratory method (News and reports)*. Washington, DC: NTL Institute for Applied Behavioral Science.

Parloff, M.B. (1970). Assessing the effects of headshrinking and mind-expanding. *International Journal of Group Psychotherapy, 20*, 14-24.

Rice, A.K. (1965). *Learning for leadership: Interpersonal and intergroup relations*. London: Tavistock Publications.

Rioch, M.J. (1970). Group relations: Rationale and technique. *International Journal of Group Psychotherapy, 20*, 340-355.

Rowan, J. (1975). Encounter group research: No joy? *Journal of Humanistic Psychology, 5*, 19-28.

Scheidlinger, S. (1967). Current conceptual and methodological issues in group psychotherapy research: Introduction to panel—Part I. *International Journal of Group Psychotherapy, 17*, 53-56.

Schutz, W. (1975). Not encounter and certainly not facts. *Journal of Humanistic Psychology, 15*, 7-18.

Smith, P.B. (1975). Are there adverse effects of sensitivity training? *Journal of Humanistic Psychology, 15*, 29-47.

Stock, D. (1964). A survey of research on T-groups. In L.P. Bradford, J.R. Gibb, & K.D. Benne (Eds.), *T-group theory and laboratory method*. New York: Wiley.

Weschler, I.R., Massarik, F., & Tannenbaum, R. (1962). The self in process: A sensitivity training emphasis. In I.R. Weschler & E.H. Schein (Eds.), *Issues in training Vol. 5. NTL Selected Reading Series (pp. 33-46)*. Washington, DC: National Education Association.

Risks We Must Take: Changes, Challenges, and Choices for Consultants and Trainers in 1987 and Beyond

Eva Schindler-Rainman

Change is ever with us, and the challenges accompanying these changes are therefore a part of our lives. During the remainder of this decade, six major changes and challenges will affect the role of the consultant and trainer. At least three threads or threats will affect these changes.

Threats and trends

1. Doing more with less. This concerns all of us, because we are seeing a tax revolt by citizen voters. The declining value of the dollar, inflation, and economic turmoil must be considered and reflected in the ways organizations, communities, and individuals do business. At the same time, the demand for services has grown, so we must now provide better services with fewer resources of materials and money and more creative use of human resources.

2. The fluctuating national mood. We have seen the national mood change from one of optimism and clarity to one of pessimism, cynicism, lack of clarity, and what Lord Snow terms "holing in." This national mood—whether it is one of optimism and faith or one of pessimism and cynicism—affects the people with whom we work, and the mood changes depending on the value of the dollar, election results, various world crises, and the level of hostility and violence in communities. Trainers and consultants must be sensitive to fluctuating international, national, local, and personal needs.

3. Speed and complexity of changes. Changes are more complex and occurring more rapidly than ever before. In view of this, Margaret Mead once

©1981, *Training and Development Journal,* American Society for Training and Development. Reprinted with permission. All rights reserved. This version slightly modified by the author.

noted that anyone over the age of 30 is seen as an "immigrant" to those under that age. We must keep this in mind as we talk about the specific changes and challenges affecting trainers and consultants. The speed and complexity of changes has led to an overload of information, and the constant development of new techniques, knowledge, and technology causes such developments to rapidly become outdated. Trainers and consultants must be able and willing to take more risks as changes occur having dynamics and consequences that cannot be predicted.

Changes and challenges

1. Demographic and population changes. One such change includes the increasing mobility of the population, especially with respect to people moving in and out of cities, countries, and rural areas. We also face a population that is growing older, resulting in a decreasing number of younger employees: By 1990, it is estimated that 63% of the labor force will be between the ages of 25 and 44 years. Thus, we will see an increase in the availability of older workers, with "older" defined as 55 years of age and above (the term is being applied to increasingly younger persons). We will also see an increased number of employed women; 60% of all new jobs are expected to be filled by women and 70% of all employable women are expected to be working by 1990. In addition, vast groups of new immigrant populations—particularly Pacific Asians and Hispanics—are entering the U.S., and their numbers are expected to increase dramatically in many urban areas.

All of the above will result in increasing competition for work by employable persons. Some feel particularly concerned about the consequences of new immigrants' competing with native U.S. citizens for jobs.

Challenges. The challenges of demographic and population changes include the following:

- finding ways to integrate new workers born abroad into the U.S. population;
- decreasing the stress felt by those working in highly competitive systems;
- training people to work with new employees as peers and training managers to supervise all employees equally well;
- getting persons and systems—and trainers and consultants—to understand and use the resources of different age, stage, ethnic, and racial groups, which are vital to a competitive world that can benefit from the use of different resources to advance product manufacturing and improvement;
- keeping consultants and trainers abreast of population and demographic changes affecting their work;
- learning how to deal creatively with unions and other organizations of employees and professionals;
- helping older workers accept and work with younger managers, and helping younger managers and supervisors learn to work well with

older employees whom they supervise or train, with whom they work, and/or with whom they consult.

2. Value changes. By this I refer to our moving from an emphasis on one set of values to an emphasis on another set. This movement epitomizes the transitions we currently face, for transition is the key to unlocking and understanding our society at this time. We are currently undergoing the following value changes:

- a change from an emphasis on a person's having only one loyalty or a few major loyalties to an emphasis on having multiple loyalties, both in one's personal and professional life;
- a change from an emphasis on permanent commitments to an acceptance of temporary bonds (previously, people considered lifelong marriages and working from the bottom up in a company satisfactory and positive, whereas now they accept sequential relationships both with personal partners and employers);
- a change from feeling one works to live and lives to work to feeling that one should demand improved quality of working life, increased participation in decision making, flexible working hours, part-time work, shared work, and the like;
- a change from little or no emphasis on health to an increased sensitivity to the importance of health and healthy environments;
- a change from respect for authority to the confronting and questioning of authority and authority figures;
- a change from conforming to established patterns of time to establishing new situations related to time and understanding new ways to use and organize time to one's advantage, including moving from day-and-night cities to 24-hour cities providing services 24 hours a day, as is the case in larger population centers throughout the world.

Challenges. The challenges of value changes include the following:

- focusing on the individual so that persons' working lives and—to some extent—their personal lives provide meaningful rewards and recognition;
- developing career ladders and life-goal planning as part of on-the-job planning, development, and training programs;
- offering opportunities for value clarification that allow persons to determine which values they wish to keep and which they wish to release;
- developing new ways to involve employees in decision making, both individually and in groups;
- providing incentives to decrease persons' alienation from their work and increase workers' motivation and satisfaction;
- involving employees in developing new work patterns and new ways to improve both working conditions and the product;
- developing new ways for workers to relate to one another across

functions—that is, more collaboratively on both horizontal and vertical levels.

3. Organizational change. As society changes, as technology revolutionizes the work load, as new information becomes available and distributed in new ways, organizations must change in response. New organizational structures are developing, from the matrix organization to the "flattened-out" organization. Some organizations are becoming more centralized, some more decentralized. But no matter what change is made, organizations are responding to some of the trends affecting our society and the world, including the following.

More multinational collaborations—among either units of the same company or units of different companies working toward similar goals and purposes—are taking place. New collaborations are also developing among business, government, and private nonprofit organizations. Indeed, some interesting networks are developing that use human resources and knowledge more creatively and with fewer resources of materials and money. Moreover, interunit competition has increased to promote better services, improved products, and higher levels of productivity.

Organizations have developed clearer emphases on their missions, clearer goals, and greater involvement of personnel in planning. Large systems have increased their emphases on social responsibility, as evidenced by participation in community life and the development of a new job category: director of community affairs or director of volunteer services. A new trend in business is increased employee participation in worthwhile community projects.

With the tightening of money, the emphasis on in-house training and upgrading has increased. This will result in a decreased need for external consultants, or—when external consultants are used—such consultants' being made members of teams of insiders and outsiders for the purpose of strengthening the insider, giving that person greater visibility and more skills, and enabling that person to carry on without help from external consultants.

Challenges. The challenges of organizational change include the following:

- helping managers develop organizational diagnostic skills allowing them not only to have many alternative methods available, but to implement these methods or know who inside or outside their system can help them do so;
- helping managers learn to handle confrontation and hostility, skills they do not generally possess;
- helping decision makers, managers, and others learn collaboration skills, which are important to allowing different individuals and organizations to work together to achieve common goals and purposes;
- having trainers and consultants help the persons with whom they work learn to understand and manage matrix organizations if that is what their systems are becoming or have become;
- increasing our knowledge of general systems theory;

- gaining crosscultural knowledge and skills, which are necessary in a society in which the influx of newcomers and equal opportunity legislation have led to many different types of people (i.e., people of different nationalities, ages, genders, races, religions, classes, and the like) working in the same units at similar jobs, requiring the integration of such diverse persons into their work groups;

- teaching workers at all levels to become more sophisticated in their communications with many different persons and groups (e.g., physicians who must communicate with patients, paramedical personnel, aides, volunteers, social workers, representatives of religious communities, and colleagues specializing in different areas of medicine);

- helping appropriate persons learn effective skills for community relations and using volunteers within their systems, and helping workers acting as volunteers for the community, not only to provide service but also to perform public relations work for their systems;

- enabling systems to develop their own training capacities and managers to develop skills as trainers as available funds for external consultants decrease;

- helping people at all decision-making levels learn to set goals, envision the future, and implement plans through a variety of methods and techniques so that they can combine these skills with strategies for action to become important assets to their systems;

- having trainers and consultants become able to be creative "on the spot," using all their knowledge, skills, experience, and sensitivity—along with a willingness to take risks in developing new ways of working, instruments, methods, and techniques.

4. Complex communications technology and systems change.

Workshops ranging in duration from a few hours to several weeks are now introducing persons with no background in machine technology to the purposes, underlying philosophy, and use of computer technology. Computers are an important part of the developing systems revolution, whether they are large main frames or smaller portable computers, and they are becoming increasingly complex and capable of performing a vast variety of tasks—provided the persons using them understand the machines' capabilities.

This information explosion is both exciting and frustrating, and it is here to stay. Therefore, we must develop a system of priorities so that we can determine which information is necessary and which is not.

The presence of new technology allows in-house training to be conducted using a multitude of media and less money when internal trainers have sufficient training. Because of this, organizations can conduct training without the costs of travel, lodging, and tuition.

These changes have caused jobs to change rapidly. Some are now obsolescent or must be done in new and different ways. People now find that keeping up with the demands of their work requires lifelong learning experiences, which they gain from inside their systems or elsewhere.

Challenges. The challenges of changes in technology and systems include the following:

- helping employees understand complex communication technology and become familiar and comfortable with new sociotechnical systems;
- creating opportunities to learn about new media capabilities, such as through computer conferences that enable units separated geographically to consult with one another regularly;
- helping clients determine which current information is important to them;
- having trainers and consultants feel comfortable about what they do not know and having them become able and willing to know and consult other experts;
- giving recognition and credit to the colleagues with whom one works and from whom one learns.

5. Changes in the use and development of human resources. The emphasis on the better use and development of human resources is perhaps one of the most exciting changes affecting trainers and consultants, providing the following opportunities.

The new emphasis allows for the development of previously underused human resources, such as women, members of minority groups, the emotionally and physically disabled, recent immigrants, persons of low status, volunteers, and older persons. In some cases, the very young have constituted part of this underused human resource population.

We also have new opportunities for developing in-house mobility as a motivation for work. Such opportunities include in-house and on-the-job training, career counseling, community-service counseling, preretirement counseling, and incentives for attending ongoing professional development courses offered either internally or externally.

Related to human resources is the concern for the improvement of the quality of work life for all workers—including professionals, custodial personnel, paraprofessionals, and clerical personnel—doing all kinds of work at all levels, from top executives to the most recently hired direct-service personnel. Such change emphasizes the participation of workers in developing and implementing the means of improving the quality of their working life, or in the recommendation and suggestions of such means when they themselves cannot implement them themselves.

People are becoming increasingly aware of the need to use many diverse individuals representing many specialties to make decisions and solve problems, rather than relying on the capabilities of only one or two persons to do so. This use of complex and diverse groups of individuals is a response to the increasing complexity of the world, which requires us to analyze problems, and make decisions affecting a vast variety of issues.

Finally, human services are now being delivered by new teams made up of combinations of volunteers, professionals, and paraprofessionals. Such teams emphasize and use the diverse resource and capabilities their members bring to this work, and are being developed in such places as probation departments, school systems, and hospitals.

Challenges. The challenges of changes in the use and development of human resources include the following:

- devising the means to use more fully human potential through available human resources skills "banks," temporary task and work forces, and different types of teams created to address a variety of purposes for both short- and long-term periods;
- learning and understanding characteristics unique to different types of people—including differences related to values and cultures, life styles, beliefs, child-rearing patterns, and family structures—and the beauty of these differences;
- learning new skills for communicating with different people than before (e.g., a physician now needs to communicate not only with patients and nursing staff, but also with paramedical personnel, social workers, occupational therapists, representatives of religions, a variety of volunteers, hospital administrators, those in the court system, members of the insurance industry, police, and unions);
- developing new systems for recognizing and rewarding workers—in addition to existing patterns for classifying and increasing salaries and wages—including skillful verbal and nonverbal forms of recognition, rewards for innovative ideas, feedback on persons' feedback, and the like;
- developing forms of continuing, lifelong education so that workers will not only be challenged but have skills necessary to remaining motivated, excited, and productive;
- developing creative, participative, experiential, and ever-changing opportunities for training and education relevant for all parts of a system.

6. Changes in leadership. More emphasis will be placed on the creativity and initiative of leaders than ever before, and leaders will need to perform functions associated with both the left and right brain if they are to lead adequately. Specifically, they must be educators and trainers as well as managers, they must learn to deal with conflict in creative and useful ways as it increasingly becomes a part of changing systems, and they must "do more with less" by understanding issues related to finance and financial management.

To do this, leaders will constantly need to update their own knowledge and skills, and make certain others in their systems also have opportunities to do so. I find it interesting that leaders will need to know the "when and how" of involvement—and whom to involve—in decision making and problem solving or in influencing these processes.

Leaders must be aware of the various types of leadership, including the following: **coleadership**, in which the powers and tasks of leaders are shared fairly equally; **shared leadership**, in which leaders agree on how they will share leadership power and tasks, which may or may not be done equally; **sequential leadership**, in which a leader assumes this role for an agreed amount of time and is followed by another person; **functional leadership**, in which someone becomes a leader because that person has some knowledge or skill important to performing a particular task and is replaced when this expertise in no longer necessary (e.g., a financial expert may be a leader when a group is planning its budget and financial future, but will relinquish this role when other work is to be done); and any temporary combinations of these types.

Challenges. The challenges of changes in leadership include the following:

- helping long-time leaders change their styles, understand the necessity of such changes, and learn skills useful for discovering and using the resources of others working with them;

- having trainers and consultants help leaders learn to detect conflict and use it as a resource—rather than view it as a sign of division or resistance—so that leaders may learn that energy used for resistance to change can be harnessed to make the change more creative and useful, thereby making the use and resolution of conflict an important leadership skill and tool;

- become more sensitive to the many realities of their systems and understand how to communicate this information to those with whom they work, learn what style of leadership to use in different situations, become comfortable with the challenges and complexities of change, and know where they can get help when needed.

What we must do

Trainers and consultants must take risks, many through the 1980s and 1990s. This will require us to do the following:

- increase our knowledge and skills with respect to future trends, trend analysis, and alternative ways of planning for the future;

- increase our training methodology "tool kits" by inventing new, creative training designs specifically tailored for individuals or organizations, thereby recognizing that each situation is unique and deserves the trainer or consultant's creativity in designing experiences to fit a particular situation and the client's purposes, needs, and financial and time constraints;

- employ the inside/outside team concept and risk teaming with someone else inside or outside a system to increase one's skills, visibility, methodological abilities, and abilities to influence, as well provide real help to the other person or persons;

- enhance what we already know about data collection and the use of resources by learning about action research methodology and techniques, simulations, multimedia instruments, group interviewing, and the like;

- be selective in our choices of new technology, packages, machines, and the like, remembering that all that is new is not necessarily better than older resources, and that technology must meet the needs of a particular situation not only with respect to training but also to money, time, and human resources available;
- learn more effective ways of involving potential participants in planning and training and having experienced participants learn how to help newcomers;
- understand and learn all about new technologies and how to choose whether or not to use them;
- find ways to use our time and our clients' time more effectively;
- learn to confront clients more skillfully when they have legitimate diferences of opinion, value, or diagnosis and to differ with our clients in constructive and creative ways;
- introduce the possibility of using volunteers in and by systems;
- make plans for ongoing professional educational development for and with all parts of a system;
- admit when we do not know something and be able to recruit additional trainers and consultants as resources;
- help clients learn modern, participative, productive ways of holding meetings;
- support clients in recognizing and committing mistakes and errors as components of being, leading, and managing, teaching that one can learn and grow from analyses of both success and mistakes.

It is exciting, interesting, and challenging to live in turbulent, changing times. As consultants and trainers, our professional skills will continually be confronted. Therefore, we must grow and change to produce the best possible "products" for delivery to our clients.

BIBLIOGRAPHY

Bennis, W., & Burt, N. (1985). *Leaders—The strategies for taking charge*. New York: Harper and Row.

Ferguson, M. (1980). *The Aquarian conspiracy: Personal and social transformation in the 1980s*. Los Angeles: J.P. Tarcher.

Fox, R., Lippitt, R., & Schindler-Rainman, E. (1976). *The humanized future: Some new images*. San Diego, CA: University Associates.

Huczynski, A., & Logan, D. (1980). Learning to change: Organizational change through transfer training workshops. *Leadership and Organization Development Journal, 1*(3), 25-31.

Lindaman, E.B., & Lippitt, R. (1979). *Choosing the future you prefer*. Ann Arbor, MI: Human Resource Development Associates of Ann Arbor.

Schindler-Rainman, E. (1981). *Transitioning: Strategies for the volunteer world*. Vancouver, BC: Voluntary Action Resource Centre.

Schindler-Rainman, E., & Lippitt, R. (in collaboration with Cole, J.). (1975). *Taking your meetings out of the doldrums*. San Diego, CA: University Associates.

Schindler-Rainman, E., & Lippitt, R. (1975). *The volunteer community: Creative use of human resources* (2nd ed.). Boulder, CO: Yellow Fire Press.

Snowden-Hopkins, F. (1981, April). Communication: The civilizing force. *The Futurist, 15*(2), 39-40.

Toffler, A. (1980). *The third wave*. New York: Morrow, Williams and Co.

Yankelovich, D. (1981, April). New rules in American life: Searching for self-fulfillment in a world turned upside down. *Psychology Today, 15*(4), 35-91.

Section II.
Trainer Development

The Trainer as Person: On the Importance of Developing Your Best Intervention

Chuck Phillips

This article is intended for aspiring trainers, developing trainers, and experienced trainers. It discusses the developmental processes that shape, form, evolve, and result in the facilitative and leadership skills of an effective laboratory educator. Most importantly, it discusses human beings and the personal traits and characteristics they embody that constitute a critical—yet often underattended—component of the developmental process of training professionals.

Marvin Weisbord once said, ". . .your own warm body is your best intervention." This article is concerned with the development, evolution, and "the care and feeding" of the trainer's "self," or person—the trainer's most important intervention tool.

The basic trainer development model contains three essential elements: theory, skills, and the self as person. This article focuses on the third element, the self. The self, however, is addressed within the context of a discussion of the complete model.

Trainer development model

The crux of this model is that one must sufficiently develop **all three** elements to become an effective trainer.

The first essential element is **theory**. A trainer should have a grounding in and working familiarity with the body of knowledge, research, concepts, and models pertaining to the field of individual and group development. These include—but are not limited to—basic psychological concepts and contexts, group development models and theories, individual development models and theories, and models and theories of change.

©1987 NTL Institute. All rights reserved.

This core knowledge, or "cognitive" area, also includes the models and frameworks representing the tools of training. Frequently referred to as the trainer's "kit bag," these are the inventory of generic and specific interventions and designs—the structures, exercises, forms, and processes—used by the trainer according to the task-oriented and/or developmental needs and objectives of a group or individual.

This first element constitutes the trainer's data bank, providing the cognitive framework from which to work.

The second essential element comprises **skills**. A skill is the practiced capability to act on, carry out, and support the actions and interventions prescribed by an analysis based on the first element—the data base.

The trainer's skills include the following.

- **Listening**: the ability to hear what others have intended to say, and the ability to let them know that they have been heard.

- **Presenting**: the ability to provide information—instructions, concepts, theories, models, feedback, data—in ways that enable others to receive and understand the information.

- **Observing**: the ability to see what is happening with an individual or in a group, to understand nonverbal cues, and to perceive and articulate changes and shifts in mood, tone, or direction.

- **Sensing**: the ability to notice cues presented through nonverbal and implicit channels, such as vocal tone, changes in energy levels, undercurrents, silences, and nonverbal exchanges among group members.

- **Supporting**: the ability to provide verbal and nonverbal indications of encouragement, validation, affirmation, acknowledgement, caring, and comfort.

- **Challenging**: the ability to confront, to interrupt, to disagree, to stop a process. The ability to use one's energy and physical self to stop action or oppose a group.

- **Diagnosing**: the ability to synthesize diverse data and cues so as to form hypotheses and constructs from which to choose interventions and actions.

These skills, which represent the second element of the model, develop out of experience, study, and practice and provide the base from which the effective trainer creates training designs and interventions. In turn, the trainer's choice of an intervention or design is informed by that trainer's data base—the body of knowledge represented by the first element in the model—and is fed by one's skills of observation, sensing, and diagnosis.

The third essential element of the model is the **self**, or person.

Self as person

Two interrelated reasons exist for making this third element in the trainer development model the primary focus of this article. First, the trainer's **self** is the most important of what are all essential elements. Second, despite its importance, this element appears to be the least well understood and, therefore, the area receiving the scantest attention in trainer development efforts.

The element of the self addresses who we are—our beliefs, values, and life experiences as they become manifest in our attitudes, needs, and motives. With regard to the trainer, the developmental concern is to determine how these attitudes, needs, and motives influence and perhaps even control behavior and thought patterns.

The importance of this element—who we are—is first shown by how we "do" ourselves and by how others perceive and receive our behavior. The effectiveness of a trainer is largely determined by how well one "is" with respect to each of the following states of facilitative leadership:

- being a model;
- being a force that is played to, off of, or against;
- being an energy field that affects the respective energy fields of a group and/or individual.

As trainers, our selves determine how we act and react to others, how much and how little we engage with and distance ourselves from others, and the like.

Trainers **always** affect the situations with which they work—whether they deal with groups, individuals, or organizations—because they are at least temporarily a part of such systems through their engagement with them. We trainers affect a system through managing our own boundaries in relation to others and to the situation.

Consultant/trainer Herbert Shepard has spoken of a concept he calls "the self as an instrument of change." It is this fundamental, immutable impact of our person and presence that he refers to as the "self." According to Shepard, who we are is **the** most significant force that we bring to training and consultation, far overshadowing in importance what we know or even what we may do.

Second, the self determines how one's collection of personal values, beliefs, attitudes, and needs affects one's ability to see, sense, and think clearly, and then to act appropriately and with relevance to one's diagnosis of the client's needs.

Robert Tannenbaum, who has been both a pioneering and a continuing advocate of the need for trainer "self-development," uses an adaptation of the leadership continuum that he has developed with Warren Schmidt to talk about this element (Tannenbaum & Schmidt, 1973).

As Tannenbaum describes it, two important continua relate to the importance of self in trainer development. The first is that of "social sensitivity," which he defines as the ability to "know" objectively what is happening in a particular situation and to know what action by a trainer would be appropriate at that point. This sensitivity may subconsciously or unconsciously be affected by one's beliefs and needs.

For example, if touching someone lovingly or comfortingly in a "professional" situation is something with which one is uncomfortable or considers "too intimate"—because of one's own upbringing, some past experiences, or the like—

the likelihood that one will notice another's hurt or pain, which often signals a call for being "held," is negligible.

The second continuum is one of "behavioral flexibility," which Tannenbaum defines as the ability to act appropriately and relevantly to one's diagnosis of the situation and the needs of group and/or individual. In the example above, then, even if one could see that the situation lent itself to a hug or some other form of loving, comforting touch, one might not have the capability to act on that knowledge with a physical response.

According to Tannenbaum, the key competency in terms of who we are and how we "do" ourselves as trainers is the ability to move freely along both continua, and therefore to intervene appropriately. In moving freely, one's perceptiveness and ability to act is only minimally blocked or shaded by one's predispositions, unconscious memories and learnings from childhood experiences and decisions, and needs. Moreover, this frees us to act according to our observations and sensations, with few restrictions on our repertoire of behavior.

Another way of looking at this element of the self, or the trainer as person, is through Will Schutz's theory of interpersonal relations, or what he refers to as the basic concerns of any group (Schutz, 1966). Schutz describes three areas of "needs" universally operative in groups and individuals. These needs relate to our concerns for inclusion, control, and affection. In the self-assessment instrument derived from the theory, varying degrees of "wanting" or "not wanting" and of "expressing" or "not expressing" each concern or need are unique to each individual.

If a trainer has high needs for control, for example, but does not express them through appropriate channels, then this trainer may overcontrol a group or end up in frequent confrontation with group members. At moments such as these, participants wonder whether or not the trainer is working on her or his own issues, rather than simply facilitating their process. Similarly, a diagnosis shaded by one's own low desire for affection could prove completely inaccurate for a group whose members are in fact desperate for a higher degree of collegiality so that they may advance their expressed goals or accomplish tasks.

Readers should thus see clearly how the trainer's personal needs—one aspect of the self—can shade, drive, or block the trainer's hypotheses, diagnoses, and interventions and thus make those facilitative and leadership behaviors inappropriate or irrelevant—perhaps even counterproductive—to the group or individual.

A truly complicating factor with respect to beliefs, attitudes, values, and needs is that not only may we be unaware of them—because we may not have made ourselves aware of them—but also that they may be operating at such unconscious and fundamental levels that they may even block our attempts at introspection and self-scrutiny. As we try to examine these parts of ourselves, we may trigger feelings of discomfort, anxiety, and even fear, which act as our defenses against the intensity of the emotions held in our unconsciousness. We respond to these more apparent, reactive feelings of discomfort, anxiety, and the like, and avoid the underlying issue, thus effectively thwarting our development.

Our unconscious, repressed experiences—probably from childhood—likely form the roots of our observational "filters" and behavioral "restrictions."

Using my own experience as an example, after a lengthy period spent in therapy I was able to encounter my feeling uncertain during childhood as to whether I was truly loved and accepted for who I was. I found a pattern of childhood behaviors subtly geared to doing and being those things that would secure the approval and (positive) attention of my father. Not an unusual history by any means, but one that contrasted markedly to the adult perspective I had had of my childhood being one of joy, love, security, and laughter in a "model home."

Only after this therapeutic consciousness-raising and even a reliving of some of these childhood experiences could I begin to see how I had continued some of these subtle childhood behaviors in my adult life and work. This occurred despite my having a relatively high degree of self-awareness, supported by extensive collegial observations and feedback indicating that I was generally a situationally relevant and behaviorally appropriate trainer and consultant.

So, what is the message? Actually, I have several. One is to urge, encourage, even "demand" that potential, or established, trainers and consultants examine their personal development processes to assess the **balance** among these three essential elements—theory, skills, and the self as person—paying special attention to the area of the self.

My second message restates the importance of the "person" element of the developmental process. Simply "knowing" multiple theories, models, concepts, and structures is not very useful if one does not have the **capacity to act**—that is, if one lacks the learned repertoires of behaviors and skills to use. Furthermore, "knowing," learning, and practicing behaviors and skills is not very useful if one's values, beliefs, attitudes, needs, and life experiences hinder and block one's ability to know or make a diagnosis and intervention.

My third message points toward some directions. As stated above, one direction is to assess the balance of one's developmental processes and to engage in activities that will tip the scales. Since one of my working premises is that the "person" element is the one most likely to be given too little attention, this message clearly implies the need for significantly more investment in activities to develop the self.

The specific type, content, or "flavor" of any developmental path will certainly have a highly individualized nature, one dependent on one's needs, inclinations, and what is determined to "fit." I caution the reader to be guided not only by what you are attracted to, but also to push yourself to examine areas in which you feel resistance, since those areas may be repelling you by stimulating some unconscious feelings, as mentioned earlier.

One may start by identifying some "approachable" outcomes. The goal is not to clear oneself of all needs, values, and beliefs, or, in the extreme, to become needless or valueless—an impossible task anyway—but to be "free" of them. When a trainer is relatively free, one's feelings, impulses, and inclinations may still be present, but the trainer is more aware of them, able to identify them for what they probably are, and able to separate oneself from their control. The trainer can then **choose** whether to be an objective observer or objective actor in the scene.

The following anecdote, which comes from my own experience, might help clarify what I have said.

I was recently facilitating a personal development group when I suddenly became aware that my breathing was shallow, my chest and neck muscles were tensing, and my heartbeat was increasing. I was on the brink of intervening in an interchange between Richard and Marilyn, intending to help them see the common ground in their argument.

As I paid attention to my physical sensations, I realized that I had tuned into a smoldering, well-masked rage in Richard, and that I had been about to **defuse** the situation because of my identification with both Richard and Marilyn. In identifying with Marilyn, I was afraid of being the object of the rage, and in identifying with Richard, I was afraid of the potential destructiveness of my being enraged.

With this awareness, I was able to separate my "self" and my own fears and needs to avoid rage from the action between Richard and Marilyn. I was then able to recognize that helping Richard to express his rage in a "safe" way would be far more appropriate and useful to both of them—and to the group.

My experience thus was one of being able to follow the clues of my bodily sensations to old feelings I had that were being triggered by the group's activity, and, then, to **choose** to be guided by what was happening in the group rather than what was happening inside of me.

The Psychosynthesis Model has as one developmental goal the capacity to separate the "essential I" from the rest of the self. This "I" operates as that part of the self that can observe or "witness" the activities, feelings, and reactions of the rest of the self without actually being, or having to be, them.

This capacity forms a significant part of the effective trainer. Developing it requires sufficient time and effort devoted to exploring and discovering one's patterns of needs, values, beliefs, and life experiences and recognizing how they play a part in one's assumptions, attitudes, and behaviors.

One important step in this self-development process is to recognize and understand that unconscious feelings and past experiences underlie many current needs and behaviors and to begin to look for expressions of that in one's own life. Discovering "clues" in this way can build a base for more systematic pursuit of the self in other ways.

I hope that this article will challenge what I perceive to be a headlong, single-minded pursuit of "tools for the kit bag" and "skills practice". I believe trainers need to take stock of the **balance** of developmental focus and produce a more significant investment in and commitment to nourishing and loving the most powerful tool we have as trainers and consultants: ourselves.

REFERENCES

Tannenbaum, R., & Schmidt, W. H. (1973, May-June). How to choose a leadership. *Harvard Business Review*, pp. 95-101. (Original work published 1958)

Schutz, W. (1966). *The interpersonal underworld.* Palo Alto, CA: Science and Behavioral Books. (Original work published 1958)

Health, Stress, and the Trainer

John D. Adams

This article has two distinct but interrelated parts. The first part discusses some of my discoveries and concerns about trainers' behaviors and life styles and the implications of these for trainers' performance and for their health and well-being. The second part outlines some of the characteristics of an effective stress management training program. Both parts are based on my experiences of the past ten years, a period in which I have designed and conducted nearly 1,000 different stress management events and trained nearly 2,000 trainers in stress management training.

I. The trainer: Protecting health and enhancing performance

In my involvement with training trainers to provide stress management training, I have been quite surprised by the high levels of stress the majority of trainers appear to live with on a chronic basis. These trainers' average stress levels are, in general, much higher than those of the clients they serve.

One of the questionnaires I have developed, entitled "The Strain Response," measures the extent to which a person's stressful experiences have taken a toll on that person's health. The questionnaire therefore measures stress-related health risks. In my "train-the-trainer" programs, I always ask the participants to fill out "The Strain Response." The results usually show that about 80% of the participants score above the 50th percentile, and such scores—according to validation and prediction studies using this instrument—indicate significant levels of health risk. As scores climb into the upper percentiles, serious illnesses are predicted.

Trainers in training to conduct stress management workshops generally identify their own "stressors," or major sources of stress, as their marginality or lack of influence in the organizations they serve. Of course, they also experience the same kinds of general stressors as everyone else. Overall, I have generally found that a surprisingly large number of trainers feel a sense of powerlessness, of "self as victim."

©1985 John D. Adams. All rights reserved.

In working with trainers in training, I always insist that we work with three operating premises. (An operating premise is an assertion that, regardless of its veracity, we choose to operate from as if it were true.) The first one I call "the peacock premise." This premise is at **any** moment you can step into your greatness—that is, you can choose to **be** the predominant creative force in your life. The name for this premise comes from a sign I saw stating that "a peacock sitting on its tail is just another turkey." You have to get off your tail if you wish to be a peacock.

The second premise I call "the self-fulfilling prophecy premise." This premise is that whatever self-concept you hold in your consciousness tends to occur in your life. If you see yourself as a victim, you will act like one and be treated like one, and the prophecy will become true. If you see yourself as self-determining, you will act as if you **are** self determining, and people will treat you as being self-determining.

The third premise I call "the higher-purpose premise." This premise is that if you base the self-determining choices you make on the highest truth about yourself you can muster at any given moment, the results you eventually get from these choices will help you clarify your true nature and purpose and your life's work.

I have consistently found that when trainers decide to adopt these operating premises for themselves, they experience less stress, get better results in life and work, and experience more frequent periods of "personal peak," or inspired performance. The interrelationships of thinking, health, and performance results is illustrated in Figure 1.

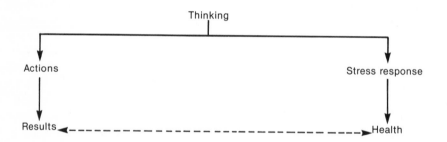

Figure 1. Interrelating thinking, performance results, and stress-related health outcomes

The basic message of the premises cited above is that you generally get what you "ask for." Clearly, we all make up our lives as we go along. Using these three premises gives you the opportunity to make up your life in the way you want it to be, rather than having external stimuli be the primary influence.

The following is a brief review of the stress response. When one experiences stress, more than 70 biological changes take place in the human body, equipping it for a quick reaction—the well-known "fight-or-flight" response. This response evolved early in human history to help hunters and gatherers handle the stressors of the usual survival crises. We have not evolved biologically as rapidly as we have socially, and the stressors of today—such as marriage, divorce, uncertainty, and project cancellations—do **not** generally create survival crises. When we do not use up the fight-or-flight preparedness our bodies have created, we establish a chronic inner tension referred to as **strain.** Obviously, punching the boss one consults with or running down the hallway screaming are not suitable responses to stressful work situations. The energy bottled up inside a person in preparation for that sort of response eventually has an erosive effect. One's health begins to deteriorate and one's ability to perform effectively declines.

Carrying around too much strain for a long period increases one's risk of becoming ill. The type of illness one contracts depends on one's genetic makeup, personality, past health history, life style habits, environment, and nature and quality of medical care. Some people develop headaches easily, whereas others develop high blood pressure, ulcers, colitis, cancer, or lower back pain.

Why do some people seem to become ill while others, who apparently experience just as much stress in life, seem unaffected? We do not yet know all the reasons. Some people **do** have stronger constitutions than others. Many people have life style habits that protect their health; poor life style habits account for more than 50% of the risks to one's health. Evidence indicates that a good network of supportive relationships also protects one's health. Apparently, one can withstand more stress and experience fewer adverse consequences if one's work—and life in general—contains sufficient **challenge**, allows one to **control** how one does things, and includes activities to which one feels **committed**.

Control, challenge, and commitment. Trainers should examine their lives and work to find evidence of these three variables. I have found that many trainers go about their jobs without much enthusiasm, whereas a few experience what they are doing as their **life's work**. The latter group, a small minority at best, consists of those who feel they have low scores reflecting strain, experience vitality and energy in their lives, and consider their training efforts to be opportunities to make their performance excellent. Those who feel they are just doing a job have high scores for strain, more frequent illnesses, and less-than-exceptional training performances.

How can you tell if you are a candidate for developing a stress-related illness and/or lowered performance capability? How can you tell how much stress is "getting to you"? Although no precise way exists for determining this—short of extensive and expensive physiological examination—the following list of conditions, taken from "The Strain Response," should help you learn your present, stress-related health risks. If you have been experiencing several of these conditions lately, you may assume that stress presently acts as a risk to your health. The more of the following items you check off as being true these days, the greater the risk:

- shortness of breath, frequent sighing;
- feeling slow, sluggish, weak;
- tiring frequently and easily;

- rapid weight gain or loss;
- changes in eating patterns or amounts;
- constipation or diarrhea;
- withdrawal from sex or overuse of sex;
- difficulty concentrating, short attention span;
- smoking or drinking more than usual;
- sleep disruption;
- headaches, physical tension;
- feeling nervous, apprehensive, or anxious;
- feeling depressed, listless, apathetic;
- irritability, misplaced anger;
- cynical, inappropriate humor;
- withdrawal from supportive relationships.

You can usually recognize a few of these as being particularly true of you during stressful periods. These are your "red flags." As a basic step in effective stress management, you should become sensitive to the occurrences of your red flag conditions. Their presence indicates that your stress levels are getting too high and that you need to avoid or remove some of the stress, cope more effectively with your unavoidable stressors, **and** build up your health to withstand stress.

Natural stress response tendencies. Unfortunately, when most people experience high levels of stress, they compound their problems by giving up their best defenses. The conditions signalling strain listed above then become self-reinforcing and extend themselves even further in a self-destructive way, further increasing the stress levels.

For example, many people withdraw from their friends during periods of high stress. When the stress is alleviated, they then "resurface" and speak, often to their friends' surprise, about what a rough period they have just completed. They seem to feel as if they must handle hard times themselves and not bother others, even if they know that effective use of support networks is one of the best stress management techniques.

Many people also allow their better nutritional habits to lapse and eat foods high in fats, sugar, and salt (i.e., highly refined or "junk" foods). At the same time, they drink or smoke more than they usually do. These behaviors, of course, create risk factors in addition to the risks associated with the stress itself.

Life style choices. Investigations of the risk factors associated with the most frequent major illnesses reveals that an average of 20% of these factors are biological, 20% environmental, and 10% attributable to health care services (e.g., drug interactions or side effects). The remaining 50% of the factors fall in the category of life style choices. That is, you can avoid or eliminate fully half of the risks to your health by making responsible life style choices. The most important thing you can do for long-term health and stress management is to control that which is controllable—your life style.

The following list notes most of the controllable risk factors:

- nutritional habits (the average American diet contains far too much fat, sugar, salt, chemicals, white flour, and caffeine);
- alcohol use (up to two drinks a day is considered moderate);
- tobacco use;
- drug use (including physician-prescribed drugs);
- amount of rest;
- relaxation habits;
- exercise (cardiovascular, stretching, and recreational);
- body weight;
- psychological outlook;
- quality of relationships;
- driving habits (seat belt use, driving speed, attitude);
- strain management;
- control of blood pressure, cholesterol, and triglycerides.

The inclusion of few, if any, of these items should be surprising. Yet most people, and trainers in particular, do not "score" very well with respect to this list. Take a few moments to assess the healthfulness of your present life style choices. When you are away from home conducting training programs, do you maintain your habits as well as you do at home? If you travel regularly, do you carry your life style with you on the road or do you use travel as an excuse to stop making healthful life style choices? Many trainers attempt to do the same things as their participants when conducting residential seminars, forgetting that the participants will go back to their normal ways of life at the conclusion of the program whereas the trainers are likely to persist in this behavior with another group of participants.

Personal planning. If you have learned that you have room for improvement in your present stress management and/or life style habits, answering the following questions will help you start enhancing your health and performance.

1. How well am I avoiding unnecessary stressors? Do I plan my time well? Do I stay away from stress carriers?
2. How well am I coping with the unavoidable stressors in my life? Do I have necessary skills for handling conflict, influence, assertiveness, and problem solving?
3. How well am I protecting and building my health? Do I promote healthy life style habits? Do I take an hour a day just for myself?
4. What do I need to continue doing?
5. What do I need to begin doing or do more frequently?
6. What do I need to cease doing or do less frequently?
7. In what specific ways can other people help me succeed in making the

changes I choose? Should I develop a buddy system, or seek challengers, encouragers, or expert advisors?

At this point, many persons decide they need to go on a total reclamation project, and end up overwhelming themselves briefly before going back to their old patterns of self-management. To overcome this tendency, keep the following in mind.

First, think of yourself as now having a project for the rest of your life: Work on one stress/health project at a time, test new ideas and habits for a month before moving on to the next project, and design each project in such a way that you know you can succeed. Second, none of the above suggestions will be of any use in the long run unless you have made a **fundamental choice** to be healthy and control your life (recall the three operating premises). Make this choice so strongly that you can actually feel yourself making it somatically. Reaffirm the choice every day. When this is done, the primary choices about life style, health, and stress management—and the secondary choices about specific behaviors, decisions, or thinking patterns—will make a huge difference. Without making this fundamental choice, you will likely experience temporary periods of gain and temporary periods of guilt, but in the long run you won't make enduring improvements in your health and stress management, and your quest for inspired performance will be frustrated.

II. An ideal work site stress management training program[1]

Undoubtedly, some of you readers are trainers who are conducting or plan to begin conducting stress management training programs. This section briefly outlines many of the key things I have learned over the years about how to make such training programs produce maximum benefits. Many of the points are, I believe, quite generic, and should enhance the success of any training program.

Whenever a training topic becomes popular, large numbers of full- and part-time trainers begin to offer such training as a part of their repertoires. Often, this results in the topic's becoming just another program of the training department. When this happens, the program generally has little lasting impact. With increasing popularity, the quantity of stress management training programs will likely increase and the quality and impact of such programs decrease in proportion. At this writing, a sizable proportion of those employed as trainers in the United States have at least a "stress module" in their repertoire, while those trained in health care are just beginning to approach the subject in large numbers.

Another serious problem is that most trainers keep themselves too busy conducting training programs to do any serious follow-up evaluations of the impact of their work. Thus, at this point, relatively little is known about the relative impact of various approaches to conducting stress management training.

One of the basic questions that should be asked of a proposed stress management training program is, "What is the true purpose of the training?" Often, these programs are created in organizations as palliatives, or as one-time efforts. They represent "the thing to do," or management offers courses on stress to do its "bit for humanity"—and therefore ceases to worry further about an unnecessarily stressful working environment. In these kinds of environments, people are forced to protect themselves from their organizations. Through six-month, post-training follow-up studies, for example, I have found consistently that following stress management training people will be getting more exercise, eating better, relaxing more, and otherwise behaving appropriately, yet feeling **less** satisfied and fulfilled at work and **less** supported on the job (Adams, Quigley, & Schmithorst, 1983, 1984). When this finding is explored further, one finds that the stress training taught people to see clearly how minor managerial adjustments could reduce the level of unnecessary stress in the work place. Yet when these people make suggestions, they are told to mind their own business or are ignored.

A large proportion of stress programs today are sold by the trainers to their companies and are offered as this year's "trick." When this is the case, the programs are most often not thought through carefully, but are merely added to the repertoire. Such programs generally have little, if any, long-range effect.

If a stress management training program is to have a strong impact on both health and performance, it needs to be conceived with and built on the clear purpose of making the system provoke less unnecessary stress, while at the same time enhancing the participants' abilities to cope and to thrive.

Each person has one of two basic life orientations, and the one that predominates among the individuals offering the stress management program will greatly determine how the program is conducted and whether or not it will be effective in the long run. The reactive/responsive orientation places the locus of control outside the individual, causing a person to react to stimuli from the environment and to respond as effectively as possible to the contraints one faces. Programs based on this orientation will teach a lot of techniques for managing stress, but will contain the implicit message that stress comes from the environment and that "you'll just have to make the best of it." Participants in such programs are unlikely to maintain long-term improvements based on this approach. Rather, the approach will ultimately reinforce their feeling they lack the power to cope effectively with a "hostile" environment.

The other orientation is the creative orientation, which views each individual as being the predominant creative force in one's own life. Programs based on this orientation focus on the underlying patterns in each person's consciousness, which greatly determine what that person gets from life. Such programs also teach participants how to develop creative orientations within themselves. Basic to this orientation is the individual's fundamental choice to be healthy. If an individual doesn't make this choice, stress management tricks will not likely be useful in the long run. A stress management program based mostly on the creative orientation is more likely to have a lasting impact on participants than is one based solely on the reactive/response orientation. (For a detailed development of these orientations, see Fritz, 1984.)

Comprehensive stress management programs must focus on both the individual and the system. On the individual level, the programs must provide an external focus on avoiding or removing unnecessary stressors and on coping effectively with those stressors that are unavoidable, or that the individual chooses not to avoid. In addition, the programs must provide an internal focus on health protection and enhancement, and on attitudinal orientation as suggested in the preceding paragraph.

These same considerations—removal, coping, health protection--also must be considered at the organizational level. What can be done within the organization to remove—or to avoid inducing—unnecessary stressors? In general, the answer is to reduce novelty (surprise or uncertainty) associated with the introduction of necessary changes and to modify stress-provoking organizational norms. What can organizations do to equip members to handle necessary stressors effectively? They can, for example, provide effective problem solving processes, training courses, and employee assistance programs. Finally, in what ways other than the stress management training program can the organization encourage good health habits? Figure 2 presents a framework for assessing stress management practices of individuals and of the organization.

Stress management responses

	The individual	The organization
Removal or avoidance		
Immediate response		
Long-term protection		

Level of response

Figure 2. Framework for assessing overall stress management effectiveness

In summary, the "ideal" stress management program receives managerial support across the organization. A feedback loop is created in which system-level ideas for reducing the number of stressors and for coping effectively with the necessary ones are encouraged and taken seriously. The training programs themselves encourage and foster the creative orientation from which individuals learn to operate from the fundamental choice to be healthy, to be the predominant creative forces in their own lives, and to have full and vibrant health.

As pointed out above, stress management training programs today often represent just another training program being offered widely. Stress management can have a major impact on individual lives and choice making and on a system's culture and functioning. The impact a stress management training program will have is largely a function of how clearly one answers the question: What results do you want?

NOTE

1. A more detailed development of this second section is available in one of my earlier works (Adams, 1986).

REFERENCES

Adams, J. (1986). Creating and maintaining comprehensive stress management training. In L. Murphy (Ed.), *Stress management training: A guide for establishing worksite programs*. Cincinnati: NIOSH.

Adams, J., Quigley, E., & Schmithorst, J. (1983). Health and stress management education in three federal agencies. *Journal of Health and Human Resources Administration, 6*(1), 100-128.

Adams, J., Quigley, E., & Schmithorst, J. (1984). Improving the health and stress management of federal workers. In D.D. Warrick (Ed.), *Contemporary organization development: Current thinking and applications* (pp. 289-307). Glenview, IL: Scott, Foresman.

Fritz, R. (1984). *The path of least resistance*. Salem, MA: DMA.

Assessment of Trainer Skills By Self, Peers, and Supervisors

Philip G. Hanson
Bernard Lubin

The increasing emphasis on continuing education during the past two decades has made professionals aware of the developmental choice of growth or stagnation. For most professionals, however, continuing education means accruing more techniques, concepts, and knowledge about their field to keep them abreast of the latest developments. Continuing education credit opportunities for trainers whose objectives are personal development and increased awareness, however, are currently scarce. This is unfortunate, as the professional who works with small groups to effect individual, group, and organizational change shares with practitioners of only a few other professions the unique need for the interaction of personal and technical skills and knowledge.

A professional trainer who has all of the technical resources for training but little self-awareness can do more harm than good when attempting to facilitate change in others. Trainers with little or no self-awareness may be insensitive to their impact on others, be unable to discriminate between their own needs and the needs of others, and lack an appreciation of their own leadership styles and how others perceive them. The professional trainers discussed here are unique in another way: To avoid burnout and to continually improve service to their clients, these trainers need periodic refreshment through experiences of increased awareness, rediscovery, and a deepening of personal insights and feedback on the development of skills that have been achieved previously. Therefore, one must maintain an ongoing, self-assessment program to increase one's awareness of self along many behavioral dimensions and to increase one's sensitivity to the behavior of others.

Fortunately, in programs to develop trainers, provided by training organizations such as NTL Institute, opportunities are provided—indeed are

©1987 NTL Institute. All rights reserved.

mandatory—for prospective trainers to experience the process of receiving feedback on their behaviors in a group setting. They do this first as participants in a T Group, receiving feedback from group members and the group leader on their effectiveness as a group member; later, as cotrainers they receive feedback from senior trainers and staff members on their leadership styles; and finally, as trainers, they receive feedback on their effectiveness as a training team member. Although these occasions provide excellent opportunities to increase trainers' awareness of themselves and their impact on others, their leadership styles, and their perceptiveness in picking up the behavioral cues of others, they are not frequent enough to allow for ongoing monitoring or self-assessment, and they usually occur only during the period of trainer preparation.[1]

The thrust of this article, therefore, is to suggest a program for self-development in which trainers can set their own personal goals and monitor their own progress. Some of our underlying assumptions (untested) are that trainers would like to learn more about themselves and to become involved in assessing their own performance, and that monitoring changes in behavior, skills, knowledge, and attitudes leads to deeper involvement in and responsibility for one's growth. The following suggestions are addressed to the person in the process of trainer development and to the trainer who wishes to become involved in a redevelopment or continued development program.

To assist in a personal learning or self-development plan, some tools are presented to aid you in identifying and thinking about significant trainer behaviors, skills, knowledge, and attitudes. Once these have been identified, you must assess where you are now and where you would like to be. Items of interest can then be checked out with peers, supervisors, and subordinates, and in training sessions with group or workshop participants. The scales can be modified or items can be added to suit your own needs and the situation in which the items are to be used. We describe three sets of scales focusing on different situations in which you may want to assess your own behaviors and receive feedback.

The first set of scales is primarily a self-assessment tool, which should alert you to various dimensions of your own behaviors and your awareness of the extent to which you practice them. The second set aims to monitor your behavior at specific meetings in which you are participating. The third set can be used to get feedback on your leadership style in T Groups, therapy groups, or other groups in which you play a leadership role. Finally, we present a format to facilitate an ongoing record of periodic self-assessments and feedback sessions.

Most people endorse the idea of increasing personal effectiveness as a goal for themselves. These goals, however, are usually vague, too global to implement, or highly idealistic—and often unattainable. A more practical and realistic approach is to specify the desired areas of personal development and particular behaviors within those areas. Once they have identified a sampling of behaviors within each area, individuals can assess their own current status with respect to these behaviors. In setting personal goals, you must diagnose your **present** status (where you are **now**) regarding an item of behavior before you can determine where you would **like to be**. Using a scale for this process helps make the assessment objective and enables the individual to measure movement toward or away from the goals. In addition, guessing how other people would see you on each item provides an anchor for your self-assessment, making it more realistic. Individuals may then choose to get feedback on these ratings from people who know them, as a way to check their own assessments. Another purpose of this instrument is to stimulate thinking and self-examination about many aspects of oneself that ordinarily might be overlooked. The sample of items in each area might serve as a stimulus to alert the individual to her or his style of interacting with oneself and the world and to some of the basic attitudes, expectations, and values behind these interactions. As a consequence, the individual develops an increased awareness of self and others and of the process of change.

Listed on the following pages is a sample of items representing goals.[2] These items should help you to think about different aspects of yourself in relation to others and to groups in which you hold membership.

Complete the scales by doing the following:

- Read through the list and **circle** the number for each item that best represents the extent to which you do the activity described (i.e., how you see yourself **now**).
- Draw a square around the number for each item that represents where you would like to be.
- Place a check mark over the number for each item that represents a guess as to how other people see you according to that item.
- In the blank items write in additional goals that are important to you but are not listed.
- Review the list and check three or four goals that you would like to work on at this time.

The word "noting" is used in many of the items of the self-assessment scales, or else it is implied. By the term noting we mean staying alert to whatever is happening in the here and now without judging, interpreting, or evaluating the experience. Noting is "being with" the experience of the present moment and attending to whatever arises during that moment. The process of noting helps to keep the "figure" sharp and clear, distinct from its surrounding "ground" (to use Gestalt terminology), and allows the experience of emerging and submerging figures to flow without hindering them.

1. Self-Assessment and Goals for Personal Development

A. *Awareness of self*	*Not at all*				*Very much*
1. Noting how I am feeling	1	2	3	4	5
2. Noting my body sensations	1	2	3	4	5
3. Noting my body postures, gestures, and movements	1	2	3	4	5

4. Noting any spontaneous or involuntary
   imagery that occurs in my "mind's eye"   1   2   3   4   5

5. Noting streams and patterns of
   thoughts as they occur   1   2   3   4   5

6. Noting what attitudes or expectations
   are present toward myself   1   2   3   4   5

7. Noting what attitudes or expectations
   are present toward others   1   2   3   4   5

8. Noting what criticisms, evaluations, or
   judgments I make about myself   1   2   3   4   5

9. Noting what criticisms, evaluations,
   or judgments I make about others   1   2   3   4   5

10. Noting whether or not I give reasons,
    explanations, or justifications
    for my behavior   1   2   3   4   5

11. Noting to what extent I am owning and
    accepting my feelings, attitudes, beliefs, etc. 1   2   3   4   5

12. Noting how I react to praise or
    criticism   1   2   3   4   5

13. Noting how I react to being assisted
    or helped   1   2   3   4   5

14. Noting how I react to being hindered
    or blocked   1   2   3   4   5

15. Noting differences when I am making
    an observation (e.g., you are frowning)
    or an interpretation (e.g., you are angry)
    of another's behavior   1   2   3   4   5

16. _____   1   2   3   4   5

17. _____   1   2   3   4   5

18. _____   1   2   3   4   5

B. *Awareness of others*   *Not at all*   *Very much*

1. Noting the feelings of others   1   2   3   4   5

2. Noting through what media feelings are
   expressed (e.g., verbal, nonverbal)   1   2   3   4   5

3. Noting differences between expression
   of feelings versus thoughts or perceptions   1   2   3   4   5

4. Noting how others handle feelings expressed
   to them   1   2   3   4   5

5. Noting body postures, movements, facial
   expressions   1   2   3   4   5

6. Noting style of verbal expression (e.g.,
   rapid, slow, soft, loud, rising, dropping,
   gesturing, incomplete sentences)   1   2   3   4   5

7. Noting shifts in style of verbal expression	1	2	3	4	5
8. Noting to what extent others use observations versus interpretations as a way of describing behavior	1	2	3	4	5
9. Noting to what extent others judge or evaluate, as opposed to describe, behavior	1	2	3	4	5
10. Noting how others receive feedback (e.g., defend or explain their behavior versus asking for clarification, checking with others, accepting it openly)	1	2	3	4	5
11. Noting most frequent reference points (e.g., self, others, past, present, future) in others' communication	1	2	3	4	5
12. Noting how others handle emotional situations such as praise, conflict, closeness, anger, affection, etc.	1	2	3	4	5
13. Noting to what extent others express feelings directly (e.g., "I like you")	1	2	3	4	5
14. Noting to what extent others express feelings indirectly (e.g., "You are likable")	1	2	3	4	5
15. Noting repetitive themes characteristic of others (e.g., always making comparisons, undervaluing self or others)	1	2	3	4	5

C. *Communication*

	Not at all				Very much
1. Telling others what I think	1	2	3	4	5
2. Telling others how I feel	1	2	3	4	5
3. Being **clear** about what I **intend** to communicate	1	2	3	4	5
4. Striving to understand others	1	2	3	4	5
5. Listening attentively to what others are saying	1	2	3	4	5
6. Hearing others out	1	2	3	4	5
7. Drawing others out	1	2	3	4	5
8. Giving an indication that I heard what was said	1	2	3	4	5
9. Asking for clarification when I'm not sure I understand	1	2	3	4	5
10. Repeating what is said to make certain I heard the communication correctly	1	2	3	4	5
11. Stopping the "noise in my head"(i.e., thinking about what I'm going to say, judging, evaluating) and focusing on the other person	1	2	3	4	5
12. Noting my attitudes and intentions when I am not communicating clearly	1	2	3	4	5

13. Noting how and when I slant my communication in order for it to be what I think the other person wants to hear	1	2	3	4	5
14. Noting how and when I slant my communication in order for others to accept the image I want to project	1	2	3	4	5
15. Noting the process (**how** we are communicating) of communication as well as the content (**what** we are communicating)	1	2	3	4	5

© 1985 Hanlu Associates, Houston, Texas

2. Personal Goals for This Meeting

Under each goal listed, circle the scale number that best describes your intention before the group meeting. After the meeting, circle the scale number that best describes the extent to which you think you met your goals. You may share these ratings (or the ones you are most interested in) with others and get their feedback. Ask how they saw your behavior, in relation to the items you selected, during the meeting.

		Not at all				*Very much*
1. Do I actively listen to others? Hear people out? Try to understand? Ask for clarification?	Before: After:	1 1	2 2	3 3	4 4	5 5
2. Do I draw others out? Help silent people come in?	Before: After:	1 1	2 2	3 3	4 4	5 5
3. Do I attend to others' feelings?	Before: After:	1 1	2 2	3 3	4 4	5 5
4. Do I tend to take charge of the group? Dominate? Crowd others out?	Before: After:	1 1	2 2	3 3	4 4	5 5
5. Do I tend to talk too much? Cut others off? Interrupt?	Before: After:	1 1	2 2	3 3	4 4	5 5
6. Do I stay with the group, and not jump to other topics or go off on tangents?	Before: After:	1 1	2 2	3 3	4 4	5 5
7. Do I tend to be silent? Not speak my mind? Not let others know where I stand?	Before: After:	1 1	2 2	3 3	4 4	5 5
8. Do I tend to speak for myself and not for others, encouraging others to do the same?	Before: After:	1 1	2 2	3 3	4 4	5 5
9. Do I express my own feelings?	Before: After:	1 1	2 2	3 3	4 4	5 5

© 1985 Hanlu Associates, Houston, Texas

---

3. Group Leader Feedback

Rate your group leader on each item below according to the following scale:

1. very little of the time
2. some of the time
3. a little less than half of the time
4. about half of the time
5. a little more than half of the time
6. most of the time
7. almost all of the time

_____ Leader attends to, and accepts, feelings that group members express.

_____ Leader appears open and receptive, is able to accept feedback about her or his own behavior.

_____ Leader listens carefully to what group members say, asks for clarification or checks for understanding.

_____ Leader expresses her or his own feelings, even when negative.

_____ Leader helps others to express their feelings, both positive and negative.

_____ Leader keeps group on target, brings group members back to topic or issue when they wander.

_____ Leader responds openly and frankly; you know where he or she stands.

_____ Leader handles conflict and strong feelings directly, does not change subject or smooth over the problem.

_____ Leader is aware of and understands what is going on in the group.

_____ Leader is willing to take risks, confronts others, takes a stand, sticks neck out.

_____ Leader is supportive of group members, checks to see where others are and how they are feeling.

_____ Leader checks to see who is not participating, encourages silent persons to talk.

_____ Leader is warm and easy to approach, does not appear distant and aloof.

_____ Leader is willing to share leadership with group members, accepts ideas and suggestions and acts on them.

_____ Leader expresses herself or himself clearly, is easily understood.

_____ Leader appears comfortable in the group, has an air of self-confidence, and appears to trust her or his own judgment.

_____ Leader is objective and nonjudgmental, does not evaluate others as right or wrong, good or bad.

_____ Leader explores her or his own feelings, values and perceptions of self when relevant to the group; processing always includes her or his here-and-now experiences when appropriate to the group.

Comments:_____

© 1985 Hanlu Associates, Houston, Texas

Review the ratings you made for yourself and the ratings you received from others. Place asterisks by those items you would like to select as goals to work on. Using the Work Sheet for Monitoring Goals given below, list these goals and rank them in order of which ones you want to work on first. Then ask yourself the following questions and note your responses.

- Is there a common thread running through the goals? Can I group them according to some underlying common features?
- Are there any that tend to be general as opposed to reflecting specific situations? That is, are they typical of me in a variety of situations, or do some crop up only in specific situations? If the latter is true, describe these situations.
- If I work on one goal, how will it affect the others?
- What are some events (e.g., a T Group, a staff meeting, an interaction with a support or resource person, a workshop, a group therapy session) coming up during which I can test some of these goals?
- Who can I use as a resource to get feedback on these goals?

Once you have listed the goals and ranked them, place an "x" on the scale reflecting how you see yourself now. Do this rating for each goal. You can judge from the three scales presented above how you rated yourself for an item (i.e., low, medium, or high).

Work Sheet for Monitoring Goals

Rank	Goal		Check points							
			Now	*1*	*2*	*3*	*4*	*5*	*6*	*7*
____	A. _____	High:	___	___	___	___	___	___	___	___
		Medium:	___	___	___	___	___	___	___	___
		Low:	___	___	___	___	___	___	___	___
____	B _____	High:	___	___	___	___	___	___	___	___
		Medium:	___	___	___	___	___	___	___	___
		Low:	___	___	___	___	___	___	___	___
____	C. _____	High:	___	___	___	___	___			___
		Medium:	___	___	___	___	___	___	___	___
		Low:	___	___	___	___	___	___	___	___
____	D. _____	High:	___	___	___	___	___	___	___	___
		Medium:	___	___	___	___	___	___	___	___
		Low:	___	___	___	___	___	___	___	___

```
_____  E. _____    High:   ___  ___  ___  ___  ___  ___  ___  ___
                         Medium:   ___  ___  ___  ___  ___  ___  ___  ___
                            Low:   ___  ___  ___  ___  ___  ___  ___  ___

_____  F. _____    High:   ___  ___  ___  ___  ___  ___       ___
                         Medium:   ___  ___  ___  ___  ___  ___  ___  ___
                            Low:   ___  ___  ___  ___  ___  ___  ___  ___
```

Identify the next event you will attend at which you can test or get feedback on some of these goals. Decide which goals will be relevant to the event. Note this event as check point 1 on the Check Point Identification Chart given below, specifying where and when the event will occur. Specify your goal(s) by placing the designated letters(s) from the Work Sheet for Monitoring Goals in the appropriate column on the Check Point Identification Chart. Note that more than one goal can be addressed during a single check point. Give a date for the event so that you will have a record of time between events.

Check Point Identification Chart

Check Points	Goals	Situation	Where	When
1.				
2.				
3.				
4.				
5.				
6.				
7.				

Develop your plan for getting feedback on your goals at the first check point. For example, use only scales relevant to the goals you are testing and have people rate you.

After you have collected the data for check point 1, judge where on the scale the data reflects your ratings and place an "x" to represent low, medium, or high.

Repeat the process for check points 2, 3, and so forth as they occur.

Finally, you need to set criteria for knowing when you have achieved a goal (e.g., two or three "high" ratings on consecutive check points). Remember: Once you have achieved your criteria for a goal, this does not mean that you can forget about the goal from then on. Ignoring goals that have been achieved can result in slipping from "high" to "low" for those behaviors. Growth is a never-ending process of setting goals, implementing them, getting feedback on them, achieving them, and continuously monitoring behaviors reflecting these goals.

The tools and format presented above may be modified to suit your particular needs. If they stimulate your thinking about your own development and act as an incentive to developing your own system, then our work will have achieved its purpose. The key ingredient is the motivation of the trainer or consultant and her or his commitment to a self-development program. Without this commitment, the most sophisticated development program is useless, and the time, energy and creativity spent implementing it is wasted. Professionals in the helping professions must subject themselves to the same self-scrutiny they encourage clients to undertake. Accepting the charge of learning about yourself and, as a consequence, increasing your sensitivity to others is a hallmark of laboratory education.

NOTES

1. Both NTL Institute, through its routine staff-peer feedback process, and Certified Consultants International (CCI) in its peer review and re-review processes, provide some opportunities for feedback.

2. The Self-Assessment and Goals for Personal Development scale used in this article are taken from our previously developed instrument (Hanson & Lubin, 1980). They represent three of ten items from the entire instrument. The other areas are: Giving and Receiving Feedback, Interpersonal Relations, Group Observation Skills, Support Systems, Handling Negative Feelings, Risk Taking, and General: A Way of Being.

REFERENCE

Hanson, P.G., & Lubin, B. (1980). *Self-assessment and goals for personal development.* Houston, TX: Hanlu Associates.

Section III.
Dynamics of Training and Learning

Elements of Laboratory Education Related to Clinical Incidents[1]

Birge D. Reichard

One of the great concerns of laboratory education is the prevention of a clinical incident during a program. Available evidence[2] indicates that only about one percent of all participants experience a distress reaction leading to a clinical incident during a program. Furthermore, a review of those incidents shows that in most cases the participant imported to the program with the ingredients for an episode rather than its being caused by the laboratory experience. Nevertheless, professional and ethical considerations dictate that every possible measure be taken to preclude such an occurrence. This article addresses such preventive measures.

The evolution of the laboratory method inevitably led to some lack of clarity about the distinction between laboratory learning and psychotherapy. The two fields are a fine example of a paradox—that is, they are separate yet related. This article focuses on how they are separate. Laboratory training is an educational methodology that has differentiated itself from a medical, curative, or disease model of change. The article discusses the importance of making and meeting learning contracts by both the sponsoring institution of the laboratory training event and the individual trainer. The article also addresses the impact of the individual trainer's style on managing stress during laboratory training.

What is a clinical incident?

For this article, a clinical incident is defined as the behavioral outcome of a distress experience, or the behavior of a group member or trainer that is not congruent with the norms of the learning program and environment. These are not mental health definitions, for the assumed purpose of laboratory training is

©1987 NTL Institute. All rights reserved.

learning rather than psychological change. Although the anxiety of a member or
trainer allows one to be aware of an impending incident, the above definitions
go beyond the simple presence of stress or anxiety.

One must consider the context of the specific behavior. An inability to have
one's needs met in the environment of a particular laboratory program does not
necessarily reflect an inability to do so in other environments. Nor do the definitions assume that a trainer is aware of all the unmet needs or incongruent
behaviors of group members. They do assume, however, that appropriate
behavior can be detemined for particular programs. Sometimes a clinical
incident arises from a person's being in the wrong place at the wrong time, rather
than from mental illness or psychopathology. One should also note that distress
is different from stress. A proper amount of stress is a necessary ingredient for
laboratory learning, and indeed for effective living.

Laboratory training versus therapy

Following the development of the T Group during Kurt Lewin's workshop on
race relations in Connecticut in 1946, laboratory training—and the T Group in
particular—evolved over time. In 1947, the Connecticut workshop participants
met in Bethel, Maine, to follow up on their experience of the previous summer,
and so National Training Laboratories (now called NTL Institute) was founded.
NTL and laboratory education became synonymous.

Among the modifications to the "original" laboratory experience was the
gradual but sure departure from Kurt Lewin's social change and larger system
orientation toward an interpersonal and intrapersonal focus. This may have
resulted because a large number of clinicians constituted much of the faculty for
laboratory education at that time, but it surely also reflected the influence of
psychoanalytic and other personality theories that were so prevalent during the
1940s and 1950s. From the early days of laboratory education, the method was—
fortunately or unfortunately—associated with individual and group psychotherapy.

Both psychotherapy groups and human relations training groups such as the
T Group deal with learning or cognitive change. In addition, therapy groups intend to deal with psychological change—that is, altered coping capacity or personality structure. Both kinds of groups work on both kinds of change to some
degree, but usually an implicit or explicit priority is given to one at the expense
of the other, and the contract between group leaders and participants is specified
accordingly. A classic article by Singer, Astrachan, Gould, and Klein (1975)
describes the kinds of groups, their goals, issues, leader behaviors, and the
overlap among the different kinds. Some groups focus more on affect or the
participants' emotions; some focus more on perception; some focus more on
values; some focus more on cognition or "thinking." The **mix** of affective, perceptual, aspirational-volitional (value), and cognitive factors varies according to the
objectives of a particular laboratory (Benne, Bradford, Gibb, & Lippitt, 1975).
For example, encounter groups focus more on affective material at an

intrapersonal level, whereas T Groups focus more on affective and cognitive material at an **interpersonal** level.

Boundaries represent the delineation point between the end of one thing and the beginning of another. Most boundaries in psychological functioning need to be permeable—that is, they need to be strong enough to delineate the entities that meet, yet permeable enough to allow entities to integrate. At an intrapsychic level, an example is the need to recognize the difference between a thought and a feeling and yet be able to integrate the two to produce congruent behavior. The trainer's job in laboratory education is to maintain the focus (boundary) of the group, yet allow for sensible overlap. For example, a program may be designed for learning about group process, yet one cannot learn about group process without understanding the impact of her or his own behavior on those processes and vice versa. Thus, a group-focused laboratory experience will inevitably include some examination of interpersonal behavior, just as an interpersonally focused laboratory experience will inevitably include some examination of group dynamics.

Given the above, one should not be surprised that the boundary between education and therapy is permeable in many kinds of laboratory training events. The premise still remains that laboratory training is an educational activity, not psychotherapy, and that it is not a substitute for psychotherapy. The term "group therapy for normals" (Weschler, Massarik, & Tannenbaum, 1962, p. 34), however, provides evidence of the difficulty in clearly dividing laboratory learning from psychotherapy.

A closer look at the schema of Singer et al. (1975) provides a starting point for exploring laboratory training as education rather than therapy. Figure 1 on the next page illustrates how the various kinds of groups relate to the continuum ranging from learning (cognitive change) to psychological change (altered coping capacity or personality structure). A Tavistock Institute program (of the nonmedical variety) would be an example of 1b in this figure, a Gestalt therapy group would be an example of 1d, and a weight watchers group an example of 1f. Encounter groups would fall under 1c, and T Groups under 1a. Because laboratory education focuses on learning more than on psychological change, groups labeled 1a and 1b are easily placed in the category of laboratory education. The kinds of groups that fit clearly in the category of psychological change are not laboratory education groups, even if they use some laboratory training methods. The greyest area between laboratory education and psychotherapy is represented by 1c—the area of the encounter group and personal growth.

Even in this area, laboratory education programs can be differentiated from therapy because participants are not called patients, the trainer facilitates learning rather than psychological change, and the action research—or "learning to learn"—concept is the principal vehicle for learning rather than, for example, a guided exploration or uncovering of one's formative years. Laboratory education focuses on the "here and now" and restricts the exploration of behavior to that particular group at that particular time. The trainer's commitment to the participants lasts for the brief duration of the program, not for the time that would

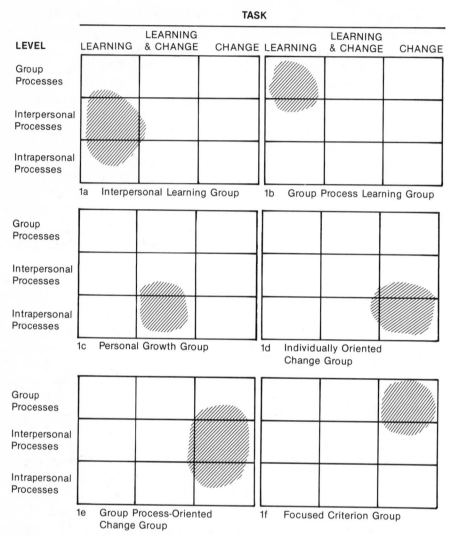

Figure 1. Task and level in the six types of small group events
(Reprinted from Singer, Astrachan, Gould, & Klein, 1975, p. 144)

be required for participants to incorporate psychological change into a repertoire of altered responses.

The importance of the learning contract

Participants come to laboratory programs for a variety of reasons, and some are as unclear to them as the middle ground between learning and psychological change on the continuum discussed above. The principal means for managing both the program and the kinds of appropriate participation in it is the contract between participants and both the sponsoring institution and the individual trainer. The contract is one of the primary means of preventing a person from being in the wrong place at the wrong time.

The importance of the administrative tasks of describing a program in a promotion brochure or annoucement is often underestimated. The description begins the development of an implicit contract for the inquiry or potential participant. Sponsoring institutions that write broad, nonspecific program descriptions—whether they do so to allow individual trainers greater personal freedom in designing and conducting the program, or so as to include all possible audiences—are, even if unwittingly, contributing to the confusion of participants who wish to place themselves and their psychological development in someone else's hands. Furthermore, unclear description and the implicit or, preferably, explicit contract are positive forms of boundary management. From the outset, some form of boundary management is important.

The responsibilities of the trainer

The individual trainer also has a responsibility to meet the contract. First, the trainer should present the kind of program described in the brochure by the sponsoring organization. Learning programs should have learning goals, and those goals—not the trainer's personal interests—should be the object of the activities. Above all, trainers should not use a laboratory training event as a means of gathering together a group of persons with whom to practice psychotherapy, even if some of the participants, for reasons mentioned earlier, are eager to do so.

Second, the trainer should act in ways congruent with the program and the predictable dynamics of groups. For example, a group process laboratory becomes insidiously confusing if the trainer intervenes mostly at the inter-personal or intrapersonal levels. Another example of incongruent behavior occurs when a trainer's own needs result in excessive affection during the inclusion stage of group development. This can exacerbate feelings of being "out of step" in some participants who may already feel unsure about being accepted.

During laboratory education, the trainer is like a manager who specifies a task to be done (learning goal), clarifies the role and responsibilities associated with carrying out the task, contracts with others on these matters, and continual-ly monitors adherence to the contract. As with any leadership activity, part of the trainer's monitoring task includes monitoring her or his own personal needs and predispositions and keeping them from transcending the commitments of the contract.

By doing the above, the individual trainer can do a great deal to prevent clinical incidents from arising during the laboratory program. These actions help a prospective participant choose programs appropriately and help the entering participant have appropriate expectations and manage her or his behavior in ways appropriate to the program.

The importance of screening

The issue of screening individuals has already been introduced above in mentioning unknown motives or goals of applicants to laboratory education programs. As noted, sponsoring institutions have a responsibility to clearly describe the programs so that applicants will know what they are contracting for and can make an informed commitment to explore specific matters. The sponsor also must help applicants articulate their learning goals, which can be useful for deciding whether an appropriate fit exists between the applicant and the program.

If an applicant has a history of undergoing psychotherapy, the nature of this therapy should be determined to decide whether the program would be appropriate for the applicant. Some believe that asking the applicant to secure her or his therapist's agreement to the applicant's participation in the program is not a good practice. This practice, however, serves both the institution's and the applicant's interests. Although some applicants may present inaccurate or even dishonest information, the requirement usually allows the institution to secure better information on which to make a decision for admission. Many therapists wish to participate in a decision to engage in laboratory education; certainly they have an extraordinary interest in their clients' welfare.

This is not simply a matter of having applicants secure the "permission" of their therapists to attend the program. Rather, they need to discuss with their therapists their learning goals. In this way contact with the therapist can help both the applicant and the institution. Learning goals serve not only to clarify the appropriateness of the program for the individual, but also begin to set the applicant's expectations, which—if identified—can be useful to the applicant, the institution, and the trainer. Properly designed application forms contain information that can genuinely assist trainers in preventing a clinical incident, and in managing the program.

The impact of the trainer's style

The variable over which trainers have the most control, and for which they must assume most respsonsibility, is their own behavior during a laboratory program. A major factor in preventing and managing clinical incidents during laboratory programs is the individual trainer's style. Lieberman, Yalom, and Miles (1973) discuss the impact of a leaders or trainer's behavior on program participants.

Deviance is commonly considered a clue useful for identifying a distressed participant. The norms from which participants deviate, however, are largely under the trainer's control. To what degree is conformity to the leader's own style a measure of a participant's fit with the program? More specifically—using the above definitions of a clinical incident—to what degree is behavior considered congruent with the learning environment actually behavior that has been subtly shaped to be congruent with the leader's? Besides failure to achieve unrealistic goals (Lieberman et al., 1973, p. 196)—which relates to the above discussion on learning goals—"lab casualties" often experience rejection (p. 195) and coercion (p. 197). How far can the behavior of participants deviate from the leader's style before it is considered inappropriate, and eventually causes participants to see themselves as deviant?

If oppressive, a trainer's style can negatively affect participants not only with respect to their learning, but also with respect to their self-management. Clinical incidents have been found to occur more often when trainers are distant, aggressive stimulaters (Lieberman et al., 1973, p. 244), or are highly controlling in their group management (p. 244). The style posing the highest risk is that of the charismatic leader who is an intense emotional stimulater (p. 245). A high-risk training style, combined with an unclear contract and a participant whose learning goals are either inappropriate for the program or unspecified (meaning they cannot help manage the participant's psychological boundary), is a powerful combination capable of producing "deviance." Under such circumstances, who can say that a deviant participant suffers from psychopathology? This is an especially appropriate question given laboratory education's orientation toward education rather than psychological change.

The laboratory setting

In addition to all the variables discussed above that relate to participant behavior, the physical setting of the laboratory program must be considered. Such programs are usually conducted in "retreat" settings that minimize distraction and let the learning environment be managed effectively. This different environment evokes different thoughts and feelings, and provides another unfamiliar experience for the participant to manage.

Summary

Clinical incidents occur during laboratory education for many reasons. Programs may not be described adequately, causing the psychological contract between the participant and the nature of the program to be unclear. The trainer may not reconfirm or carry out the program contract. The trainer's style may result in norms to which an individual cannot, or will not, conform. The individual may import inappropriate issues before the group that were not screened by the institution, or which the trainer did not screen properly. When the "unfreezing" part of a laboratory program occurs, the previously "healthy" participant may exhibit behavior incongruent with the norms of the learning program and environment.

Rarely does a clinical incident result from any single ingredient. Rather, an incident is more often the confluence of several factors. Most of the reasons for a clinical incident, however, can be identified and prevented. In addition, the trainer has available numerous strategies for managing disruptions—such as recontracting, setting goals, or modifying the participant's style—and thereby enabling the program and laboratory education to continue for everyone.

NOTES

1. This article stems from a book in process by B. D. Reichard, R.C. Lippincott, P. Rodenhauser, and C. M. F. Siewers, *Understanding and Managing Stress in Laboratory Education.*

2. The source for this article consists of records for NTL Institute program participants for 1984.

REFERENCES

Benne, K. D., Bradford, L. P., Gibb, J. R., & Lippitt, R. (1975). *The laboratory method of changing and learning.* Palo Alto, CA: Science and Behavior Books.

Lieberman, M. A., Yalom, I. D., & Miles, M. B. (1973). *Encounter groups: First facts.* New York: Basic Books.

Singer, D. L., Astrachan, B. M., Gould, L. J., & Klein, E. G. (1975). Boundary management in psychological work with groups. *Journal of Applied Behavioral Science, 11*(2), 137-176.

Wechsler, I. R., Massarik, F., & Tannebaum, R. (1962). The self in process: A sensitivity training emphasis. In I. R. Wechsler & E. H. Schein (Eds.), *Issues in training.* Washington, DC: National Training Laboratories.

Game, Schmame!
What Have I Learned?

Lawrence C. Porter

A good friend and colleague of mine tells this story:

> A number of years ago, when I was teaching in the public schools, I
> decided to try using some of these "teaching games" I'd heard about. The
> students loved them, and my classes were always among the most popular
> at the school. Then one day I heard one of my students talking to another
> student, who asked her what we did in my class. "Oh," my student
> replied, "We have a great time. We do a lot of really neat things. I don't
> know what we're supposed to learn, but we have a terrific time!" That's
> when I decided I'd better learn something about what I was doing with
> all these "neat" games!

In short, the extraction-of-learnings/applications segment of any structured
activity is essential to—indeed, not to be separated from—the thinking of any
competent trainer. Still, all too frequently inexperienced trainers will focus on the
activity itself to the extent of using up all or most of their available time, leaving
little or no time for deriving learnings and applications from the activity.

In the early days of my training, I **would** leave time for processing learnings
and applications because I had been well taught that this was important—but I
had not been well taught **how** to do this. I had no formal, conscious model for
helping persons derive learnings and applications from their workshop experiences. As a result, sometimes the processing went just fine (I suppose at those
times I unconsciously "did it right"), whereas at other times it went badly,
rambling because it had no clear focus, directions, or outcomes. Moreover, I
never knew why it went well one time and badly another.

What I lacked, of course, was a clear idea as to how people learn and a
conscious, valid process based on this that produces insights, the confirmation
of previous learnings, and a sense of how these can be used in participants' lives.
Patience, determination, and a willingness to work hard were not enough; I
needed a model, and the ability to use it.

©1987 NTL Institute. All rights reserved.

I now am convinced that three things are absolutely necessary if one is to use "experience" legitimately as a learning vehicle.

- The trainer must have a clear idea as to the learning objectives of the activity and be committed to those objectives.
- Enough time must be allotted for participants to derive learnings and applications from the activity.
- Participants must be conscientiously guided through a series of steps that are consistent with how most persons learn through experience.

I emphasize this in this article by using the term "structured activity" to refer to the **entire** learning process and the term "experience" to refer only to the first phase of the process. I hope that inexperienced trainers will thus be encouraged to view a "learning activity"—a structured experience, role play, or activity using an instrument—as an entire **learning cycle** rather than merely the first segment of such a cycle.

The learning cycle

Many models describe the learning process.[1] The one with which I am most familiar, and use almost exclusively in my own work, is that developed by Bill Pfeiffer and John Jones (see Pfeiffer & Jones, 1983, pp. 3-8). In the remainder of this article I refer to this model, although I change some of the terminology to employ words that I find more suitable than those employed in the original publication discussing the model.

Figure 1 on the next page illustrates this model. Following this figure, I explicate each of the steps to the model.

Phase I: Experiencing

The five-phase model commences with some kind of experience, which is intended to "generate data." This might be what is commonly called a "structured experience," a role play, or completion of an instrument (e.g., FIRO-B). Selection of the experience, of course, is determined by the learning objectives. Just what does the trainer want the participants to learn from this activity?

In establishing the timing for the entire learning activity, the trainer must assess in advance the duration and "power" of any given activity so as to ensure that participants will have sufficient time to "process" it well. No correlation necessarily exists between the amount of time required by the experiential portion of the learning cycle (Phase I) and the amount of emotional, intellectual, and or psychological energy it may generate in participants. Some brief experiences can generate high affect, as most trainers have learned during their work. The trainer must use her or his own experience to assess how much processing time will be needed, or else depend upon the experience of others.[2] One should never skimp on processing. If time is limited, it is much more effective—and responsible—either to modify the desired experience to shorten it, or to choose instead an experience that is shorter or produces a lower affect.

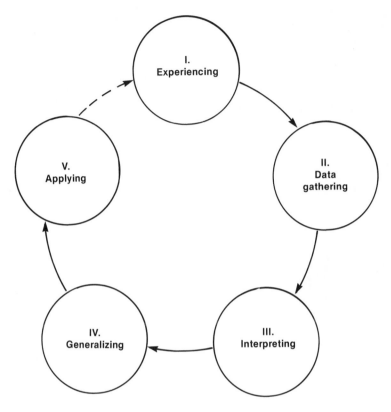

Figure 1. The learning cycle model

Phase II: Data gathering

When the experience is completed, the data-gathering phase (Phase II) begins.[3] During this phase, participants are asked to report **what happened** during that activity—and only what happened (i.e., thoughts, feelings, what persons did and said, and the like). This can be done in any way the trainer considers suitable: Persons can call out data, participants can be assigned to small groups to report data to one another and then share this with the entire group, persons can write down their "experience of the experience" and then report this, or other methods.[4] Typically, this information is recorded on newsprint on a flip chart, because it becomes the basis of what follows.

During this phase it is important to retain one's focus. If this is not done, the process may get off track, making it difficult to help participants discover learnings and applications. Remember: The intent of this phase is to get the participants to recall and report **what happened** during the learning activity, and

only this. Persons will commonly either move back to the experience and begin discussing it, or leap ahead to interpretations, learnings, and the like. When this happens the trainer must help return the participants to the matter at hand. A constant swinging back and forth among the various phases will muddy the entire learning process.

Gathering **sufficient** data is also important, for this phase provides the building block for learning. Skimpy amounts of data will make succeeding steps difficult or impossible, so gather as much as possible without running the process into the ground. Record it using your best trainer style. Make sure it is data, not interpretations. Make sure it arises from the experience, not from theories. Write down exactly what the participants say, not your own interpretations or modifications (the participants, not the trainer, should "own" the data). The data will come forth more easily if trainers don't interfere in the process by trying to make interpretations or by worrying about getting "just the right word." Play Sergeant Friday of "Dragnet"; seek "just the facts, Ma'am."

At the same time, trainers may need to help participants to ensure they provide **all** relevant data. For example, if the first two or three pieces of information are positive, with the group following this lead, the trainer may need to make a statement such as, "I see a lot of 'positive' reactions here. Were there any 'negative' ones?" In another example, the group may only provide the thoughts and feelings of individuals, and so the trainer should ask such questions as, "What did you observe happening with other persons?" The facilitator can also help shape data for the next step. For example, if the group has just experienced a "blind walk," the trainer may begin Phase II by displaying a flip chart with headings asking for four kinds of data: "sighted, negative," "sighted, positive," "unsighted, negative," and "unsighted, positive." For some other experience, the chart could solicit "what I thought," "what I felt," "what I saw and heard."

One cannot provide a complete or "correct" list of the ways trainers can obtain data.[5] The main principle is that the trainer is always free to assist participants as they provide data, but the data must always represent their **own** experience.

Phase III: Interpreting

I call the next phase (Phase III) "interpreting" because I believe this word best captures the essence of what is done during this step.[6] During this phase the trainer should intend to help participants make sense of the data reported in the preceding phase. This is an important step—for many trainers and participants the most difficult one—and probably the one most commonly not done well or even taken at all. Even though the trainer may see "latent" learnings running through the data like a thin layer of gold in a chunk of ore, he or she must resist the temptation to move directly to learnings before helping participants put the raw data into meaningful forms by perceiving patterns, sequences, trends, dynamics, or groupings.

In addition, the trainer must sometimes keep participants themselves from leaping prematurely into Phase IV, the "generalizing" phase. They should not make this move until they have as fully as possible explored and understood ("interpreted") the dynamics of the experience. The more the experience has involved participants—that is, excited them—the more impatient they may be with going through all the steps leading to learnings and applications. Therefore, ironically, the better the choice of learning experience and the more participants have been seized by it, the harder trainers may have to work to help the participants derive learnings and applications from it.

In this phase, the focus moves from what happened to how one makes sense of what happened. Examples of relevant questions include the following: "As you look at this data, what patterns do you see?" "What do you make of that?" "How can we account for that?" "What 'pops' off the page for you?" "Into what meaningful 'bins' does the data fit?" "What matches do you see?" Other questions may occur to the trainer as he or she looks at the accumulated data.

The trainer must avoid asking leading questions—that is, questions that move participants to make interpretations the **trainer** has in mind. The participants should provide **their own** meanings for the data, so that the learnings they derive will be theirs also. Trainers inhibit this if they operate from their own interpretations.

I cannot emphasize too strongly that this phase, "interpreting," provides an important bridge that takes participants away from the experience itself—thus providing a necessary change in focus—and toward the learnings and applications to be derived from it.

Phase IV: Generalizing

After the trainer has conducted the experience (Phase I), drawn out and posted (usually) participants' views of what happened (Phase II), and involved them in making sense of this data (Phase III), the time has arrived to move to Phase IV and "generalize," or draw out what participants have learned and relearned. Typically, the trainer's work becomes easier during this phase. If Phase I created a relevant, powerful experience for participants, if sufficient, valid data was gathered during Phase II, and if meaningful patterns were developed during Phase III, some generalizations will likely jump off the charts. Drawing out others may require patience and skill from the trainer.

During this phase—as a last resort—if I see some learning in the interpretated data that the participants do not, or that they see but have trouble articulating, I feel free to help them perceive this learning by speculating aloud, asking questions, or even making suggestions as to learnings not yet listed. As I do this, I recognize the risk of "ownership slippage" of the learnings, but I feel freer to act in this way than I would in an earlier phase because this step is further removed from the participants' experience. Furthermore, if I have not contaminated the data-gathering process of Phase II or the participants' perceptions' interpretations (Phase III), I am less likely to impose learnings on persons during

Phase IV. Questions trainers might ask during the generalizing step include the following: "What learnings or relearnings are there here for you?" "What here helps you make sense out of the experiences you've had?" "What associations do the data help you make?"

If I should find myself arguing with participants over what learnings stem from the data, then much of what appears on the flip chart is likely to be mine rather than theirs. Similarly, the data gathered during Phase II may not have been sufficient to warrant significant generalizations. Often, we erroneously consider such situations to represent "participant resistance" to learning. I emphasize firmly that each step in the learning cycle has important implications for the steps following it.

Phase V: Applications

This phase deserves as much attention as the others, but—since it comes after much hard work and is last in order, and therefore presses against to the boundary of time—this step is the one most likely to be given short shrift. This is too bad, for Phase V is generally the most significant of the phases, providing the very thing we want participants to take away from the activity: ways to **use** the learnings.

Questions to ask with respect to applications include the following: "How can you use this learning (or relearning) at home?" "Given this learning, can you name something you can start (or stop) doing next week?" "How can you build this learning into your long-range work-improvement plans? "If these learnings are important to you, how can you best hold on to them?" "How can you use this learning to make your work life (or personal life) better?"

Sometimes trainers find it useful to structure this step so as to help participants make commitments to what they will do with their learnings back home. Examples of structures include applications contracts with other participants, promises written out by the participants for themselves, and a "letter to myself" written by each participant during the program and mailed by the trainer (or a learning partner) some time after the program's end. Whatever a trainer can think of that will make the applications phase "live" for participants will bring them payoffs.

Conclusion

I believe that "processing" learning experiences is one of the most subtle, demanding, and important "art forms" of training. Processing requires most of the skills and knowledge a trainer possesses, including those related to framing correct questions, listening carefully, persisting despite participants' desires to move on, maintaining a focus, remaining clear about aims, and working carefully and creatively.

In my experience, processing is the single most difficult area of competence for trainers to learn. As they do learn processing, in stepwise fashion, trainers sometimes grow impatient with its seeming stilted quality, with the degree to which the "machinery" shows. Once learned, however, the model provides excellent service, for—as is true with any sound model—it enables trainers to know at any moment where they are and what must be done next. Once they have mastered it, trainers find that their awkwardness in using the model disappears and that they use it as a seamless whole rather than as a series of lurching steps. They eventually find their **own** best ways of using the model, and thus enjoy the freedom that comes with mastering any form.

NOTES

1. Albert Palmer discusses six such models, which overlap a good deal with one another (Palmer, 1981).

2. For example, one might seek help from a more experienced colleague. In addition, some books discussing learning activities give this information. University Associates' *Structured Experience Kit*, for example, rates each learning activity according to three dimensions: affect, structure, and materials (Pfeiffer & Jones, 1981).

3. The model by Pfeiffer and Jones calls this step "publishing." I prefer instead to refer to it as data gathering, as the term publishing already has a firmly entrenched, common use that differs from data gathering.

4. At each step in this process the trainer can gather needed information from the group in numerous ways. For more details on this, see "The Experiential Learning Cycle" (1985, pp. 5-8).

5. Readers should note that for each phase discussed in this article, the various examples provide more questions than the trainer will need to ask in any one workshop.

6. The model by Pfeiffer and Jones calls this step "processing." I do not wish to use this word to refer to this phase because the term is so commonly used to refer to all the phases following Phase I.

REFERENCES

The experiential learning cycle. (1985). In J. W. Pfeiffer (Ed.), *Reference guide to handbooks and annuals* (1985 ed.)(pp. 5-8). San Diego: University Associates.

Palmer, A. B. (1981). Learning cycles: Models of behavioral change. In J. E. Jones & J. W. Pfeiffer (Eds.), *The 1981 annual handbook for group facilitators* (pp. 147-154). San Diego: University Associates.

Pfeiffer, J. W., & Jones, J. E. (1981). *Structured experience kit*. San Diego: University Associates.

Pfeiffer, J. W., & Jones, J. E. (1983). *Reference guide to handbooks and annuals* (1983 ed.). San Diego: University Associates.

Trainer and Trainee: What Role Theory Can Teach You About Training

Katharine Cole Esty

The word "trainee" is not an everyday term among those of us who are human relations trainers and organization development consultants. Although "trainer" is in common usage, "trainee" is not part of our common parlance. One reason for this is that many trainers focus primarily on their own content specialty—whether this is leadership, management skills, or conflict management—and only secondarily on the participants' needs, wishes, level of skill, or past experience. Moreover, trainers usually give even less thought to the quality of the interaction between the trainer and participants as they design their programs.

It is most enlightening to reconceptualize training programs as performances that involve two sets of actors: the trainers and the trainees. This model, which grows naturally from role theory, leads to many insights into the training process that otherwise would not be so salient. This article begins with an outline of the basic tenets of role theory, and then examines what trainers can learn about training from role theory.

Role theory

The term "role," borrowed from the theater, denotes—according to Sarbin and Allen (1968) in their classic article on role theory—conduct that adheres to certain "parts" (or positions) themselves rather than to those playing them (p. 489). The first and major tenet of role theory, then, is that many behaviors are determined less by the internal traits of persons than by the roles that people play in their lives. Everyone is born into some roles or positions, such as those of daughter, American, black, or Catholic, and thus some of the many roles one plays are "given." Others are assumed as one moves through life. A few of these assumed roles are rather long-term positions—such as that of father—but the vast majority

©1987 NTL Institute. All rights reserved.

are temporary, such as those of college student, supervisor, tourist, or representative.

A second tenet of role theory is that role behaviors exist only within given social systems. When a person leaves a system, he or she usually sheds the associated role behaviors. For example, at work, as Director of Human Resources, Hilary is organized, highly articulate, and fast moving. When she comes home each night, she finds herself speaking in baby talk for hours on end as she enacts her role as mother.

We like to believe that people behave the same way in every setting. Because situations rarely call upon people to play two conflicting roles simultaneiously, we are rarely confronted with the reality of how differntly the same person can behave depending on the role one plays.

Roles derive not only from specific social systems, but also from the role behaviors of others occupying a given social system. Roles are nearly always reciprocal and complementary. A university professor enacts her or his role in relation to the way roles are enacted by the university president, the department chair, the trustees, colleagues, students, and the dean. The totality of complementary roles is designated a **role set**, and how any one person's role is played is shaped by how others play their roles.

Many roles consist of complementary pairs, such as parent-child, doctor-patient, teacher-student, coach-athlete, and manager-employee. One cannot play one of these roles without someone else's playing the role of the "other." For example, although one can be sick all alone, one cannot become a "patient" without the presence of medical personnel—that is, without calling a doctor or going to the emergency room.

Not only are roles complementary, but in most role sets there is a power differential between roles, with one role of the pair wielding more power than the other. One person tends to be bigger, older, and stronger, the other smaller, younger, and weaker. One is the expert, the other the novice. True parity between roles in a role pair is uncommon.

According to Sarbin and Allen (1968), a universal tendency among performers is to try and play their roles well, based on basically three criteria for judging the enactment of a role.

- Is a person in the right role?
- Does this person display the correct behaviors for the particular role?
- Is the performer giving a convincing performance?

Role expectations are cognitions about the rights, privileges, duties, and obligations of an occupant of a social position in relation to the other persons in that system. Fuzzy and ambiguous role expectations can lead to behaviors that are judged inappropriate, improper, and unconvincing. Various persons in a single role set can have quite different expectations, leading to conflict, strain, and tension. Whether problems exist or not, most persons try to conform to the role expectations they perceive and to meet all of the role demands. Often, role occupants do not realize that they have the option of leaving a role set.

Another important aspect of role theory is the metaphor of the theater embedded within the theory. The word role suggests an actor playing a part, and derives from the sheet of parchment turned around a wooden roller on which a script—or actor's part—was written. The metaphor is expanded to suggest, as Shakespeare put it, that "all the world's a stage," conjuring up a theatrical context that includes the idea of a performance, staging, sets, costumes, directing, and special effects.

Implications of role theory for trainers

Trainers tend to think about participants in terms of their individual characteristics and their positions in their work organizations. They think less often about probable effects of the participants' position as trainees upon their behavior in the program. Yet, as Philip Zimbardo's experiment in roles at Stanford University illustrated (Haney & Zimbardo, 1977), the power of role designations cannot be overestimated.

Having recruited a good number of college students for a two-week study of prison life, Zimbardo randomly assigned them to the role of either prisoner or guard (participants were chosen because they were judged emotionally stable, based on extensive tests.) Zimbardo converted part of a classroom building at Stanford into a mock prison and charged the "guards" with the responsibility of watching over the "prisoners." What happened next surprised everyone. During the next few days, each of those playing guard exhibited some kind of aggressive behavior toward those in the prisoner role, including verbal or physical abuse. The prisoners became extremely passive and withdrawn; one began crying uncontrollably and appeared so severely depressed he was released from the experiment immediately. Three other prisoners developed similar symptoms and were released as well. The experiment clearly showed that role is a strong determinant of behavior, even when a role is known to be randomly assigned, to have a short duration, and to be merely part of an educational event.

Zimbardo's experiment underscored the impact of the power differential contained within most role sets. Some trainers are oblivious to the effects of these power differences. They need to realize, however, that all the participants have chosen to play a subordinate role. Many trainers, ideologically committed to minimizing their authority, take various steps to narrow the power gap between them and the participants. These trainers wear "nonpower costumes," especially when training outside the corporate setting. Wearing blue jeans, T-shirts, and running shoes, they look indistinguishable from the trainees. Typically, they encourage trainees to challenge the trainer's point of view, and may even negotiate changes in the program to meet the participants' emerging needs. Having done this, the trainers may be unaware of the remaining power gap and the "demand" situation of the trainees.

Milgram's (1963) experiment, as did Zimbardo's, shed more light on roles. Milgram, a Yale psychologist, told subjects they were taking part in an experiment on learning, rewards, and punishment. He instructed them to administer an electric shock to a "learner" whenever the learner made a mistake in a learn-ing task. (In actuality, the learner was an actor who pretended to suffer from elec-tric shock when the subjects pushed the designated buttons.) When the learner began to scream with pain, the subjects were told by the experimenters to con-tinue administering shocks. As they continued to shock the learner, instruments indicated that the shocks were of a dangerously elevated voltage level. At this junc-ture most of the subjects became visibly upset, perspiring profusely, trembling, and turning pale. Yet all of them continued to shock the learner. **They stayed in the role**. Afterwards, they offered a host of reasons for why they had obeyed. They explained that once they had agreed to participate—to be subjects—they hesitated to disobey, to appear uncooperative, to ruin an exercise, or to say "no" to the researcher.

Knowing how difficult it is to break out of a role, trainers must be realistic in evaluating what "going along" with their program design actually indicates. They must be extremely cautious about interpreting compliance as commitment, when all it may signal is role enactment. An important training task may be to teach participants how to develop the skills required for refusing unreasonable role demands and how to give honest feedback on the spot.

Role theory also helps us differentiate between training within the context of an organization versus training on "neutral turf." Participants of a training program sponsored by their employer usually remain in their organizational roles throughout the program. The role of trainee is superimposed upon the job role and therefore its demands are rather faint in comparison. Indeed, some trainees may contnue to be primarily in their job roles. Typical behaviors indicating this are tardiness in arriving at training sessions, running back and forth to their of-fices for phone calls, and careful scrutiny of the reactions of the higher-ranking participants. In addition, the internal trainers themselves are part of the organiza-tion role set and usually have far less power than those from outside the company. Their place—usually not too high—in the organizational hierarchy allows the participants to consider them to be peers, perhaps subordinates. The usual "transference" is diminished.

A quite different experience occurs when employees are sent away for train-ing to a residential setting such as a university or an NTL Institute program, especially when they go alone rather than as members of a team. In that context, they may discard their work roles rather quickly, and their role as trainee becomes more significant. Some participants expend much energy explaining to the group of strangers the importance of the roles they may play in their back-home organizations. Others find liberation from their usual roles to be a heady experience; they can appear quite adolescent as they experience their new-found freedom. It is not unusual for a trainer to realize that some of the participants are counting the minutes until the sessions are over so that they can return to their main concern with developing new relationships or working out.

More light is shed upon the training process by examining the accepted role expectations for trainers and trainees. Trainers are generally expected to provide a variety of structures for learning, such as lectures, exercises, discussions, case analyses, demonstrations, simulations, instruments, and small group work. The trainer develops the activities, plans the sequences of events, and controls the pace. Often trainers are expected to provide feedback to the participants as they master the workshop material.

Less clarity exists, however, with respect to expectations for trainees. Brochures and other materials describing programs often mention the obligation to attend all the sessions, and usually describe the kinds of events to expect. Trainers often expect, though they state less frequently, that the trainees will participate fully in the entire range of activities. Because, in some cases, the learning is an outcome of the participants' interaction, an implicit expectation is that the trainee will interact with and give feedback to the other trainers.

Beyond these implicit expectations lies another level of role expectations that is even more subterranean. These are often unstated and sometimes outside the awareness of both the trainer and trainees. For example, some trainers expect participants to behave "authentically"—that is, they want trainees to express their opinions with candor and their feelings from the heart. This can put the trainees in a bind, especially those in programs at their work sites. They have often invested much time and energy learning to manage corporate politics, to say the "right thing," and to cover up and play down their own opinions. Is it unrealistic to expect them to suddenly become open and honest if the corporate culture has not encouraged critical comments all along?

Some trainers have other secret expectations. They may want their trainees to meet the trainers' personal needs. They may want their trainees to affirm them as helpful and competent. Or they may send subliminal messages that the participants should praise them lavishly, and should not challenge the trainers' ideas.

Trainees, too, bring unstated expectations about their role to the training event. Some participants sign up for training events so that they can be entertained. They expect to be fed predigested nuggets of expertise and to learn by "being there." This can directly conflict with trainers' expectations for participant involvement and commitment to experiential learning. At the other extreme, especially for training programs held at conference centers in resort areas, trainees may see themselves as "on vacation" and develop elaborate plans to enjoy tennis, golf, sightseeing, and meeting old friends. For some "workaholic" persons, attending a training program is the nearest thing to a vacation they can allow themselves. The clash of expectations can lead to an invisible tug of war between the trainer and trainee.

Trainees also have various unstated role expectations for the trainer. Sometimes they seek a "quick fix" for their complex professional and personal dilemmas. When they are given anything more ambiguous than a "cookbook recipe" for action, they perceive this as a sign that the trainer is incompetent. Other trainees seek a successful role model—a person who has truly "gotten it all together." They come to the workshop hopeful that, at last, they will find a trainer without "clay feet." As the trainer's imperfections inevitably become exposed, the trainee feels dissatisfied and slightly betrayed.

A trainer must do more than simply ask at the start of a training program, "What are your expectations for this program?"—although that is a good and necessary step. Determining "covert" or "secondary" expectations for programs usually nets a richer yield, especially, if in the process, the trainers themselves surface one or more of their own unstated expectations. But no easy solutions exist for uncovering such expectations, and they must be dealt with continuously throughout a program—person by person.

Remember: **Training is show biz**. This is another important insight derived from role theory. Rather than dismissing the participants' wish to be entertained, the trainer would do well to accept this covert expectation as legitimate. Successful persons in every field recognize the role of theater in communications. Skilled trainers develop their trainer role into an interesting character role partly by what they do, and partly by what they choose to disclose about themselves. They have a well-rehearsed repertoire of war stories, jokes, and illustrations to breathe life into their material. Some trainers are especially creative in their use of "special effects," providing unusual exercises to emphasize a point. Others use brief displays of anger or employ the Socratic method of questioning on occasion to raise the training program to its full potential as theater. They pay attention to beginnings and endings, and even plan the curtain call.

Although role behaviors are typically inferred from the behaviors of others, trainers can accelerate the learning process by coaching their trainees about how to be "good trainees." Some trainers present their trainees with a list of behavioral norms or guidelines to set the stage. I have found guidelines such as "you are responsible for your own learning," "feelings are facts," "risk taking is encouraged," and "mistakes are part of learning" to be effective. Even more important is handling the first challenge of inappropriate behavior skillfully.

The final lesson I present from role theory concerns follow-up. If we accept that when people leave a social system they shed the roles associated with that system, then we should not be surprised at the difficulty trainees have incorporating their new learnings into their back-home settings. It is natural for them to encapsulate the training experience.

Several tactics should help trainers deal with this tendency. First, scheduling a follow-up training session and building this into the program from the start is useful. Sometimes, when this is not possible, trainees can be offered an hour's consultation on the telephone. Even better is developing "support" groups for ongoing consultation among the participants. In my experience, participants respond positively to this structure, and have reported that these groups have continued to function usefully for years after a training program has ended.

The best way to make training "stick," I believe, is to train teams of employees within an organization. Even a single team enhances the likelihood that the training will carry over and change the organization to some degree. When a significant mass of employees—perhaps as few as 30%—has been trained in a particular program, then the material presented stands a good chance of transforming the entire organizational culture. This is an exciting but rare phenomenon—for it means that a systematic approach to training has been employed, and that top levels of management have supported the training effort. It also means that behaviors encouraged for the trainees are increasingly similar to those expected of employees.

In conclusion, role theory may manifest both the realities and the potential of training. By raising awareness of the unacknowledged aspects of training situations, trainers can become increasingly skilled in managing the subtle issues of authority. The theory also informs them how to design their programs for lasting results.

REFERENCES

Haney, C., & Zimbardo, P. G. (1977). The socialization into criminality: On becoming a prisoner and a guard. In J. L. Trapp & F. L. Levine (Eds.), *Law, justice and the individual in society: Psychological and legal issues* (pp. 198-223). New York: Holt, Rinehart & Winston.

Milgram, S. (1963). Behavioral study of obedience. *The Journal of Abnormal and Social Psychology, 67*(4), 19-33.

Sarbin, T. R., & Allen, V. L. (1968). Role theory. In G. Lindzey & E. Aronson (Eds.), *Handbook of social psychology* (Rev. ed.)(Vol. I)(pp. 488-567). Reading, MA: Addison-Wesley.

Using a Stage Theory Model To Understand and Manage Transitions in Group Dynamics

Jane Moosbruker

This article seeks to take developmental theory of small groups another step by adding the component of the group leader's dilemma in facilitating the group's progress through each stage. As applied to groups, the term "developmental" means that the concerns and needs of each stage must be dealt with before the group can move on to the next stage. As this occurs, group members progress in their ability to relate to one another and to work together.

A generalized, four-stage model, applicable both to self-study groups (T Groups) and to task groups, provides the framework. In discussing the evolution of the model, the literature on stage theory is reviewed, with particular attention paid to managing transitions from one stage to the next and to the type of group.

The four stages of the model are the following:

- I. Orientation,
- II. Conflict,
- III. Solidarity,
- IV. Productivity.

I use this framework to describe the leadership dilemmas faced in facilitating the group's progress. I argue that these dilemmas are the same for both task groups and T Groups, but that the solutions—or constructive behaviors for the group leaders in solving dilemmas—vary according to the type of group.

Stage theories: Literature review

By 1965, at least 50 articles had been written about stage theory (Tuckman, 1965), and much has been written since them. The number sand names of specific stages

©1987 NTL Institute. All rights reserved.

vary, but those writing about stage theory generally agree as to the flow. Table 1 provides a comparison of similar theories. The first, by R. D. Mann (1967), provides a more clinical model, emphasizing the individual's concerns. Both Mann's and Schutz's (1958) models are based on observations of self-study groups. Tuckman's (1965) is a general model, but is based primarily on articles about self-study groups and therapy groups.

Table 1
A Comparison of Stage Theory Models of Group Development for Task Groups and Self-Study Groups

	Mann	Schutz	Tuckman	Fisher	Bales and Strodbeck
Type of group	Self-study	Self-study	General	Task	Task
Stage I	Nurturance	Inclusion	Forming	Orientation	Orientation
Stage II	Control	Control	Storming	Conflict	Evaluation
Stage III	Sexuality	Affection	Norming	Emergence	Control
Stage IV	Competence	(Affection)	Performing	Reinforcement	—
Additional stages	—	(Control)	Separation	—	—
		(Inclusion)			

The similarity of Fisher's (1970) model to the others presented in Table 1 is noteworthy because it is based on content analysis of the verbal interactions of task groups in the process of making decisions. Fisher's "reinforcement" stage refers to the reinforcement of the decision made by the group.

Despite the use of different terms for this article's model, it also parallels closely that of Bales and Strodbeck (1951) which stems from an empirical study and is based on tasks. To them "evaluation" means the group is dealing with differences in values, interests, and judgments, which other models refer to as "conflict." To Bales and Strodbeck "control" refers to the regulation of group members and their common environment; other models call this "norming," or norm setting.

A major difference among stage theory models is in the extent to which they pay attention to transitions from one stage to the next. Those presented in Table 1 pay little or no attention to the actual process of development. What must happen for the group to progress? Will this happen automatically? Can the leader do anything to facilitate this process?

One early model does deal with the movement of the group from one stage to the next: that of Bennis and Shepard (1956). They attribute a group's movement to "unconflicted" members who serve as catalysts. These members are unconflicted with respect to issues of dependency or intimacy, based on their individual personalities. The leader is not perceived as having an active role in facilitating the group's development.

There are other theories, similar to Bennis and Shepard's, that follow the analytic model, such as those of Bion (1961), Slater (1966), and—in general—the

Tavistock approach to groups. The leader is not an active force for moving the group in these models, but rather something of a blank page on which members project their feelings about authority.

More recent writings on stage theory acknowledge the leader's role in facilitating the process of group development and provide some prescriptions for effective leadership behavior. Bradford and Cohen (1984) do this in the context of a manager's building her or his own "shared responsibility team." Nielson (1984) addresses the empowerment of the group by its leader, also in an organizational context. Both theories use a similar model, based on the work of Obert (1979). Unfortunately, this particular model is complex, having five stages, two of them transitional.

Table 2
Stage Theory Models of Group Development that Consider the Process of Moving Through the Stages

	Bennis and Shepard	Bradford and Cohen	Nielson
Stage I.	(1) Member-leader relations	Membership	Dependence
Stage II.	Dependence/submission	Subgrouping	Similarity versus dissimilarity
Stage III.	Counterdependence, resolution/independence. (2) Member-member relations	Confrontation	Support versus panic
Stage IV.	Enchantment	Differentiation	Concern versus isolation
Stage V.	Disenchantment: overpersonals versus counterpersonals. Interdependence: consensual validation	Shared responsibility	Interdependence versus withdrawal

Table 2 presents the models of Bennis and Shepard, Bradford and Cohen, and Nielson. The three models have some interesting similarities. First, they all deal with the process of the group's transition from stage to stage. Second, they all carefully address the member-member and member-leader relations separately. Their latter difference increases their complexity, requiring additional stages. I do not consider the payoff worth the cost.

Dimensions of small group behavior

Another approach to an understanding of group dynamics has grown out of attempts to discover the underlying dimensions of interpersonal behavior. Some major research has been done in this area, and the resulting dimensions—which are also themes in group life—show a striking resemblance to the issues the group faces as it moves through developmental states. The major dimensions are the following:

- dominance versus submission (Bales, 1970; Chapple, 1940; Couch, 1960; Leary, 1957),
- positive versus negative (Bales, 1970; Couch, 1960; Leary, 1957),
- conforming versus nonconforming (Couch, 1960; Hare, 1982),
- serious versus expressive (Couch, 1960; Hare, 1982).

Based on this research, the following parallels can be drawn: (1) the prevalence of behavior along the conforming/nonconforming dimension at the beginning or first stage of the group, (2) an emphasis on dominance/submission during the conflict stage, with the negative axis of the positive/negative dimension also being salient, (3) a preponderance of positive behavior during the integration or solidarity stage, and (4) the serious versus expressive dimension surfacing most frequently when the group is fully productive.

Because only minimal research data support stage theory, the dimensional approach helps confirm that stage-related behavior is real.

Relationship with systems theory

Stage theory also parallels the functional perspective in social systems theory (Parsons, 1961). In particular, four basic problems must be solved if a system is to survive:

- pattern maintenance or some common identity and shared commitment;
- exercising sufficient control over its membership to reach its goal effectively;
- having enough shared norms and a feeling of solidarity to stay together to do the group's work;
- sufficient adaptation to the group's environment to be able to survive— or example, by defining a goal and obtaining needed resources to accomplish it (Effrat, 1968).

Thus, viewing the small group as a social system, as the basic unit of an organization, provides a convincing argument that a four-stage model more pragmatically describes reality than a model with three, five, or six stages. This is why the model I propose has the following stages: I. orientation, II. conflict, III. solidarity, and IV. productivity.

Anyone concerned with ending the group would require a fifth stage: termination. The issues of terminating the group are not dealt with in this article.

The remainder of this article attempts to provide useful application strategies for group leaders. The generalized model is discussed to facilitate leaders' efforts to develop their groups into fully effective teams. By "generalized" I mean that the dilemmas confronting the leaders in this process are similar for both task groups and T Groups. The actual leadership behaviors appropriate for each situation, however, usually vary according to the type of group.

Group facilitation model

In discussing each of the model's stages, the article addresses the likely feeling of the group members, the most salient or observable member behaviors, and the group level phenomena characteristic of that stage. More important, I treat the leader as the **major** agent for the group's transitions. For each stage the particular leadership dilemma the leader must successfully resolve for the group to reach the next stage of its development is presented and discussed. The importance of other mechanisms related to transitions—such as individual members and events, or situations external to the group—vary according to the stage, and I mention only the most salient.

Stage I: Orientation

Potential group members (i.e., those present) will likely feel isolated and alone, somewhat fearful, and perhaps excited in anticipation of what is to come. Self-confidence is usually at a low ebb, and some "members" may feel worthless, or at least useless, until they can figure out what to do in this situation. The members may be comparing themselves to one another along such superficial dimensions as looks and dress, or on the basis of known or assumed roles and status outside the group. These comparisons may result in jealously, insecurity, or a sense of superiority.

The need exists for people to become acquainted with one another as individuals in the interest of developing some common identity. A concrete task can provide the group's identity, at least temporarily. This formation around a task, which most groups do or attempt to do, can assist development for a while. If the group is to stay together and become fully productive, however, individual acquaintance is also necessary, and this may be hindered by premature attempts to solve problems.

The behavior by which a group in Stage I is recognized includes a large amount of interaction directed toward the leader, a lack of listening, a lack of support for others' agenda, superficial politeness, a low level of openness about one's personal needs or feelings, and a preference for using "we" instead of "I."

The leadership dilemma during this stage concerns how much structure to provide the group. This dilemma is the same for an unstructured self-study group or a T Group and for a task group, but the appropriate solution may differ considerably. Lower amounts of structure provided in a group generally result in higher anxiety levels in members. The optimum anxiety level for effective performance varies according to the task.

Although technical—in the broadest sense of the word—work is achieved successfully in a relaxed situation, self-study is better accomplished when enough anxiety exists to enhance self-awareness.

In a T Group, the leader can easily err by providing too much structure— for example, by offering a lot of good ideas for helping people become better acquainted. Too much direction can result in a leader-dependent group, whose members neither focus on their own needs nor learn to take responsibility for meeting those needs. The leader's overly helpful suggestions come to be regarded as "games," and the group may go on just playing games. The long-term result can be low cohesiveness and a lack of productivity (Lundgren, 1971).

On the other hand, the leader can provide too little help, or offer only obscure pronouncements on group level phenomena, thus appearing cold and distant. Behavior at this end of the continuum can result in member regression and a lack of group progress. Task group leaders most often err in the direction of providing too little structure or the wrong kind of structure. For example, managers attempting to be "participative" can fail to provide and follow meeting agenda. Structure is needed to facilitate the group's work on its process task of getting acquainted and its content task of developing goals and assigning roles. The "wrong kind" of structure includes formats for meetings that are rigid and do not allow for what people wish to contribute, calling on members, telling people how to do things, and using other forms of control.

Stage II: Conflict

The most prominent feelings at this stage are frustration and anger. If unexpressed, or if they occur in cycles of unproductive expression, these feelings can turn into futility, apathy, and impotence. Competition among members may occur; some members may compete with the leader, and some of the anger and frustration may be directed that way. Leadership may be challenged, covertly or overtly.

At this stage behavior is variable, because conflict may occur among members or with the leader, or both; it may be overt or covert; it may vary according to the issue. The most complex behavior patterns often are present. As noted above, several models expand this stage to two stages in order to deal with the multiple issues.

Where the conflict resides depends on the combination of member personalities and leadership style. For example, overt conflict with the leader would occur if at least some group members were counterdependent and the leader's style was directive. Conflict with the leader would be covert in the case of dependent group members and a leader who fails to provide sufficient structure.

To resolve member-leader conflicts, understanding and acceptance of issues of power and authority are needed. Such issues include individuals' (i.e., members' and the leader's) feelings toward authority, needs for power, and the appropriate role of the leader in the particular group.

To resolve member-member conflicts, members must be able to talk openly about the differences among them with respect to opinions, values, approaches, life styles, and the like—and **listen** to one another. Agreement is not always necessary, but understanding is.

The leadership dilemma centers on how and how much the leader should facilitate the group's utilization of the conflict, or how much to open up the conflict. "Conflict" does not mean physical contact; the expression of anger is not even necessary. The term "conflict" simply means the expression of differing viewpoints, the ability to disagree openly.

In task groups, "conflict" may take the form of general dissatisfaction with the group's progress. The task is likely to be still unclear and in dispute. Morale may be low compared to earlier high expectations.

In a T Group, conflict is often useful for facilitating self-insight and building relationships. The amount of conflict that is productive is far greater for a T Group than for a task group. A guideline is to open as much of the conflict as necessary for enabling the group to work together effectively, while maintaining the awareness that some of the issues needing attention may not be related to the task at all.

In both task groups and T Groups, setting the norm that disagreement is permissible lays the groundwork for conflict utilization. Asking questions about persons' ideas, values, ways of approaching problems, and the like supports this norm. Demonstrating an ability to tolerate disagreement with one's own views adds credibility. In this way a leader can act as a transition mechanism. Other potential mechanisms include individual members who are comfortable with conflict. There are also some groups whose members are so uncomfortable with conflict that they will not do the work of this stage no matter what the leader does.

Once disagreements are out in the open, the leader can play an important role in helping persons discuss them and listen to one another in ways that can lead to understanding the issues and appreciation of the person. The leader's activity level is a factor in that too high a level can suppress participants and too low a level can result in destructive escalation of conflict or withdrawal. An orchestra conductor provides a useful, elegant model for conflict facilitation— although at times the model of an air traffic controller is more appropriate, as leaders must prevent several members from ganging up on one, interruptions, unfinished business, and the like.

The bottom line in Stage II is that conflict is generated by individual needs for control and by concrete issues. The leader must be able to help members work out patterns of reciprocal control with one another and with the leader that will allow the members to meet enough of their needs to keep on functioning as a group.

Stage III: Solidarity

The salient feelings characterizing this stage are harmony, sympathy, support, and caring. In some sense, the group is resting from the conflicts of Stage II, and in another sense it is celebrating the resolution of many of those conflicts. The group clearly has developed its own identity: "We" is now accurate, and does not merely represent an avoidance of expressing individual needs.

Having fought hard for control in Stage II, the group members give up control in Stage III and become overly conforming. Members may not challenge one another. There may be little expression of individuality.

Most often the need for leadership is less intense by Stage III, and the leader can participate fairly freely in the group's process, whether this is task

centered or person centered, using whatever individual talents and abilities he
or she possesses.

In Stage III, the leadership dilemma is determining when to live within the
norms the group is setting (i.e., play a membership role) and when to influence
these norms and how to intervene when doing so (i.e., play a leadership role). The
group at this stage pressures the leader to behave as just another member of the
group, and the leader may find this tempting because the members are now
capable of having much fun together.

The group itself faces a dilemma, which the leader may share to varying
degrees, of determining how close members want to get to one another and to
the leader. The issues of interpersonal attraction are more salient for a T Group
than for a task group. For example, interest in and concerns about sexualtiy are
often on persons' minds at this stage—both the leader and the members—if there
is any similarity or overlap in age and life style. The group may need to have the
leader help it talk openly about positive feelings and find an appropriate level for
expressing these feelings. Differences among members as to what level of
expression is acceptable need to be discussed. The leader is part of the group on
this issue and needs to be aware of her or his own feelings toward other members.

Some of the same concerns may also arise for task groups. These are usually
discussed outside the group's formal sessions, and many individuals find them
more difficult to deal with than conflict. The group may need to have the leader
help members acknowledge the positive feelings they have for one another and
give them approval. There may be a time when it is appropriate to discuss the
group's—or the company's—norms about socializing outside of work.

Dealing with issues of interpersonal support can be productive for a group
whose members do not challenge one another or have a lower standard of
productivity than the leader would like.

Stage III is also a time of feeling superior to other groups. In fact, the mere
presence of other groups with which to compete can serve as a transition
mechanism for moving into Stage III. Intergroup competition can be a source
of rich learnings in a T Group environment if the leader can stay out of the
competition and facilitate the learning. In the work place, a leader who keeps the
good of the company as a whole in mind can help the group find the right balance
between cooperation and competition--not an easy task, as the competition may
be over survival.

Stage IV: Productivity

The dominant feeling at this stage is one of comfort, but feelings are not
dominant at this stage. Even in self-study groups Stage IV is task oriented.
Feelings are primarily related to task issues, for interpersonal issues have largely
been resolved. The group is achievement oriented, but behavior is often creative
and can be very playful. There is "base line" of trust, warmth, and openness that
is not usually violated, even when task-related conflict arises.

The leadership dilemma is deciding when to appreciate and support members and when to challenge, confront, and find new opportunities for the group as a whole and for individual members. Individuals now emerge from the group and display their own styles and needs, and—because the group now does most of its own maintenance work—the leader is freer to facilitate the growth of individual members. The right mixture of warmth, positive feedback, and genuine appreciation on the one hand, and insightful, challenging, or somewhat negative feedback on the other (or, in the case of a task group, challenging assignments) can help each person become all he or she is capable of becoming.

Regression may occur at this or any other stage of the group's development. Indeed, the progression through these stages is not usually a neat, orderly process, but rather is a series of approximations on a general sense of development. Regressions may occur in response to crises in the external environment—such as the organization in which the group is operating—or when the group loses or gains a member. Time and distance between group meetings can result in brief reenactments of the stages at each meeting.

Conclusion

The theory that small groups evolve through developmental stages can provide important assistance to the leaders of groups and teams. The literature on stage theories reveals more similarities than differences in terms of specific, identifiable stages. A gap exists in this literature, however, concerning the transition mechanisms or processes by which groups are actually developed. Leaders of formal groups have an important role to play in their groups' transitions.

Leaders of both T Groups and task teams face the same significant dilemmas as they attempt to facilitate group development. These dilemmas are how much structure to provide during the orientation stage, how much and how to open up differences and disagreements during the conflict stage, when to act as a member versus a group leader during the solidarity stage, and, finally, when to appreciate members and when to challenge them during the productivity stage.

REFERENCES

Bales, R. F. (1970). *Personality and interpersonal behavior*. New York: Holt, Rinehart & Winston.

Bales, R. F., & Strodbeck, F. O. (1951). Phases in group problem solving. *Journal of Abnormal and Social Psychology, 46*, 485-495.

Barnlund, D.C. (1959). Comparative study of individual, majority, and group judgment. *Journal of Abnormal and Social Psychology, 58*, 55-60.

Bennis, W. G., & Shepard, H. A. (1956). A theory of group development. *Human Relations, 9*, 415-437.

Bion, W. R. (1961). *Experiences in groups and other papers*. New York: Basic Books.

Bradford, D. L., & Cohen, A. R. (1984). *Managing for excellence*. New York: Wiley & Sons.

Chapple, E. D. (1940). Measuring human relations: An introduction to the study of interaction of individuals. *Genetic Psychology Monographs, 22*, 3-147.

Couch, A. S. (1960). *Psychological determinants of interpersonal behavior*. Unpublished doctoral dissertation, Harvard University, Cambridge, MA.

Effrat, A. (1968). Applications of Parsonian theory (ed. intro.). *Sociological Inquiry, 38*(2), 97-103.

Fisher, B. A. (1970). Decision emergence: Phases in group decision-making. *Speech monographs, 37,* 53-66.

Freud, S. (1913). Totem and taboo, *Standard Edition, 13,* 1-161.

Hare, A. P. (1982). *Creativity in small groups.* London: Sage.

Leary, T. (1957). *Interpersonal diagnosis of personality.* New York: Ronald.

Lundgren, D. C. (1971). Trainer style and patterns of group development. *Journal of Applied Behavioral Science, 7,* 689-708.

Mann, R. D. (1967). The development of the member-trainer relationship in self-analytic groups. *Human Relations, 19,* 85-115.

Nielsen, E. (1984). *Inducing shared responsibility through empowerment: A strategy and its prospects.* Symposium on the Functioning of Executive Power.

Obert, S. L. (1979). *The development of organizational task groups.* Unpublished doctoral dissertation, Case Western Reserve University, Cleveland, OH.

Parsons, T. (1951). *The social system.* New York: Free Press.

Schutz, W. (1958). *FIRO: A three-dimensional theory of interpersonal behavior.* New York: Holt, Rinehart & Winston.

Slater, P. (1966). *Microcosm: Structural, psychological and religious evolution in groups.* New York: John Wiley.

Tuckman, B. W. (1965). Developmental sequence in small groups. *Psychological Bulletin, 63,* 384-399.

Moving Toward the Client/ Learner

Ronald Lippitt

During the past decade we have heard the phrase "participative management" more frequently than we have heard the term "participative training." But the growth of influence of the trainee is an even more widespread phenomenon than is employee involvement.

The consumer revolution of the 1960s, 1970s, and 1980s has spread to "the learning situation." Pupils, students, and trainees have discovered that they have the right and power to have some influence over their needs and interests. What they will be taught, and how they will be taught, have both become the focus of evaluation and decisions. Many teachers and trainers of "required" learning activities have discovered that learners have increased their abilities to "turn off" or avoid directive teaching efforts. A facade of compliance may shield a range of turning off, foot dragging, avoidance, and other strategies, or even an overt refusal to participate.

Norman Cousins summarizes this consumer revolution beautifully:

> People today want a larger share in the decision-making about their lives. However, much as they may have respect for the superior learning of their teachers, they believe they themselves have something of value to offer in the determination of what it is they should be taught and even how they are to be taught. They see themselves not just as receptacles for instruction, but as essential participants in the educational experience. They mirror the central tendency of this age—which is the quest for individual respect. Finally, they shun those for whom thinking is reflexive, rather than reflective, and increasingly subject to computerized decisions. (1981, p. 37)

The sponsors of education and training are also increasing their demands for accountability, asking such questions as, "What hard evidence of accountability is there? Is there evidence of concepts and skills learned? Are these used to improve productivity? Skill? Competence? Commitment?"

©1987 NTL Institute. All rights reserved.

The challenge for the teacher/trainer of the 1980s

Confronted by this, teachers on campus and trainers and consultants in organizations are facing—often painfully and reluctantly—such important requirement as the following.

- They must work out some kind of voluntary teaching/learning contract with pupils and/or students.
- They must understand and consider differences in learning style and rate of learning among members of the same learning group when they design their teaching/training programs.
- They must clarify and demonstrate the relevance of what is being taught to valued payoffs in the lives of the learners.
- They must understand and use the major influence of peers as sources of and support for learning.
- They must understand and use creatively the appropriate media and experimental designs that facilitate different types of learnings.
- They should realize that the external authority of the guru role—the definer of what should be learned and how this should be done—has diminished in importance to successful education/training.

The unit of learning activity may be a person, a group, an organization, or a human collective (such as a national society or international institution). In this article, I focus on the person as the learner, and the trainer as a teacher. I analyze the teaching-learning process as a series of linkages, using the schema of the internal linkages model shown in Figure 1. The linkages consist of trainer interventions and learner tasks, which are necessary for a full training process to occur.

Linkage 1: Input communication

A wide range and variety of resources exist external to the learner's senses, such as research findings, demonstrations of practice, case studies, experiences of others, nonverbal communication, documentary movies, and more. The trainer can potentially link the learner to these resources, provide input, stimulate inquiry, and act as a model of motivation to learn. As a result of this linkage, the trainee/learner acquires information.

Linkage 2: From information to understanding

The trainer/teacher or consultant is challenged to help the learner or client process the information into understanding (generalizations, insights, and the like)—that is, to give meaning to the data. Most educational testing aims toward assessing either information or one's understanding of it. In our orientation, this is just the first phase of the process of real functional learning.

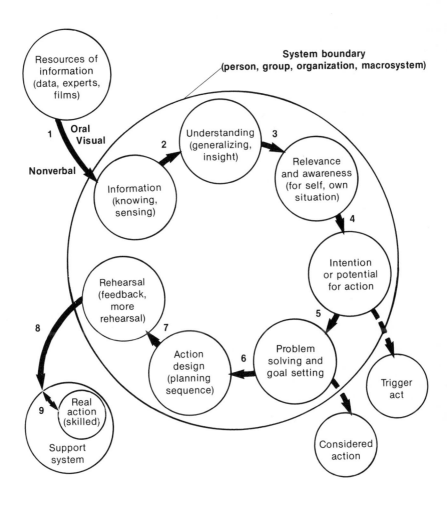

Figure 1. Model of process linkages for learning and problem solving

Linkage 3: From understanding to relevance and awareness

A large proportion of information never gets as far as becoming relevant to one's own life, or to the operations of an organization. One of the most important challenges for a trainer or consultant is to help link perceptions and feelings of relevance to the specific interests and problem-solving needs of the learner/ participant. Relatively few lecturers or presenters of information stop regularly to ask the listeners to reflect on the applications of the ideas presented to their own situations and needs.

Linkage 4: From relevance to intention or potential for action

The trainer or consultant is challenged to help bridge the gap between relevance and the potential use of the knowledge through action. One of my colleagues, a European professional and intellectual, looked at my linkage model diagram and said, "I grew up in the coffee houses of Vienna. We could solve any problem of the world in any three hours of any afternoon. We had very sophisticated awareness and could make any data relevant to our situations."

"So," I responded, "when you left the coffee house, I assume you had some intentions of doing something?"

"No, never! We had solved the problem in our heads. That was enough for us."

Much case analysis and group discussion stops at this point, without any linkage to an intention to do something concrete. Often, I find it important at this point to legitimize ambivalence about risk taking as normal for either intrapersonal or interpersonal situations. I use various techniques to encourage an "internal dialogue" between the cautious, protective and the risk-taking, "pro-action" sides of ourselves.

The diagram illustrates a problem associated with this linkage. Sometimes an intention to act emerges as a spontaneous, impulsive "trigger act." Such actions usually do not succeed, because they are triggered by impulse and lack guidance by problem-solving deliberation and a sensitivity to others. The trainer or facilitator must seek to provide a linkage to exploring alternatives before the learners jump into action.

Linkage 5: From intention to problem solving and goal setting

"Before swinging into action on that idea, let's test other alternatives to see what possible action might ensure the best chance of success." Such intervening statements are important in many training and consulting situations. They may lead to exploring existing innovative solutions, to assessing the consequences of alternatives, and to conducting feasibility analyses with available "reality testers." From this process emerges a considered goal decision—that is, a decision as to what to do.

At this point in many learning and problem-solving sequences, a "considered action" emerges. This certainly has a higher probability of success than does the trigger act, but it still sadly reflects a lack of work on the "how-to" aspects of quality action. The supportive trainer or consultant still must offer much help to ensure a successful action by focusing on how it should be done.

Linkage 6: From goal setting to action design

Goal setting provides the launching pad for creative and realistic, step-by-step action planning. This planning process includes not only the projected action sequences, but also consideration of "who else needs to be involved," and how this should occur. Following this should be a focus on evaluation—that is, on evidence of progress toward action, and the important consideration of how to celebrate the steps of progress, which supports the motivation to continue putting energy into the effort.

Linkage 7: From action design to rehearsal

In learning any how-to skills, one must practice in a risk-free situation—rather than one of "playing for keeps"—and have the chance for feedback and more practice. The techniques of role playing, simulation, and imagery provide important rehearsal tools. This is one of the most important—yet most neglected—areas of training and consultation.

Linkage 8: From rehearsal to real action

Just when a person or group is ready to move from rehearsal to the risks of real action is not always precisely clear. The practitioner must feel ready, and the teacher/consultant must be willing to help with and support the decision. One learning to play a musical instrument finds that much rehearsal, feedback, and follow-up rehearsal is crucial; we all can see this clearly. Similarly, in making our presentations of recommendations to top management, practice and feedback on our errors is also important.

Linkage 9: From real action to the support system

A good teacher/trainer helps the learner identify necessary support systems for the contemplated action, and helps develop strategies for involving those in such systems in the action. Many times as a consultant I found one of my most important linkage activities to be that of orienting top management toward receptive listening to and collaboration with those presenting ideas. A consultant will find it important to help prepare potential support systems to be receptive to the initiatives of those taking risks.

Using this model

I consider this series of linkages to be a holistic process for learning or problem solving, a helpful check list for creating a learning design, or useful for assessing the quality of the learning opportunity one is designing.

If you assess—either by yourself or with others—the various interventions that might be appropriate or feasible for each of the nine linkages of the model, you will discover the richness of your own training/teaching repertoire, and also the points at which you should seek new methods and practice new skills.

I find this model helps me develop and assess teaching designs and consulting relationships with individuals, groups, organizations, and even community systems. You may develop your own adaptations and modifications to the model, which you may wish to share with your colleagues, and enrich this idea.

REFERENCE

Cousins, N. (1981). *Human options.* New York: Berkeley Publishing Group.

BIBLIOGRAPHY

Lippitt, R. (1975). Linkage problems and processes in laboratory education. In K. Benne, L. P. Bradford, J. Gibb, & R. Lippitt (Eds.), *The laboratory method of changing and learning* (pp. 172-188). Palo Alto, CA: Science & Behavior Books.

Lippitt, R., & Schindler-Rainmen, E. (1978). Knowing feeling, doing. In A. W. Foshay & I. Morrisett (Eds.), *Beyond the scientific: A comprehensive view of consciousness* (pp. 93-108). Boulder, CO: Social Science Education Consortium.

Schindler-Rainman, E., & Lippitt, R. (1975). Awareness learning and skill development. In K. Benne, L. P. Bradford, J. Gibb, & R. Lippitt (Eds.), *The laboratory methods of changing and learning* (pp. 213-239). Palo Alto, CA: Science & Behavior Books.

Increasing Awareness of Self and Others: A Perspective Through Which To View Group (or Life) Events

Philip G. Hanson

When we talk about awareness of self and others—which involves awareness of such processes as communication, giving and receiving feedback, interpersonal relations, risk taking, and handling conflict—we need first to address the issue of reality. That is, we must ask ourselves two questions.

- When we describe, label, interpret, judge, or evaluate an event, from whose perspective are we talking—yours or mine?
- When two or more of us observe and react to a particular behavior or event, do we experience it the same way?

For the purposes of this article, I deal with two kinds of reality: the kind of reality created through agreement, and the kind that constitutes one's own experience of persons, things, and events. The first is called **social reality,** and is public, and the second—**personal reality**—is private, until one shares it. A third kind of reality, which is referred to occasionally, is the **ultimate reality** underlying the other two realities.

Social reality

Social reality is (relatively) external to one and deals with a reality that has been agreed upon by many, and which can be changed through agreement. Why do we call a chair a chair and a table a table? Some persons, somewhere, at some time agreed to call these items a chair and a table. We collectively agree—that is, hold a general consensus—on what is right and wrong, good and bad, beautiful and ugly, legal and illegal, fair and unfair. This agreement extends even to such conventions as to how many degrees a circle has, how long a foot is, how heavy a pound is, and the like. We set standards and then make judgments based on

©1987 NTL Institute. All rights reserved.

these standards. In disagreements, persons can be right or wrong, can win or lose arguments. Social reality can also be called "cultural" reality, because it is a kind of reality that is influenced—or dictated—by the particular culture and the period of time in which one lives. This is the kind of reality one must be in touch with to function and communicate effectively in society. Not being in touch with it constitutes a serious threat to the survival of the individual.

Personal reality

Personal reality is one's own experience. This experience represents what is real for one at any given moment and includes one's feelings, body sensations, thoughts, perceptions, beliefs, values, imagery, and attitudes. Each person's experience (personal reality) differs from every other person's, and is a consequence of and is influenced by one's personal history. This personal history influences how an individual experiences the world, and how the experience of the world influences the individual's own history. One's personal reality, therefore, is peculiar to that person.

Because we have been trained throughout our lives, to perceive the world in certain ways and to adopt commonly shared values, however, our personal reality overlaps others' personal reality so that we may have similar reactions to the same event. Most of us may laugh at a joke, feel horrified by a killing, get angry when we feel put down. Even if people have similar reactions to events and persons, however, their experience of these events is never identical. Indeed, one can never really know another person's reality, nor can one ever experience, directly, the reality "out there" because it has always been sifted through (influenced, distorted, or changed by) one's own experience. To experience directly, external reality, one would have to empty oneself of one's thoughts, concepts, values, judgments, beliefs, and other "mind" or "ego" processes making up a person's perceptual screen. The problem of "what is real" preoccupied many ancient philosophers and is still a much-discussed issue. Kant epitomized this issue in his statement, "You can never know the thing in itself *(ding an sich)*" (see Durant, 1954, p. 271).

Your own experience does not have to agree with another person's experience. The peculiarity of one's personal reality, however, does not mean that persons cannot reach an agreement as to how they perceive others. One problem frequently encountered is that of determining whose reality "is real." We tend to apply the same kind of reasoning, when considering social reality reached through agreement, to personal reality that is one's person experience. As a result, persons argue over whose experience is correct, when this type of reasoning is inappropriate. The most any individual can say is that he or she experiences something differently from another person, or that one person's experience of an event seems to agree with others' experience of the same event. You cannot say that one person's experience is right and another's is wrong. Personal reality is neither right nor wrong, good nor bad—except as you evaluate it that way. **Any reality—excluding ultimate reality—is only a point of view.**

The problem of what is real also arises when considering theoretical points of view. Many professionals become so identified with a particular theory that they treat the theory as if it were ultimate reality itself. When pushed, they will say they consider a theory "true" to the extent that it approximates reality, with each professional considering her or his theory a close approximation of reality, and therefore viewing all alternate points of view of an event to be incorrect, or—at best—inadequate. The question is: How can one approximate something about which one has no direct knowledge? Much "heat" is generated in arguing over whose theory is right, rather than seeing each theory for what it is: a useful description, explanation, or symbolic representation of something one can never know directly.[1] A theory's "truth" depends on its popularity—that is, on social reality reached through general agreement. What is the risk of putting aside one's point of view to understand another's? The risk is that you may thus be influenced to change your mind about your own point of view.

If I accept my personal reality, whatever it is, as true for me, and if that reality is only a point of view, what then guides my behavior? At this point, I am aware that my values guide my behavior, and my behavior—that is, what I do rather than what I say—reflects those values.

Personal reality and responsibility

Personal reality—one's own experience—is a reality one creates, for which one is responsible and which one can change over time. This statement is difficult to accept. Most of us would like to lay the blame for our experience on others and make them responsible for the way we feel. Each person has been creating her or his own reality, however, since birth—perhaps prior to that.

The mind is not a passive recipient of all incoming stimuli, but actively sorts what it will or will not respond to (through selective attention and inattention) and organizes events to make "sense" in order to survive, cope, and grow. What people teach us or train us to do is their responsibility. For example, one may perceive identical twins as receiving the same kind of treatment from their parents. Yet if one turns out to be "successful" and the other "a failure," everyone wonders what happened, especially because heredity is constant with identical twins. From the perspective of the twins, however, they may have different experiences of their relationships with their parents. For example, both may ask their father to play with them, but he says he is too tired. One twin's experience may be that the father has had a hard day and is tired, and so that twin does something else. The other, however, may experience the father as not wanting to play with them, and feel rejected. If the twins' realities continue to develop in the directions indicated, their experiences of the same events will continue to diverge.

Your experience of events is the only reality you have, and that reality is true for you at that moment. Stated another way, nothing outside of you **causes** your experience.[2] For example, if other persons caused your feelings, then everyone would have the same feelings (or reactions) to an external event, such as a joke or an insult. This would thus make you the victim (the effect) of other persons' behavior. If others caused your experience, then you would have to get them to change so that you could change.

You cannot change others or the world so that you can change, but you can change your view of the world if you accept responsibility for creating your own experience. If you create your experience, you can then recreate (or change) your experience—a much more powerful position than that of being a victim of circumstances. Furthermore, if nothing outside of you causes your feelings, where do they come from? Your feelings, of which you have many, have been with you a long time; they are always there, representing an ongoing internal state of affairs. Most of your feelings, however, are dormant until some event triggers them and they surface: At that moment you become aware of your feelings.

Other persons can provide the stimulus to which you react—usually automatically, not intentionally—by evoking these feelings. Indeed, the person to whom you are reacting may be far less important than the behavior that person manifests. If I am overly sensitive to rejection, then I may react to a variety of behaviors that I perceive as rejecting, regardless of who is displaying them. If I can become aware of the behaviors to which I am sensitive, how I interpret them, and how my reactions reflect my interpretations, I may then be able to respond appropriately—both internally and externally—to the person involved. If I accept responsibility for everything I am and how I behave, feel, and think, then it follows that I am the creator of my own experience (personal reality).

Completing an experience

Most of us do not allow ourselves to experience fully what happens in the here and now, particularly if the experience is negative. Instead of staying with the experience (i.e., attending to or noting our feelings, body sensations, thoughts, images, and any emerging attitudes), we suppress the experience by avoiding, denying, covering over, substituting a weaker feeling, or shutting it off by evaluating it, by trying to make sense of it, or by assigning to it a cause-and-effect relationship. By using these avoidance maneuvers, we keep the experience in a state of incompletion, where it continues to exert pressure toward completion. We allow the experience to maintain its energy to draw our attention toward it, which then requires more energy to resist the pull. If the energy level is strong enough, it prevents us from giving full attention to matters at hand.

Each person is a reservoir of incomplete experiences (or tasks) continuously exerting tugs and pushes. Fortunately, most of them lack sufficient energy to immobilize one and keep one from attending to daily activities. The incompletions do, however, increase the difficulty of focusing fully on one's present experiences, free from intrusions and distractions. For example, think of the times you've tried to concentrate on what you were reading when you knew a promised letter waited to be written, when you had had your feelings hurt earlier that day and had tried to rationalize the hurt feelings away, or when you had had an argument and left the issue unsettled. Staying with the experience—completing it—allows other aspects to emerge until one has the "whole picture." This process drains the energy from the experience and decreases its power to draw one's attention unwillingly. Moreover, this completion then frees more energy for the present situation, as one is not spending energy resisting the expression of the incomplete experience.

The situation becomes even more complicated through the collusion of others in helping you avoid the experience—for example, by cheering you up when you feel sad, cradling you when you're hurt, and telling you not to feel angry. To focus on what is happening **now** and to accept the experience as real one at that moment increases one's awareness of the total situation.

To complete an experience is to be done with it. When one does not fully acknowledge an experience, it stays with that person. If I deny or suppress my anger, it does not really go away; it creates physiological and psychological tensions and continues to influence my behavior. People tend to want to hang on to many experiences by trying to prolong or relive them if they are good, or by becoming obsessed with them if they have not been resolved satisfactorily. Resisting an experience as a means of getting rid of it is really a way of not changing. Completing an experience leaves an empty space into which one can invest (create) another experience free from the remnants of a previous experience, which can persist or interfere with the new experience (as when the incomplete experience of anger lingers to contaminate the appreciation of a warm embrace). Completing an experience enriches contact with all the elements of an experience and increases an awareness of self in general.

The following four steps facilitate the development of awareness.

Step 1: Witnessing

To facilitate the process of increasing one's awareness of events—both internal and external—one will find it helpful to develop the role of witness. Witnessing is a Buddhist concept in which the individual observes oneself as one acts, reacts, and interacts in one's daily activities. In each of us exist many roles one acts out every day. These roles may also be thought of as "I's" or "you's"—the angry I or you, the loving I or you, the I that wants my own way, the I the father, the I the jogger, and the like. Central to, and distinct from, all these roles is an I that sees or notes what is going on. This is one's center, the physical and psychological point of equilibrium that is calm, dispassionate, and aloof from one's desires, feelings, thoughts, and acts, and that views even these events as objects. The subject is I, the object consists of desires, feelings, thoughts, and acts.

The act of witnessing or observing oneself involves **only noting** what is happening in the here and now, without evaluating, judging, or interpreting. Diekman (1982) uses the term "the observing self." Most of us conduct this kind of self-observation to some extent when we occasionally watch ourselves playing out some interaction, or note how we feel about something; we may say, "Here I go again, wanting things my way" (in my case, "Phil is feeling irritated because he is not getting his way"). Most of the time, however, we forget our self-observations by identifying with our desires, feelings, thoughts, and behaviors, focusing on the other person, on the content of the transaction, on our need to win or be right, or on our judgments and evaluations. At these times, one is not centered; the witness is obscured and one is asleep. As one begins to cease identifying with these other roles (I's), witnessing becomes less obscured and more frequent, and one becomes more centered in one's daily activities.

The act of self-observation can change an experience. Even in quantum physics, this is true. Quantum physicists have found that the act of observing subatomic particles influences the movement of these particles and changes the nature of the interaction between the observer and the observed—that is, the observer "participates" in the change rather than remaining an unobtrusive, external observer. In witnessing oneself, the "external" event may not change, but one's **experience** of it changes. You begin to know the laws by which you operate and live more of your life on the **causal** plane.

Step 2: Awareness

Most of us live our daily lives in a state of unawareness, occasionally awakening to experience what is happening with us and with others. Awareness is that level of consciousness prior to judging and conceptualizing. Awareness is not a matter of judging or perceiving, but of just being aware. It gradually takes on the characteristics of attention and interest. Awareness involves attending to what is going on with you **now** in terms of your feelings, body sensations, thoughts, images, and attitudes, and being attuned to what is going on with others by actively attending to them (i.e., listening and seeing). Awareness is a here-and-now phenomenon that does not occur in the past or future.

The past is a memory and the future is a hope or fear. One finds it difficult to be aware of what is happening now when one's attention is focused either on the past or the future. Most of us avoid the present moment by continually dealing with things that happened yesterday, last month, or last year, planning for things that will happen in the coming minutes, hours, days, or years, and focusing on what is happening elsewhere in the world. In addition, we spend much of our time wishing things were better or different, desiring this or that experience, thinking of how we'd like to be and how we'd like others to change. Indeed, much of our present-day attitudes concerning growth and goal setting foster a future-oriented focus of attention. The idea of "searching" or "seeking" for a better way of being, enlightenment, or whatever implies that what one is looking for lies somewhere else at another time, rather than within oneself at the present time (here and now). In addition, always being in the future or always planning for the future robs one of the pleasure of attaining one's goal. That is, if you get what you planned for, you cannot enjoy the achievement or experience the fruits of your planning in the here and now—in the present—because you are still in the future: planning, imagining, and hoping. You never catch up with yourself. Being aware requires a willingness just to be with oneself, with others, and with the experience as it occurs here and now.

Step 3: Acceptance

Once you are aware of an experience, the next step is to accept it as true for you at that moment. What is, **is.** Ways of not accepting an experience include evaluating or judging how it should or should not be, whether it is right or wrong, or good or bad, and trying to justify, rationalize, or make sense of it. Not accepting the experience is another way of resisting or avoiding it. If I can accept my anger without evaluating myself as good or bad, or justifying my behavior in terms of the situation or some historical antecedents, then my awareness of that experience increases. By staying focused on the experience and letting it flow through me, other aspects of the total experience may emerge—for example, feelings of fear and unworthiness behind the anger.

Acceptance of one's experience is also important to changing behavior one wishes to change. You cannot change behavior that you do not "own" or that you continuously defend. I cannot work through my anger if I do not accept or own my angry feelings. Being aware of my anger and accepting it as true for me without judging myself or evaluating the feeling changes the nature of the experience itself. Sometimes one deals with an unpleasant situation or feeling by saying, "I'm not going to let that bother me," thinking one thus accepts the situation. This rejection of the experience ties up energy and is really another strategy to avoid the unpleasant feeling or experience. True acceptance is a more passive, open way of letting an experience become part of one's own reality, noting the event, and then moving on to whatever else one must do. In broader terms, acceptance allows me to be what I am at any given time and enables me to allow others to be or not be what they are.

Step 4: Sharing

Two kinds of sharing exist. One involves sharing some experience so as to get other persons' reactions and feedback on their feelings and perceptions. The other kind of sharing—the one I address here—seeks to enlist other persons to listen to and understand what one attempts to communicate. The goal is not to get others to agree or disagree with—or evaluate or react to—what one is sharing, but to have others participate in the experience by trying to obtain clarity as to what the experience is. During the process of sharing, feelings and perceptions may change solely as a consequence of the physical act of talking about the experience (describing it), hearing oneself talk about it, and experiencing the act of communicating. The experience is further enhanced when others try to understand you and facilitate your exploration of the experience by helping you stay focused on it.

What you do not share tends to remain inside in a state of incompletion. What you share openly helps to complete the experience and creates a sense of closure. This is particularly true for experiences that involve negative feelings. For example, recall interactions that you found frustrating or upsetting. They usually involved something that you did not share with the other person with respect to your feelings, expectations, or thoughts. What usually happens then is that you obsess about with what you should have done or said, or you continue to work out the interaction to a satisfactory completion in your fantasy. The process of sharing helps you become more aware of yourself and your intentions in the interaction—and, as a consequence, completes the experience with the other person. You can then communicate more clearly because the completion of the experience leaves no clutter.

A model for increasing awareness of self and others

Increasing awareness of self and others is best done when the focus of your attention is on your own behavior and how it affects others. Ram Dass (1976, pp. 91, 115) offered good advice when he said that if you have any problems about how things are, "work on yourself." We tend to work on others, trying to get them to change or to be more sensitive (to our own needs, of course). You can, however, enlist the aid of others to increase your own awareness. Each of us has two facets of ourselves that inhibit our potential for increased awareness. One facet deals with the extent to which we are **unaware** of many **of our behaviors** and how they affect others—that is, we do not **sense** their reactions (an external experience). The other facet deals with the relatively small amount of **sharing** we usually do about our **own experiences;** we therefore shut off potential information concerning how others may react to our "internal" experiences.

For this article, I use the terms "internal experience" and "external experience" in the following way. One's internal experience is privy only to oneself, and does not become available to others unless one chooses to share it. Internal experience includes desires, attitudes, feelings, body sensations, motivations, thoughts, and the like. If one shares one's internal experience and others react to it, the transaction affects one's external experience, including how one sees, hears, smells, touches, and tastes. As long as one keeps one's experience private (internal), one cannot know its effect on others. External experience is one's perception of how others react to what one has shared (one's internal experience). External experience enables one to become aware of one's impact on others.

One's private reaction to one's own impact is also one's internal experience, and it remains private until one shares it. In addition to others' reactions to one, external experience involves one's perceptions of others persons' behavior in general. Both internal and external experience require attending to one's own physical and psychological states and to what one's senses pick up from the environment, particularly the interpersonal environment. A cycle becomes repeated again and again: Have an internal experience, share it, perceive how others react, have an external experience, react privately (an internal experience), share that internal experience, and so forth.

Although I present the cycle as consisting of discrete events—for the purposes of clarity—I must emphasize that considerable overlap and simultaneity to these processes happen. A powerful mutual influence exists between the internal and external experience. What one senses or does not sense is strongly influenced by one's internal state of affairs, which in turn is strongly influenced by what one senses. Information through both these sources is observed by the witness. What information is available to the witness, however, is a function of the level and scope of awareness of the individual, and, at the same time, awareness is increased through the act of witnessing.

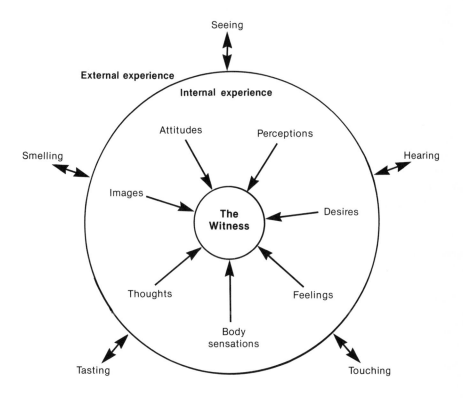

Figure 1. Anatomy of experience

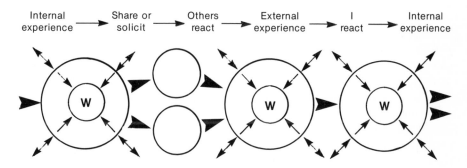

Figure 2. The cycle of experience

The two activities of the cycle through which increases one's awareness of oneself and others—which are elaborated upon below--are (1) attending to and sharing one's internal experience, and (2) obtaining and attending to others' reactions to oneself. The model is an "intentional" model—that is, the individual actively pursues the goal of increasing awareness of oneself and others by sharing and soliciting personally relevant information. Other ways of increasing awareness, of course, may be more passive, such as observing (witnessing) and attending to both internal and external affairs of the moment—that is, just noting without doing.

One way I can increase my awareness of myself is to obtain feedback from others (an external experience) about my behavior and how it affects them in terms of their perceptions and feelings. This process requires a receptive attitude toward others and a willingness to clarify what others are communicating to me without dampening their impact by evaluating their reactions or defending my behavior. At the same time, my awareness of them is increased in two ways. First, my attention is focused on them, rather than myself, and what they are trying to convey to me (and how they are doing this). Second, their feedback about my behavior also communicates to me what their areas of sensitivity are. If I get upset when you interrupt me and I let you know my feelings, I am also letting you know that I am sensitive to that kind of behavior. Remaining in contact with the other person during the interaction also includes observing (witnessing) my own reactions (internal experience, such as the extent to which I am judging or defending something) without getting embroiled in them. I just note that they are present and, at the same time, keep my attention focused on the other person.

To increase others' awareness of me, and at the same time increase my awareness of myself and my impact on others through their eyes and through the act of sharing, I must **share with them my own** feelings and reactions (internal experience) to their behavior. That is, I must let them know that my experience is of myself and of them. When I share myself, I have less need for others to interpret my behavior or to project their own personal issues onto what they think I am or am not communicating. When I do not share, I can only guess what others' reactions might be to my internal experience. Like persons who never test their assumptions, I may be building myths about the persons around me and behaving as if these myths were true.

I must offer a note of caution. I do **not** mean that people should always share their personal experience of what is going on with them or that it is better to be self-disclosing all the time. One some occasions it is far wiser to keep your feelings to yourself, such as when you are angry at your autocratic boss, when you perceive someone as too fragile or too self-deprecating to hear your feedback constructively, or when you realize you are dumping your own issues on someone else. Self-disclosure may also be inappropriate or disruptive in some situations— such as some staff or faculty meetings—in which powerful norms restrict this kind of behavior. Knowing when not to share may also indicate a high level of awareness. Even when it is wiser to withhold your feelings, however, two consequences still exist in terms of increasing awareness: You do not really know what the impact of your sharing would have been (how others would react is, and will remain, only a guess or fantasy), and you do not experience what your feelings, body sensations, and thoughts would have been during the act of sharing. What this article addresses is one's general interpersonal **style** with respect to sharing and soliciting personally relevant information, **not** those incidental occasions when one must choose whether or not to disclose one's personal reactions.

The extent to what one does or does not work on one's internal and/or external experience results in three levels of potential for increasing awareness:

- the lowest level, which indicates little or no attending to either internal or external experience,
- the moderate level, which suggests unilateral attention to internal **or** external experience (one or the other),
- the highest level, which indicates attending to both internal **and** external experience.

An individual may move up and down these levels depending on the relationship one has with the other person, the situation, and one's psychological state at the moment. A particular level, however, may be more characteristic of some individuals than of others—that is, some persons are more open that others. The levels are described in detail below.

Level I: The lowest level

The lowest level of potential for increasing my awareness occurs when little or no sharing of my experience takes place with others or when I do not solicit others' experience of me. What is real for me is not shared; what is real for others is not solicited. The lowest level may represent an unproductive turning inward toward myself, in which the primary focus is not to gain greater awareness of myself and others, but to defend against information not consistent with the image I am maintaining or projecting. Energy used to maintain these communication barriers is not available for creativity, exploration, or personal growth. As a result, untapped resources remain under wraps. The lens for a clearer, broader picture of myself in relation to myself and others is kept out of focus and narrow. By not sharing my own experience and testing it against the experience of others, I may develop private representations of the world around me that are somewhat out of focus with what is really there. Not knowing who I am, I do not know what I can become. Not knowing who others are, I am unwilling to risk the openness necessary for mutually enhancing one another's awareness. This low-level exchange of personally relevant communication decreases my potential for increased awareness and keeps me "stuck" where I am.

Level 2a: Self to others

This style of sharing indicates that I am expressing my reactions to others (internal experience), but not soliciting or attending to their reactions to me (external experience). That is, when their feedback to me is not given, I do not seek it, or when they do react I do not perceive what and how they are communicating. As a consequence, I may not be aware of my impact on others and appear insensitive to their feelings. Expressing my feelings about their behavior may take the form of dumping rather than sharing my experience. Information from others, critical to increasing my self-awareness and sensitivity, is not available to me. Not listening to others, I am tuned in to my own noise, which further interferes with listening and provides no external criteria against which to assess the impact of how my needs and reactions are expressed. Much of my feedback, therefore, may come across as evaluative and judgmental, or as expectations and demands on others. My insensitive style may alienate others and further increase my isolation, making unavailable to me the corrective function of feedback from others. By interacting with others, I may—to some degree—increase my opportunities for developing greater awareness, an improvement over Level 1. By keeping the flow of personal information moving in one direction, however, I do not learn the experience others have of me, thereby decreasing my potential for greater awareness at the same time. As a result of this one-way communication, I may continue to behave in ways that keep communication barriers up and that provide no data for changing my style and increasing my awareness of myself and others.

Level 2b: Others to self

This is another style of one-way communication, and suggests that I am not sharing my own experience of myself and other persons (internal experience), but rather am spending time soliciting and attending to feedback or information from others (external experience). My not sharing my own experience with others may arise from an unwillingness to risk exposing myself to criticism or to hearing feedback that would violate my self-image. As a consequence, I must first ascertain what others think and feel or have some notion of how they will react before I will commit myself. Because I do not share what is going on with me, I am frequently stuck with an incomplete experience. For example, if I handle an interpersonal conflict situation unsatisfactorily and do not communicate my feelings or thoughts at the time, my experience of the situation remains unfinished. I am then forced to complete the experience in fantasy or in repeated ruminations of what I have should have said or done instead. My awareness of that interaction is curtailed by not knowing what the consequences would have been had I shared my experience.

Focusing only on soliciting or attending to feedback from others enables me to increase my awareness of the feelings and perceptions that others have of me, an improvement over Level 1. This awareness, however, may be biased by others having a limited experience of me because of the facade I maintain. Not knowing what I am thinking or feeling, others may project their own personal needs and fear onto my blank screen. As a consequence, I may find it difficult to sort out what is coming from me rather than from them. In addition, the awareness that accrues from the very act of sharing my own experience is unavailable to me.

Level 3: The highest level

The highest potential for increasing my level of awareness occurs when I share my own experience of myself and others and solicit from them and attend to the experience they have of me and of themselves. This mutual exchange of feedback increases my awareness of how others experience me (external experience) and how I experience myself (internal experience). This kind of mutual sharing also enables me to get "unstuck" from my own point of view (personal reality) and to get a sense of the other person's personal reality. My willingness to share facilitates a greater acceptance of what is real or true for me. As a consequence of greater acceptance of what is real for me, the potential for change and increased awareness is greater. A major "payoff" of accepting and sharing is that I am able to complete experiences rather than remain stuck with them. I can then move on to create new experiences.

Individuals can move from Level 1 to Level 3 through a self-initiated program geared to increasing their awareness of themselves and others, such as workshops, self-development through reading and practice, and getting involved with a teacher, group, or school. As mentioned above, increasing awareness is a function of both intention (taking an active role) and just witnessing (taking a passive role). The active role, as discussed in terms of this model, requires some sensitivity and selectivity with respect to whom you choose for sharing or soliciting personally relevant information. Sharing and soliciting feelings and reactions indiscriminately will scare off most persons. In some settings, however—such as T Groups, therapy groups, and encounter groups—this kind of mutual sharing is the norm. Outside of these settings, we can select persons in our interpersonal environment who care for us and who are willing to exchange this kind of information to our mutual benefit. In any event, deciding upon the kind of person one wants to be—whether this is open and available or closed and unavailable—is a crucial choice that involves a lifelong commitment.

Conclusion

In summary, awareness can be enhanced in two ways. First, one can passively but alertly scan both the internal and external environment, maintaining a receptive openess to experiences. The other route is more intentional and requires an active involvement with others in collecting feedback and in sharing one's personal experience of what is happening to oneself and others. Awareness is a here-and-now phenomenon that can occur only in the present. To focus continuously on the past, future, or something other than the here and now is to maintain the status quo. By attending only to the forest, you miss the exquisite delicacy and fragrance of a single wild flower. The key to awareness and change, therefore, is to be in the present, to experience what is happening, and to chose the quality of your life. To quote the Indian sage Rajneesh (1976), "Awareness is a mind flowing in all directions simultaneously. Nothing is excluded and nothing is a distraction. All things exist together, and if you can listen, just be aware, everything becomes part of one harmony."

NOTES

1. This statement is reflected in the world view of many Quantum physicists, such as Eddington,

Bohr, Schroedinger, and Jeans, and is best summarized by Sir James Jeans (quoted by Wilber, 1984, pp. 9-10):

> The essential fact is simply that *all* the pictures which science now draws of nature, and which alone seem capable of according with observational facts, are *mathematical* pictures . . . . They are nothing more than pictures—fictions if you like, if by fiction you mean that science is not yet in contact with ultimate reality. Many would hold that, from the broad philosophical standpoint, the outstanding achievement of twentieth-century physics is not the theory of relativity with its welding together of space and time, or the theory of quanta with its present apparent negation of the laws of causation, or the dissection of the atom with the resultant discovery that things are not what they seem; it is the general recognition that we are not yet in contact with reality. We are still imprisoned in our cave with our backs to the light, and can only watch the shadows on the wall.

2. This statement does not imply that nothing exists "out there." How one experiences what is out there is the contribution of one's mind. This idea is not new; Kant (see Durant, 1954, p. 272) turned the world of science and religion around by distinguishing between the world one constructs—phenomena—and the thing in itself, noumena. What is out there cannot be experienced directly; how it **is** experienced is the construction one makes from the stimuli one's senses receive. "Sensation is unorganized stimulus, perception is organized sensation, conception is organized perception, science is organized knowledge, wisdom is organized life . . ." (p. 271). This point of view—that what we experience is our own creation—is still current among many in the scientific community.

REFERENCES

Diekman, A. J. (1982). *The observing self: Mysticisms and psychotherapy.* Boston: Beacon Press.

Durant, W. (1954). *The story of philosophy: The lives and opinions of the world's greatest philosophers.* New York: Pocket Books.

Rajneesh, B. S. (1976). *The hidden harmony: Discourses on the fragments of Heraclitus.* Poona, India: Rajneesh Foundation.

Ram Dass (with Levine, S.). (1976). *Grist for the mill.* Santa Cruz, CA: Unity Press.

Wilber, K. (Ed.). (1984). *Quantum questions: Mystical writings of the world's great physicists.* Boulder, CO: Shambhala Publications (New Science Library).

ANNOTATED BIBLIOGRAPHY

Bentov, I. (1977). *Stalking the wild pendulum: On the mechanics of consciousness.* New York: E. P. Dutton. (Very readable and illustrated with delightful cartoons.)

Brandon, N. (1971). *The disowned self.* New York: Bantam Books (with arrangements with Nash Publishing or Los Angeles). (Description of awareness includes conceptual awareness.)

Capra, F. (1977). *The tao of physics.* New York: Bantam Books. (Capra has modified his views since this book was published. He presents a readable summary of Eastern mysticism and Quantum physics. Read within the framework that physics neither proves nor disproves mysticism. Statements that are similar on the surface do not necessarily reflect an underlying connection.)

Hanson, P. G. (1981). *Learning through groups: A trainer's basic guide.* San Diego: University Associates. (Note particularly Chapter 3 on feedback.)

Heider, J. (1985). *The tao of Leadership: Lao Tzu's Tao Te Ching adapted for a new age.* Atlanta: Humanics. (Group-oriented leadership.)

Pagels, H. (1982). *The cosmic code.* New York: Bantam Books. (An excellent review of quantum physics for the layperson.)

Ram Dass. (1974). *The only dance there is.* Garden City, NY: Anchor Press/Doubleday. (Eastern mysticism and Western psychology discussed.)

Smith, W. L. (Ed.). (1976). *The growing edge of Gestalt therapy.* Secaucus, NJ: The Citadel Press. (One section integrates concepts with Gestalt therapy.)

Courses and Working Conferences as Transitional Learning Institutions: A Tavistock Institute Approach to Training and Development

Harold Bridger

> "A fish only realizes that it lives in water when it is already on the bank."
> —old French saying

> "If we do not learn from history we shall be doomed to repeat it."
> —George Santayana

> "A basic principle of groups . . . how any given person was reconciling personal ambitions, hopes and fears with the requirements exacted by the group for its success."
> —W. R. Bion

> "The main emphasis today is that people want to arrive without the experience of getting there."
> —Daniel Boorstin

Introduction

In one sense the four quotations above, taken together, express the purpose and problems of the kind of training with which I have been associated. The first relates to the complexity and uncertainty associated with our environment. It implies that we have much to learn about ourselves and the immediate systems and relationships in which we live. The second bids us to take note of the "there and then," while the third draws attention to the issues of the "here and now." The fourth warns us that attempts to take into account the "what is to be" will not only be hampered by those who want to retain or return to the "there and then," but also

©1987 NTL Institute. All rights reserved.

by expectations derived from technological advance rather than from an appreciation of learning and development processes.

In such a context, courses and working conferences (other than those devoted to simple instruction or to inculcating skills and techniques) should be able to act as communities and organizations for self-study when providing participants with experience and concepts related to processes operating in task-oriented groups. Further emphasis in this regard derives from the realization that the groups and organizations from which the participants come are largely "open systems"—that is, highly interactive with their environments. This is equally true for the Tavistock Institute, which is an independent, "not-for-profit" social research organization that, contrary to U.S. impressions, is primarily concerned with action research endeavors.[1]

While NTL Institute and T Group training were founded in 1947 by Leland Bradford and his colleagues, the Tavistock Institute (founded in 1946), following its wartime innovation of the use of groups for selecting officers (Sutherland & Fitzpatrick, 1945) and development of therapeutic communities (Bridger, 1984, 1985), resisted what was felt would be a distraction from learning more about the nature of organizations and the problems they were facing in the postwar era. Bion's constantly reiterated theme, to which I have always adhered, was the group's "study of its own internal tensions in a real-life situation." The importance he gave the last phase—a real-life situation—which most other Tavistock approaches neglect, derived from his further criterion: that "the study had to commend itself to the majority of the group as worthwhile and for this reason it had to be a study of a real-life situation" (Bion, 1946).

It was not until 1957, therefore, that Eric Trist and I designed, with the assistance of Hugh Coffey of NTL (on a two-year sabbatical at the Tavistock Institute), the first "Group Relations Training Conference" (Trist & Sofer, 1959). It must be said that the idea of sensitivity training (NTL's T Group) was felt to be quite inadequate because it concerned the study of interpersonal relations in a group setting and also allowed for interventions by the group "trainer" (a term we felt was quite inappropriate) on an interpersonal basis. The psychoanalytical orientation of Tavistock, together with our experience of group-centered (or group-level) interventions, derived from Bion's approach to group therapy (Bion, 1961), precluded any replication of NTL's methods. The conference design did, however, adopt the idea of following what we called the "Study Group" sessions with Application Groups. In addition, based on our wartime and later action-research training experiences, we introduced external operational tasks, in the course of which participants engaged with local bodies (i.e., police, industry, and local government) in exploring some specific problem or issue. The problem had to be real, and had to be identified by the "client" as one currently being examined by that client.

It was not until much later, however, that I discovered a fallacy that I feel related as much to NTL's approach as to ours. The sequential steps of Study Groups, Application Groups, and even external real-life assignments do not really fulfill Bion's criteria. The idea that the group of conference participants has the "task" of "learning about groups by being a group" only really meets the conditions for "the study of its own internal tensions" when the participants are patients prepared to join such a group—with the expectation of "getting better"—when the real-life task is seen as joining a group to get well. Although such a task can be seen as "worthwhile" for patients, it had different effects on the conference participants. This we discovered in a systematic follow-up study about a year later. Most of those (though not all) in the "business" of therapeutic or applied psychological activities felt that the Study Group experience had been both relevant and useful, both personally and professionally, whereas of those concerned with organizational and operational affairs a small number had derived personal insights, but only a few found the Study Group experience of value in either the Application Groups or for their work back home in their organizations.

We decided not to repeat the conference design until I had visited the NTL conference center in Bethel, Maine, discussed matters thoroughly with Lee Bradford and his colleagues, and tried out our approach in the NTL setting. I spent most of the summer of 1959 at Bethel doubling as Counselor for the community as a whole (quite a busy job in those days!) and as a "group trainer"—much as I disliked the term. Up to that time, a "group" for me had meant a body comprising 7-10 members. Imagine my surprise when I learned that the group consisted of 18 seated at a large, round table. I was reminded of King Arthur and his knights, but without his power and authority, and had only my group-centered interventions—if I could find one to make. Fortunately, the group members all started to introduce themselves to one another after I had stated the purpose of the group and of my own role. Then there was a silence, followed by a further spate of concern for me as someone who was so strange to the country and the culture and who must be experiencing great difficulties in understanding the U.S. way of life and finding my way around. Having learned from their exchanges of the wide variety of professions, roles, and organizations the members represented, and of the many different states from which they came, I was able to point out that "while it was quite true that I was a foreigner and learning to find my way around, perhaps I was also being used to cover both the individual members' feelings at entering Bethel and entering this group in particular, and that the group as a whole was feeling like a stranger, not knowing what it was or where it was." I have given this example not simply as a personal reminiscence of a significant point in time for me, but also to indicate the nature of the intervention itself.

Later, with the agreement of this group and others, I was able to invite other T Group trainers to observe the group at work while I was given a similar opportunity to observe their groups' activity. In particular, I was fortunate to be able to work with Jack Glidewell and take part in his role-playing, intergroup exercise that he had designed as an "application experience." It was this opportunity that led me later to introduce an intergroup component into our conference, but with the difference that it was part of the actual psychodynamics of the conference "institution" itself. Its objective was a task "that was real" within the conference setting (in effect to design a program of special interest sessions that would be relevant to the conference participants in the second week). The impact and potential for learning, however, both in the "large group" of the members and staff and for the conference as an "institution," enhanced and enriched the conference design.

On my return to England I took over the directorship of the "Leicester Conference" (as it came to be called) from Eric Trist. I redesigned the working conference to include the large-group/intergroup experience. A research component was built into the conference to study the intergroup phase and its effects (Higgin & Bridger, 1964). The improvement was marked in terms of both short-term and longer-term evaluations. In my view, however, the Study Group was far too close to a therapy group model to relate adequately to the rest of the design. There were still differences of view about this, even after two further conferences. It had seemed to me that the Study Group members, although they agreed to attend the conference itself, had no choice but to take part in an experience that, in effect, largely deprived them of utilizing powers and competence derived from real-life external roles and functions. In effect, the design and the consultant role **provoked** authority issues that might then be interpreted as such.

Actually, reports from those attending A. K. Rice Institute group relations events, as well as those using the current "Leicester" model, suggest that this phenomenon is still part of their current practice. I had proposed a relevant, task-oriented approach for the study group that would give a "worthwhile" relevance to the need for studying intragroup tensions—without, as we have discovered since—detracting one iota from the opportunity to explore the processes underlying the groups at work. In fact, the learning derived from that "double task" and group purpose and group process becomes more evident and more available for application in other events—and back home.

The technical and professional differences on this score were not resolved, because far more disruptive Institute events overtook and overwhelmed the Conference issues. In fact, there was an obvious connection between them. During Eric Trist's sabbatical at Palo Alto, A. K. Rice attempted—with the tacit agreement of a few—what can only be described as a "takeover bid" for Institute control. Although we were able to prevent this, it led, finally, to an agreed split in the Institute. This must be mentioned because the particular department head at Leicester University who was primarily concerned with the field of group relations and who "hosted" the conference had allied himself with the Rice group. As part of the overall division of affairs, therefore, the "Leicester" conferences were handed over to this group. I was then free, however, to redesign and develop the conference elsewhere.

Contemporary events and developments

During the latter half of the 1950s, Eric Trist, in collaboration with Ken Bamforth, an Institute Fellow with a mining background, had formulated the concept of the sociotechnical system (Trist & Bamforth, 1951). I had been conducting an action research study with Philips, the multinational electronics firm, which in effect was concerned with "interface" and boundary problems between two divisions of the company—that is, a "live" intergroup situation. As we began to make headway (to which the experience of the conference intergroup work had contributed a good deal), two other areas opened up: the initiation of autonomous and semiautonomous work group experiments, and the development of managers to meet the challenge of change in their roles and operational tasks. This is not the place to discuss these fields in detail, but I will say it was the combination of all these elements, almost coincidentally with the Institute split, that provided me the opportunity to rethink and develop an improved design in collaboration with a company whose management felt it "worthwhile" to review its strategic, management, and operational approaches selectively. There was what I later referred to as a spirit of being "bothered"—in the best sense of the word—about accelerating technological advances and the implications for operations, for management, for organizational choices, and for marketing (environmental) policies. Of course there were many others—one thing led to another—but it was through the investment in selected field work and in training that the commitment was most evident. It was, therefore, in the context and demands of the work place that the opportunity occurred to rethink the conference design—but from a quite different viewpoint. This time, the job was to develop training designs relevant to distinct organizational needs—but ones that entailed considering the organization as a whole, its environment, boundaries, and interdependencies—and its changing managerial and operational modes. Such designs, naturally to be adapted to different memberships, would also have some more general basic applications. In collaboration with key training and technical people, I shared in identifying some basic considerations.

Essentially, each facet of the pilot course was to be concerned with "managing groups at work"—which entailed **understanding** groups at work—hence the need to appreciate the essence of informal systems and other processes affecting a group as a sociotechnical system. Both in trials and in discussion, it became clear that the **consultative** aspects of management were becoming increasingly significant, whether for more sophisticated and satisfying appraisal methods and career development, or for reaching the most effective outcome with a work force. I came to see the consultative process as a "basic building block" in the development of a group as well as an important element in its own right within any training for organizational effectiveness (Bridger, 1981). The Study Group became a "Work Group," but with a double task.

- The group had to work on selected issues of importance for group members in their organizational settings and in their roles. The group was to "manage" its own selection of topic(s) and to manage itself. It always, implicitly, posed to itself the problem—and the challenge—of being able to face differentiation within itself, thereby enabling leadership and other capabilities to be demonstrated according to the pertinent circumstances.
- The group had to identify the processes operating within the group at different times, especially the way the group as a whole (the group entity), with its particular set of values and norms established at any time, was influencing events and modes of working.

It was recognized that by developing its capacities for the second task and recognizing the group working "as if" it were carrying out its appointed task and managing itself appropriately, the group could[2] more readily address its objectives and become more effective. With respect to individual group members, each would be able to draw personal observations and inferences for himself or herself from ongoing group experiences, conducting a "private task," whose product could either be offered to the group—in part or as a whole or, indeed, not at all.

The "intergroup" could be developed in a variety of forms, but in early models of the training design (Low & Bridger, 1979) it also had as its task an interim review of the course about two-thirds of the way through the week.[3] Each Work Group would review the experience thus far and prepare recommendations for amending the remainder of the proposed program so as to better meet the original or changed expectations of the Work Group members. In addition, each group was to select an appropriate group member (or two) to represent the group at a meeting with the staff representative and jointly make some proposals. "Talk-discussions," which gave a conceptual framework to the experience and self-review, were a feature of the course, and were placed at points when they were most likely to be relevant.

The placing and interlocking of these aspects, together with transitions for entry and departure, were carefully thought through to ensure that both the "real-life situation" and the "study of processes" (internal tensions) involved were operating for each component dynamic of the course, as well as for the whole.

The Tavistock Institute/Bath University and international designs

As the internal courses for various designs, length, and complexity were established for different levels, functions, and sides of this company and others, it became possible to identify those who could take over such training and fill the appropriate staff roles. This has always been a feature of the action research approach. To fulfill this development effectively, specially designed external programs were developed, both internationally and in the United Kingdom.

For many years, collaboration with Bath University replaced the development that had been halted by the break with the "Leicester" model, and eventually four years ago that too was replaced by an international design that can also more readily study cross-cultural processes. This basic action research endeavor has now found a permanent "home" at Minster Lovell, near Oxford, England, in the heart of the Cotswold country. Although this article must be restricted with respect to history, growth, and various directions of further development, it must be said that the annual visit to Bethel has been a feature of trans-Atlantic development. This mutual enrichment, begun in 1959, has continued on both sides of the Atlantic, and innovative designs—which have included combinations of sociotechnical and psychodynamic approaches, NTL member colleagial models, and, even more recently, collaboration with executive and staff development designs with Birge "Ric" Reichard in Canada—have demonstrated their transnational quality and capacity for diffusion. Although there are basic elements, there is no single pattern. The particular participants and staff for each program determine the outcomes and learnings gained. To encourage that perception, a "Personal Mapping" experience is provided some time ahead as part of the preconference phase and to introduce the transitional approach well ahead of the conference itself. Personal mapping is not a questionnaire, but an opportunity for the participant to reflect on a wide variety of issues pertinent to her or his participation and own "private task"; it is not intended to be communicated to anyone else. It is entirely up to the individual to judge what he or she does or does not refer to it. One small section toward the end also provides some guidelines for preparing the issue or problem that the participant may want to use in the consultative group work.

In the last resort, however, the critical judgment is the extent to which the individual can mobilize collaborative—not just advisory or supervisory—support or reinforcement. We usually suggest that two colleagues should attend such courses or conferences, unless colleagues are already available in the organizational or work setting who have attended such events.

A conceptual basis for further consideration and development of the Tavistock Institute approach

Although it is unusual to outline an approach and design before providing the conceptual frame, I do not apologize for doing so because it is as a result of creating such designs that the relevance to future developments has emerged.

If we are to design appropriate training and—above all—equip consultants to meet the demands of future change, we had better realize that it is not only the organizations that need help to change. Increasingly, consultants get out of date without realizing it, and the first signs of this are the frenetic chasing after the latest "techniques" or "exercises." Suffice it to say it is important not only to understand and become equipped to deal with trends, but also to recognize how and why these trends are developing in this way—and why we need better understanding and competence to cope with both the transition and eventual outcome.

I therefore outline my way of looking at such trends and conclude with a set of "paradigm shifts," many aspects of which are already in being.

Characteristics of change in society and organizations

The accelerating rate of change in social, educational, technological, economic, and other fields—and, above all, the way these interact—has forced communities, organizations, and individuals to seek a greater understanding of what is going on within and around them. Reciprocally, this intensifies the difficulty of planning, coordinating, and controlling activities to achieve effectiveness. In learning to cope with and understand the various environments affecting them, all bodies have had to become more "open" to those environments, but also more exposed and vulnerable. To better understand the relevant forces and factors and to appreciate their implications for such bodies, specialities and expertise of many different kinds have been introduced to help regulate (control) those open boundaries and reduce uncertainty. In turn, this has significantly affected the nature and character of leadership (and management) at all those boundaries, whether at the periphery or within the community or organization. In particular, this has led to an increasing emphasis on the need for consultation and collaborative modes that "manage" both external and internal complexity and conflicts of interest for those who are now having to experience much greater interdependence in fulfilling their roles and responsibilities.

Professions, academic institutions, and public and private bodies of all kinds—including unions—are in a situation corresponding to that of communities and organizations in these respects. All have begun to question their values, methods, and practices and their relevance to those they lead, influence, teach, or seek to advise in facing the issues of today and tomorrow.

It is just when a greater emphasis on collaboration and interdependence is needed for transforming current or traditional ways and means into more appropriate directions and dimensions that the contradictory tendency of groups and individuals to fall back on their own particular areas of competence and tried structures from earlier times often asserts itself. This paradox must be understood as a more complex, important issue than "resistance to change." In addition, attempts to counter the paradox, or other reactive tactics, most frequently lead only to more involved, intractable problems in the medium or longer term. Increasingly, the choice of more appropriate organizational design, form, and ways of working, planning, and control required to meet changing conditions, technologies, environmental turbulence, and so forth has to be made from a wide range of options. These options must be identified and their fuller implications explored and compared before that relevant choice can be made.

In the highly charged environment of today, it is easier to state and acknowledge such a principle than to act on it and work it through. Even the exploration of options and their implications can arouse pain, stress, or impatience and result in more simplistic but more comfortable rationalizations. This will especially be the case when change involves "unlearning" earlier-held values and ways of thinking and acting. Such a change is likely when in the course of sharing responsibility in decision making and attempting an appropriate balance of consultation and negotiation. In the process of unlearning and learning while developing new forms of working, those concerned must find within themselves a readiness and capability of understanding and working through both conscious and more unrecognized attitudes and preconceptions. These are most usefully identified and explored while developing and sharing the ways by which any system is planned, regulated, and managed. The interdependence of objectives, activities, structure, people, technologies, and other supporting resources must be balanced appropriately. Coping, testing, and working through experiences of this kind are becoming a sine qua non for those having to live and work in turbulent, complex, uncertain environments. Thus, reducing any so-called resistance to change is far less a problem than acquiring a capability for recognizing and relinquishing—or unlearning—established and valued, but outmoded, forms of working while using insight to face tendencies toward rivalry and envy, which increasingly accompany a greater emphasis on interdependence.

New forms of organizational design and working do not inevitably result in "happier" or "easier" solutions, but rather in a different set of "prices" and "costs" for appropriate choices of options. These often are a source of disillusion if the implications of such designs and their potential implementation are not anticipated in the planning process. It therefore becomes important to find ways and means of establishing what may be called "catalytic" experiences, methods, and collaborative forms that provide all concerned with the opportunity to unlearn approaches and build new ones for more relevant strategic and operational modes. In this context, all concerned must also develop internal institutional resources for maintaining and reviewing the new state and ensuring continuous commitment and planning. This trend can also be perceived in the tendency of younger persons to develop capabilities for crossing boundaries of many kinds and internalizing those features of their environments that enable them not only to cope with changing conditions but to use them to deal with changing characteristics in social, vocational, and career patterns. In general, therefore, humans may be releasing themselves from a dependence on hierarchical forms and be moving toward being more active, self-reviewing, and ecological.

Implications for organizations

Most organizations and institutions have been managed in a form whereby the pattern of authority was relatively clear cut, hierarchical, and within the institution itself—whether it was authoritarian or benevolent in nature. In other days, too, the environment was a much smaller influence on or force affecting the organization; government intervened to a much smaller degree; unions had less impact; persons applied competitively to institutions for employment; and—in general—change was recognizable but less turbulent than today. Schools mostly maintained their "monastic" walls; hospitals were powers unto themselves—as were the professions and universities.

Today, however, the government intervenes increasingly, and unions, consumers, competitors, suppliers, the technological explosion, and other forms of social, international, and economic change impinge on all institutions.

Originally, few advisors were required internally. Today, to help organizations interpret and cope with growing external problems—with all their internal derivatives—far more internal specialists and advisors are employed. This requires that control and management must, both now and for the future, reconcile institutional needs and environmental forces to a much greater extent than ever before.

This is a tremendous change. Not only must one spend much of one's time and effort considering and operating external affairs and developments, but there is the need for continuously re-educating professionals, specialist advisors, and managers who must ensure the viability of the institution or enterprise.

Figure 1 is a model of a predominantly "closed system," in which subordinates have been more concerned with minding their own share of the business. It is characterized by a relatively stable environment of institutions and other public or private bodies, communities, and the like. Control and coordination both consist of accountability and responsibility and simpler forms of internal advisors and specialization to assist in "managing" a more stable boundary. Values and standards are more defined and clear, the wider organizational environmental allows for more conscious and deliberate transactions across boundaries, the forms for management and determining careers are hierarchical, and identity, worth, and value are more readily recognized but "dependent" in character. Subordinates assist their superior in fulfilling her or his responsibilities; opportunity for independence arises within a dependent context, with interdependence regarded as desirable rather than essential.

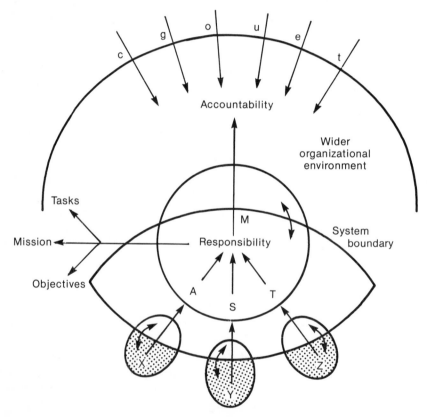

Figure 1. A predominantly closed system*

Legend: c = consumers, g = government, o = other organizations, u = unions, e = educational development, t = technical explosion and informal systems, M = leader, A = accounting functions and specialists, S = secretarial functions and specialists, T = technical functions and specialists, X, Y, and Z = subordinates.

*Adapted from Bridger (1980a).

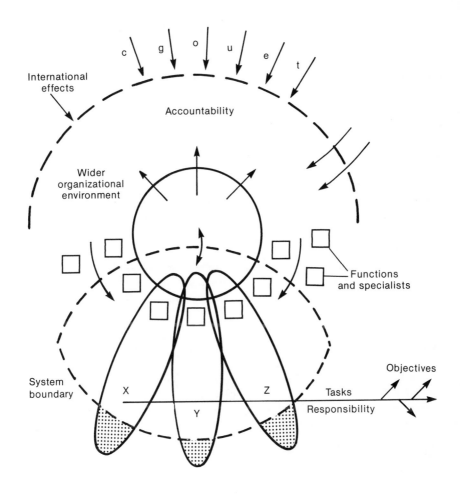

Figure 2. An open system*

Legend: c = consumers, g = government, o = other organizations, u = unions, e = educational development, t = technical explosion and informal systems, X, Y, and Z = subordinates/colleagues.

*Adapted from Bridger (1980a).

Figure 2 depicts a model of an "open system," which requires its members to share more closely in managing the internal system (Bridger, 1980b). Subordinates manage their own environment to a greater extent, as is typical throughout the organization. Thus, we have to learn to change from the classic "family tree" type of organizational structure for authority patterns to a new form of "boundary" leadership: the management of external uncertainty and internal interdependence. Continuing this process means that erstwhile "subordinates" become "colleagues" whose commitment is required to share the accountable leader's and other team members' efforts at achieving group objectives. This can be regarded as an operational definition of participation, which differs from an older pattern of delegating tasks by "hiving off" defined areas of work with more limited scope for direction to different members of a team. Thus the management of complexity and interdependence is more important for today and tomorrow than are some of the simpler prescriptions for leadership and management with which we have been brought up. The environment is relatively unstable, comprising other organizations and arrays of unknown and predictable effects produced by accelerating technological, social, and economic change and by an interaction of these and other environmental forces. With respect to control and coordination, the organization is compelled to emphasize environmental forces, reviewing them and taking accountability for responsibilities, decisions, and actions taken by others—that is, it must manage the boundary of the system and the environment. Values and standards vary according to functions and courses, the wider organizational environment is complex and uncertain, and identity and roles require more group components. Employees tend to have interdependent responsibility for operations and consultative/collaborative relations with respect to the organization's mission and objectives; interdependence is considered essential, not just desirable, and may include "collaborative competitors"—both internal and external.

Open systems and the management of their boundaries

A distinctive difference between the two models (Figures 1 and 2) occurs with respect to control and coordination operations. It will be apparent in the open-system model, for example, that in addition to a changed "boundary" position for control and coordination, a critical difference has developed between **accountability** to external authorities (Figure 1) and **responsibility for achieving objectives** (Figure 2). This is also a feature of most of the subsystems of the open-system model.

In contrasting the two models, another difference is that the open-system model also includes the special feature of a greater group or network component required to fulfill the control and coordination function. As a consequence, managing interdependence and conflict or stress begins to replace or modify the more dependent, conflict-dominating modes inherent in a more closed, strictly hierarchical model.

The model in Figure 1 depicts a relatively clear-cut hierarchical pattern of authority, in which the control and coordination vested in the "manager" can be directed largely to the internal world of the manager's unit. Historically, of course, this was more feasible when government intervened less often, unions had less of an impact, consumers of a production-oriented society received less attention, and so forth. The model in Figure 2 reflects that, however, in more recent years not only have the technological and information systems explosion and other accelerating social, international, and economic changes affected the main focus of the executive role, but so have an increasing array of specialism and functions that are drawn upon either internally or externally. To enable the "accountable authority" of any bounded system to fulfill its task, the particular manager or group must be able to regulate and cope with reciprocal interactions **across** the boundary and try to gain some understanding of the cumulative interactions between forces in the environment of external affairs. In doing so, that accountable authority must recognize—not deny—its own authority and power. Equally, it must reach a working rationale for the interdependent operational mode within the boundary of the system, which exercises responsibility for the fulfillment of tasks. Such tasks will also likely be affected by the work and objectives of other bounded systems of the wider organization.

It will be seen that both externally and internally other forms of interdependence are required for the open-system model to enable its boundary to be "managed." The location, numbers, and quality of advisors, functions, and services required to balance and fulfill the tasks of the bounded system have a material effect on the nature of interdependent working. Thus, in general this model (see Figure 2) shows that whatever form of organization may be set up to suit the parameters and conditions, the key organizational areas of competence—such as control and coordination, planning, decision making, and action—demand that institutional needs and tasks, and environmental forces and resources, be reconciled to a much greater extent than ever before. In turn, therefore, what we have called the "accountable authority"—in whatever **relevant** form it is designed so as to achieve the objectives of the institution—has had to develop some ways of working that differ from those appropriate for the model shown in Figure 1. Some of these ways will show a difference in degree, others will be different in kind. For example, giving and taking advice was a **desirable** characteristic of closed-system managing; it is an **essential** characteristic of working in open systems. In a closed system, subordinates are more concerned about minding their own shares of the "business"; in open systems they manage their own environment to a much greater extent—throughout the organization—while relinquishing (as do their superiors) relevant control of planning, decisions, and actions for levels below them. Thus, the range of organizational forms has widened considerably from an almost-exclusive concentration of the classic "family tree" type of organizational structure and authority pattern to various combinations of the models shown in Figures 1 and 2 for managing external uncertainty and internal interdependence. In addition, both collaboration and uncertainly have also become—to a greater or lesser degree, depending on circumstances—features of external and internal working life, respectively.

Before proceeding further, it should be mentioned that there is a tendency to label the model in Figure 1 as old-fashioned and "wrong for today," and the model in Figure 2 as modern and "right for today." Such an assumption is wrong, and denies the importance of relating activities, persons, technologies, structure, and operational subsystems to the objectives to be attained. It may well be that, in light of changing values and circumstances, the objectives themselves and even the boundary of the organization itself may need review and change along "certain" ways, but the **relevance** of the pattern of working according to tasks and objectives will remain paramount. Increasingly today, complexity of organizational life takes the form of being asymmetrical, not only in its structures, but also in models of managing that must be accommodated and interrelated to achieve a greater whole. Thus, variations of the models displayed and of managing appropriate to them should be expected, even within the same organization.

Some of the trends deriving from this analysis are set out below (see Table 1). We need to take this paradigm shift into account when dealing with the psychodynamics of groups and organizations considered as systems—whether they are "open" or "closed."

Table 1
Implications for Change in Roles and Functions

Change from *(relatively closed system)*	*Change toward* *(relatively open system)*
Control and coordination retained in the superior managerial role	Control and coordination retained in superior role for policy, but shared with relevant staff for operational goals
Prescriptive tasks for subordinates with with some delegated authority	Decision making and discretion devolved to relevant staff when responsible for the action involved (i.e., executive and consultative mode)
Managing mostly within the confines of the system	Managing at the boundary (i.e., reconciling external and internal resources and forces)
Allocation of jobs to persons and "knowing one's place"	More interdependence in working groups, **but** more anxiety about one's identity and independence
Managing to eliminate conflict	Managing the conflict by exploring its nature together
Accountability and responsibility located together	Accountability and responsibility may be separate
Single accountability	Multiple accountability
Hierarchial assessment and appraisal (often uncommunicated)	Self-review and assessment plus mutual appraisal of performance and potential
Career and personal development dependent on authority	Mobility of careers and boundary crossing for development, greater responsibility for own development
Power rests with those occupying certain roles and status in hierarchy	Power rests with those having control over uncertainty
Finite data and resources utilized toward building a plan	Nonfinite data and resources leading toward a **planning process** and maintaining a **choice of direction in deciding among options**
Periodic review and tendency to **extrapolate** (projection forward)	Control and planning requiring continuous attention to review (i.e., **prospection** as well as **projection** forward)

Risk related to an information **gap**	Risk related to information **overload**
Long term/short term based on operational **plans** (periodic)	Long term/short term based on **continuous adaptive planning process**
Concentrating on "getting on with the job" and "trouble-shooting" activities	"Suspending business" at relevant times to explore work systems and ways of working
Difficulty with "equality" and "freedom"	Difficulty with "fraternity"

It will be seen that any consultant engaged in a joint endeavor with a group or organization to understand and use the processes occurring in—and at the boundary of—the system must be prepared to assess the degree of shift over a range of dimensions (Bridger, 1980c). Not least, the specific attention paid to the group-centered intervention enables group members to observe and assess **for themselves** how much they recognize or agree with what the consultant has **offered** them for consideration.

When participants can also share and compare their perceptions of such processes and reach an agreement as to their awareness of their effect on the particular tasks and problems—and **act on** this—the consultant can begin to work on her or his own process for leaving.

It has been said that to give groups a "real-live task"—however relevant to the environment, both within and at the boundary of the course or conference itself—is to "dilute" or offer opportunities to avoid facing intragroup tensions. Actually, as Bion has also shown, the reverse is the case. In my experience, the quality of work in intragroup tensions—the psychodynamics—that can be confronted by "live-task" groups far surpasses that in other designs. At the same time, "casualties"—not unknown in those methods—do not occur. One important consideration, however, must be taken into account: The consultant needs more training and experience in developing the capability to work with such methods and interventions. The work is harder, but it is hoped that participants may find the work more rewarding.

NOTES

1. This impression was probably gained from the inappropriate use of the "Tavistock" label by the A. K. Rice Institute for its own brand of group relations conferences.

2. I use the word "could" rather than "would" because it is so often the case that insight can also be used as a defense against action. This syndrome is one I have observed all too frequently in organizational and professional life.

3. Reducing the program to one week has both advantages and disadvantages, but it had to be faced if one wanted to have the relevant participants for a course.

REFERENCES

Bion, W. R. (1946). The leaderless group project. *Bulletin of the Menninger Clinic, 10,* 77-81.

Bion, W. R. (1961). *Experiences in groups.* London: Tavistock Publications.

Bridger, H. (1980a). The contributions of OD at the level of the whole organisation. In K. Trebesch (Ed.), *Organisation development in Europe* (Vol. 1A). Bern, Switzerland: Paul Haupt Verlag.

Bridger, H. (1980b). The kinds of "organizational development" required for working at the level of the whole organization considered as an open system. In K. Trebesch (Ed.), *Organisation development in Europe* (Vol. 1A). Bern, Switzerland: Paul Haupt Verlag.

Bridger, H. (1980c). The relevant training and development of people for OD roles. In K. Trebesch (Ed.), *Organisation development in Europe* (Vol. 1A). Bern, Switzerland: Paul Haupt Verlag.

Bridger, H. (1981). *Consultative work communities and organizations: Towards a psychodynamic image of man* (the 1980 Malcolm Millar lecture). Aberdeen, England: Aberdeen University Press.

Bridger, H. (1984). *The therapeutic community: Groups in open and closed systems.* Rome: Centro Italiano di Solidarieta.

Bridger, H. (1985). Northfield revisited: A review of Wilfred Bion's unique experiment at Northfield Military Hospital—Some antecedents, implications and successors. In M. Pines (Ed.), *Bion and group psychotherapy.* Boston: Routledge & Kegan Paul.

Higgin, G. W., & Bridger, H. (1964). The psychodynamics of an inter-group experience. *Human Relations, 17,* 391-446. (Reprinted as Tavistock Pamphlet No. 10, 1965.)

Low, K. B., & Bridger, H. (1979). Small group work in relation to management development. In B. Babington Smith & B. A. Farrell (Eds.), *Training in small groups.* Elmsford, NY: Pergamon.

Sutherland, J. D., & Fitzpatrick, G. A. (1945). Some approaches to group problems in the British Army. *Sociometry, 8,* 443-455.

Trist, E. L., & Bamforth, K. W. (1951). Some social and psychological consequences of coal-getting. *Human Relations, 4,* 3-38.

Trist, E. L., & Sofer, C. (1959). *Explorations in group relations.* Leicester, England: Leicester University Press.

Section IV.
Applications

Laboratory Training and Microcomputers

Tom Armor

The microcomputer is here to stay. Its impact is already quite evident in most professions and is now being felt in the field of laboratory training.

By microcomputer, I essentially am talking about the "personal computer" as exemplified by the IBM-PC and many similar computers designed for one person to use. Various configurations extending from this starting point are legion. The software programs discussed in this article are all produced to run on this level of technology, and for the most part strive to be usable by the novice with little or no previous computer experience.

Two emerging schools seem to exist concerning the role of this technology vis-a-vis laboratory training. The first, and most visible to date, is characterized by the numerous new computer programs being marketed to training professionals or other "users." The quality and utility of these programs vary greatly, but the common characteristic seems to be that the program, once selected, has limited—if any—adaptability. Most are usually electronic forms of paper-and-pencil "self-report" instruments that do not accommodate interactive or "other-reported" data.

A second perspective on the potential microcomputer technology and laboratory training is focused upon a more generic role of the technology and the resulting interaction of professional creativity, laboratory training theory and practice, and a new synthesis of experiential learning with this technology. In exploring this perspective, I first address the role of microcomputers in supporting the planning and design of laboratory training, then the role of microcomputer applications within such programs, and finally some implications of this for the way we perceive laboratory training and this technology.

The microcomputer as a support tool for laboratory design

The planning and design process for any laboratory training program will naturally vary considerably depending upon its purpose, staff, participants, time,

©1987 NTL Institute. All rights reserved.

and context. In many situations, microcomputer applications can help one perform these tasks in various way.

Data collection

In those training activities in which data about the specific context or issues is to be collected and used in formulating the training design, the microcomputer has proved its value. Not only does it allow interview data to be collected by different staff members in a form usable by all the staff, it permits these data to be organized using the methods of data base management (DBM).

Briefly, DBM means that data—of whatever kind—are collected and stored in the smallest, most discrete pieces having inherent meaning or value. These data are "cross-referenced" to one another in one or more ways that allow them to be retrieved based on many criteria. They can be counted, sorted, searched, combined, and otherwise manipulated to yield a great variety of information about the underlying source of the original data. For technical reasons this ability has not been widely available for "free-form" text material until recently.

The following example of how this was done using a portable, lap-sized computer in conjunction with a microcomputer illustrates the above method.

As part of a foreign assistance project in Pakistan, two consultants were asked to conduct a "needs assessment" to help restructure a training program focused on rural development for senior civil service personnel. This needs assessment was to include interviews with a cross-section of relevant government staff, the actual participant of the particular training program, and staff of the institution in which the training would take place. Based upon this needs assessment, a revitalized and experience-based training would be designed and carried out some weeks later.

The consultants traveled to several different cities and interviewed approximately 25 persons. Paper-and-pencil notes were made during all interviews, and these notes were entered into the portable, lap-sized computer later each day or evening.

A typical interview session, as reflected in the computerized notes, contained 15-25 separate, one- or two-sentence "items" that each captured an important point made during the interview. These "items" were then electronically transferred to the microcomputer and stored in a "text data base." As they were stored, each was cross-referenced with several important "key" terms that would allow it to be retrieved. Some of these terms identified attributes such as the subject's name, administrative position, department, and the like. Other terms were assigned by the consultants according to their professional judgment of the importance of the issues raised by the items.

For example, one such item read: "Many feel there must be a rural development policy statement to guide them. Such a statement will be difficult to find, perhaps it has to be evolved by each for himself." This was cross-referenced by name (Aqbal), position (director), political body (national), administrative body (Center for Rural Development and Local Government), and several issue terms (policy, individual, course objective).

When the team sat down to design the training program, the first thing it did was to have the computer print a list of the "issues" that had been noted during the data collection and entry process. Similar or related issue topics were then used to retrieve the original statement items. By this interactive and iterative process at the keyboard, the team was able to review the interview data and outline a design for learning activities that best met the relevant needs reflected in the data.

In addition, the resulting training design made specific use of some of the interview data within the design itself. Several important issues raised during the interviews were used as points of departure for learning activities. These data were more credible to the participants because of the methodical process for collecting and recording them.

Data base of exercises and activities

Experienced trainers have a wealth of exercises, simulations, and other activities that they have developed and/or used previously. At some point, the sheer number of these activities causes one difficulty in effectively considering appropriate past experiences for use in new contexts. The computer's ability to cross-reference such activities can greatly enrich the design process of any training program.

Using the storage and retrieval capacity of a microcomputer only becomes valuable as descriptions of exercises and activities are entered into an expanding data base. Thus, a commitment to this approach will require an early investment of time and effort well before much benefit is derived. This argues strongly for a collective approach, not unlike the extensively indexed publications of "structured experiences" now available.

In practice, a laboratory design team would obtain from the computer a list of activities that fulfilled a set of criteria, using such terms as "intrapersonal," "gender awareness," "stranger group," and "no materials." This would result in an annotated list of potential activities that were intrapersonally oriented, raised issues of attitudes toward gender differences, could be used by a group of strangers, and required no previously prepared materials. Such a list would spark the creativity and professional judgment of the staff and make their planning and design effort more productive.

Modification of materials

Closely associated with the storage and retrieval function of a microcomputer is its ability to quickly and effectively modify existing exercises and activities to better fit the current needs of a laboratory training design. In its simplest form, this is merely word processing. More comprehensively, this might allow new designs that in themselves permit materials to be modified **as a result of actions within the training event**. For instance, a group problem-solving or priority assignment task might be designed in two parts. In the first part, subgroups could be asked to generate lists of important issues or topics according to some relevant criteria. The trainer could then combine these lists, put them in random order, and insert them into a previously prepared set of instructions for the second part of the exercise, all within minutes. Printed instructions containing the new lists would result. This ability to produce a clear, specific task assignment could expedite the training activity, with much less confusion and time spent explaining the elements and steps involved in such a compound activity.

The microcomputer as an element within laboratory training

As suggested, the potential of microcomputers must be understood in terms of supporting social processes, not replacing them. Much as music, art, videotapes, and similar innovations have been used appropriately, so can the microcomputer. Data and information can only help persons understand their own experiences; they are no substitute for experiential learning. The challenge lies in making the best use of this technology for collecting and organizing data and information to facilitate experiential activities.

The workings of this technology in laboratory training activities is illustrated by the following simple and familiar example.

Consider the venerable Johari window, with its four quadrants for entering information about oneself. If each individual in a laboratory made entries into the proper quadrants of her or his own "computerized" window, a common data base could be produced. Now, through some simple instructions to the computer, a single list of all the entries made by all the participants into the quadrant (e.g., "known to self/not known to others") could be produced. This common list, computer generated quickly and ensuring anonymity, could then be used in a general discussion.

Similarly, in small groups that have been working together, each person could be asked to contribute something to each other person's quadrants. The computer could then produce for each person a collation of entries targeted to one. Variations on this methodology are easy to envision. The computer simply allows information to be recognized quickly and easily.

The major constraint to such usage is that of keyboard entry. Currently, it is not practical for each member to have separate access to a keyboard. The use of inexpensive lap-sized computers or simple multiuser systems are potential solutions. Many of the most useful applications of this technology, however, may not require simultaneous individual access to a computer. Some of these are described below.

Important and well-recognized social and psychological theories that have been applied to instruments or otherwise made operational are being adapted to microcomputer methods. Some are specifically designed for use by small groups, with the computer analysis providing timely, sophisticated feedback for direct use within the group. One example of such an application is SYMLOG, based on the work of Robert Bales (1985).

Many times small groups are called upon to "brainstorm" about ideas or issues. Often, the items on the resulting lists are then reorganized onto different topical lists according to some emergent schema. Although this often needs to be done as a shared process, the laborious mechanics of redrafting the items and moving them to newly identified categories can be done more quickly and easily by a "documentarian" from the group who works at a keyboard. This process usually requires collapsing initial categories or spinning off new ones, which can both be done easily with just a few keystrokes. Sometimes this can be done with a large video display that makes the process visible to all. The resulting lists can be immediately printed and distributed as needed.

Exercises that require original input to a prestructured format can be done in ways that enhance both the process and the product. For example, a force field analysis approach to understanding change would lend itself to this methodology. The "forces" could then be entered quickly as they are identified, and easily recognized according to priorities, valence, categories, interrelationships, or any other useful criteria almost instantly as they are analyzed by a group or individual.

Many activities are based upon separating subgroups to work on the same or different aspects of an issue, then comparing or integrating the results. Microcomputer methods make the differentiation and integration of textual material much quicker, easier, and more flexible than does the use of newsprint pads in many situations.

Some exercises or simulations require complicated scoring or recording of results or decisions. This may sometimes be readily adapted to computerized formats that can save much time and confusion. One example is the often-used exercise designed to illustrate the value of consensus decision making.

A new synthesis

The most exciting implication of microcomputer technology and laboratory training is the fundamental change it portends for how we think about such training. This has usually been considered a social process, often augmented with sophisticated technical support (e.g., videotapes). Something akin to a sociotechnical systems model for understanding laboratory training and microcomputer technology might now be useful.

This perspective would focus on the mutual and interactive influence of the social subsystem and the technical subsystem. The boundaries and core processes of the laboratory training activity are now open to a new analysis that integrates these subsystems and seeks to understand something wholly new.

Consider current and potential applications of microcomputers to laboratory training in light of the following.

The power and speed of current microcomputer technology is close to "real time" for most of the applications discussed above, meaning that re-analyzing data with new assumptions, changing the sources, targets, or issues of an analysis, obtaining scores and interpretations for instruments, and identifying complementary, conflicting, or supplementary relationships on the basis of complex instrument scores (e.g., the Myers-Briggs Type Indicator) can all be done essentially instantaneously. The simultaneous generation of such feedback with the experiential opportunity to act upon it is a new phenomenon.

Microcomputer applications within laboratory training can be expected to have an impact beyond that of other "adjunct modalities," such as music/body movement, art, or videotapes. These modalities are limited because they are not usually part of life outside the laboratory. Microcomputers, however, are becoming a regular part of life for most of us. The extension of this technology to and from other learning and life contexts for participants can make the laboratory experience more relevant.

Data collected and analyzed with the use of microcomputers is inherently credible. Persons generally know that to make a computer operate, one must use precise, well-thought-out instructions. The use of technology to support the feedback process requires more explication and clarity, not only of the mechanics of the process (e.g., a computer program, algorithms, decision rules, data formats, and so forth), but also of underlying principles and concepts. The resulting information about behavior, values, and attitudes is thus less clouded by a perceived subjectivity of analysis.

Related to this inherent credibility is the potential for direct participation in the analysis of such data. The computer allows anyone to try different or selective rearrangements of data with ease. Persons more truly participate in and control the processes of the laboratory training experience.

Not only is time collapsible within the laboratory setting, but neither time nor place constrain laboratory learning to the extent that they formerly did. Computer communications make extending the experience practical, both before and after face-to-face group meetings. Data can be collected by menu-driven programs "accessed" at a terminal by participants well before a laboratory. Initial sharing of feedback, expectations, and other nonconfrontational information may even take place in this manner before the meeting. At the laboratory training meeting itself, the design might incorporate planning and commitments among and between participants for actions that would be supported by computer communications well after the meeting ends.

The biggest challenge of using microcomputers with laboratory training is to develop innovative designs based upon a new and integrated view of the technical and sociopsychological phenomena unfolding. Marshall McLuhan gave us a new way of understanding electronic (and other) media. As yet, we do not have a new, accepted paradigm for understanding the interrelationship of computer technology and sociopsychological dynamics. Perhaps this will emerge from our experiences using this technology in laboratory training.

REFERENCE

Bales, R. (1985). The new field theory in social psychology. *International Journal of Small Group Research*, *1*(1), 1-18.

Realistic Simulation: An Alternative Vehicle for Laboratory Education

Robert E. Kaplan
Wilfred H. Drath

The idea behind laboratory education is quite simple: To provide a setting in which participants can exhibit behavior and, in turn, reflect on and learn from that behavior. Laboratory education emerged as an alternative to didactic methods that specialized in having a content expert present information to an audience whose members bore the burden of applying the information to their own experience. Laboratory education is also an alternative to the case method, whereby an instructor leads a group of students through a postmortem of an unusually complex situation in which the students played no part. The didactic approach and the case method leave much to be desired when the purpose is to educate people about their own behavior and leave them with indelible lessons about human behavior in general. Laboratory education was invented expressly to serve this purpose by creating a living laboratory in which participants put their own behavior under a microscope.

Everything depends on the design of the laboratory—that is, how the sample of behavior is produced. The prototype of a device for producing behavior was the T Group, invented in Bethel, Maine, in 1947. The T Group was the training method around which National Training Laboratories (now NTL Institute) was built. The T Group assembles 10-12 persons in a room with a nondirective facilitator, who sparks interaction by improbably leaving group members with nothing to do but examine their own behavior in the group. Attempts to fill the void created by the trainer's unconventional laissez-faire style and to cope with the ambiguity of the task assigned to the group creates the laboratory "specimen" that comes under scrutiny. As the group continues, behavior and analysis of that behavior becomes interwoven and inseparable.

The T Group has much to recommend it; testimony to this is that, after 40 years, it is still going strong with NTL (we will not speak of the image problem

©1987 NTL Institute. All rights reserved.

the T Group movement has developed during this same period). The T Group does, however, have certain built-in disadvantages for training managers. These include the unlikely self-analytic task, the distinct lack of structure, and the highly emotional and personal content of the learning.

The realistic behavioral simulation, which has only recently come onto the scene, represents an alternative technology for laboratory education. Because it produces behavior in an organizational setting and examines that behavior in a more structured, less personal way, it escapes some of the limitations of the T Group and finds greater acceptance among managers.

Behavioral simulations fall squarely in a tradition of "experiential" learning in management education. What distinguishes this type of behavior from other experiential exercises is its degree of involvement: Participants are drawn powerfully into their roles and into the larger organizational setting. Thirty minutes after such a simulation begins, most participants are thoroughly involved in the business. Because participants lose themselves in the simulations, they tend to act naturally while participating, thereby producing representative and reasonably accurate samples of how they normally perform.

Realistic behavioral simulations recreate the experience of daily life in organizations by placing approximately 20 persons in interrelated roles in a particular type of organization such as a bank, hospital, or manufacturing organization, by staging the simulation in an office-like setting, and by allowing the simulation to run for several hours. The events of the simulation become the shared experience that participants examine—usually in small groups cor- responding to work units in the simulation—for insight into themselves, their relationships, and organizational dynamics (Drath & Kaplan, 1984; McCall & Lombardo, 1982). Prime examples of such simulations include Looking Glass, Inc. (described below) and FSI. Looking Glass, Inc. was developed by Morgan McCall, Michael Lombardo, and David DeVries at the Center for Creative Leadership from 1976-1979 (see McCall & Lombardo, 1979). The FSI (Financial Services Industry) simulation was developed by Steven Stumpf, Thomas Mullen, Karen Hartman, Roger Dunbar, and Bill Berliner at the Graduate School of Business Administration at New York University from 1982-1984.

Looking Glass, Inc.

Looking Glass was developed for research purposes by the Center for Creative Leadership. The simulation's developers set out to create a laboratory setting in which leaders could be studied in a realistic organizational context—not in isolation, as leaders often have been studied. As were many other innovations, the discovery of the simulation's potential for needs analysis and training were serendipitous.

Looking Glass is a hypothetical, medium-sized glass manufacturing corporation (McCall & Lombardo, 1982). For a simulation, Looking Glass is quite realistic. Complete with annual report, plausible financial data, and various glass products, the simulation creates the aura of an authentic organization. Participants are often placed in an office-like setting, complete with telephones and an interoffice mail system. The positions actually filled in the simulation are those of the corporation's top management, including the four levels ranging from president to plant manager (see Figure 1 on the next page). The fictitious company consists of three divisions whose environments vary according to the degree of change, with one division's environment being relatively placid, another's being turbulent, and a third's being a mixture of the two.

The simulation lasts six hours and is intended to represent a typical day in the life of the company. It begins by placing each participant face to face with an in-basket full of memoranda. Together with background information common to all participants, this information—which differs somewhat from division to division, level to level, and position to position—constitutes the stimulus. Participants spend the rest of the day responding to these interlocking sets of stimuli, acting and interacting as they choose. Contained in the collective in-baskets of the 20 participants are more than 150 different problems that participating managers might attend to. The problems vary in importance, and—realistically—in how they are apparent or hidden to the one or more individuals who should be concerned about them. Also true to life, the number of problems far exceeds the time available to deal with them.

The simulation is involving, and most managers find it accurately represents their daily work lives. Research has also revealed a close resemblance between patterns of activity of managers taking part in Looking Glass and patterns of daily activity of managers at work in organizations. Based on direct observation of Looking Glass participants, this research tracked such activities as the amount of paper work, time spent on the telephone, and time spent in meetings (McCall & Lombardo, 1979).

The "debriefing"—conversations after the simulation ends—takes a day or longer, and follows a format that pools the observations of the staff members, the experiences of the participants themselves, and feedback obtained using instruments, which uses the results of previous runs of the simulation as a standard of comparison. This allows participants to make sense of their experience as a team, as individual contributors, and even as part of a management culture. In concrete terms, they learn in which respects they performed ably in the simulation and in which respects they could have done better. The simulation and debriefing are typically embedded in a larger program that includes careful attention to how participants will apply what they have learned to their work, careers, and lives in general.

In the following section, we seek to answer questions frequently asked about the use of realistic behavioral simulations by presenting an account of one manager's experience in the Center for Creative Leadership's program entitled Workshop in Organizational Action. This workshop is built around the Looking Glass, Inc. simulation itself and the debriefing sessions following its use.

Allen Bruce

Allen Bruce was a successful manager with bright prospects in a fast-growing company. He had always thought of himself as a person who made friends readily

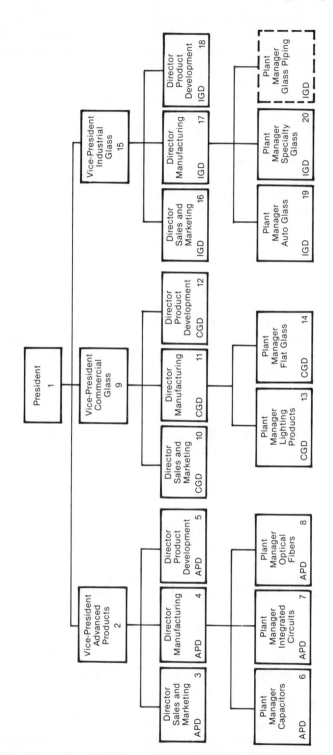

Figure 1. Position chart for Looking Glass, Inc. simulation
© 1978, McCall, Lombardo, & DeVries
(reprinted with permission)

and who was good at "interpersonal relationships." He therefore experienced something of a shock when an associate at work had confided to him one day that Allen had a reputation for being "threatening" to work with. What did he do to make people feel that way? Why had no one said anything before? The answers were vague, couched in general terms. By implication, however, the associate depicted Allen as being an overly ambitious, somewhat self-serving person who cared little for the feelings or legitimate concerns of others. This issue—the perception of him as threatening—was what Allen brought to the workshop.

During the simulation, Allen recreated six behaviors (this, of course, is an after-the-fact analysis) that helped create his "threat" to others.

1. Tendency to manipulate others. Allen was assertive and controlling when working with others, even when making the simplest kinds of arrangements. For example, during the night before the simulation he considered it a good idea for his division for the simulation—the general products division—to gather for a meeting. He was not to play the division vice president; calling such a meeting was not really his responsibility. Allen was a go-getting kind of manager, however, who when he got an idea "ran with it." He talked about it with the other division members, got the vice president's approval, and set up the meeting. It was his meeting—held in his hotel room, with his agenda. All of this occurred before the simulation had actually started.

At another time during the simulation, he manipulated the meeting time at his convenience, and was somewhat dishonest in doing so. He told one of the persons involved that another could not meet at the suggested time, a "white lie." The meeting was rescheduled to a time that better suited Allen.

2. Acute responsiveness to the interests of superiors. When the simulation officially began, with telephones ringing and a general sense of frenetic activity, Allen's first act was to call the president and accept an invitation to play tennis at the president's home. Allen firmly believed one was never hurt by making oneself visible "upstairs."

The main agenda item Allen chose to work on was triggered by an issue raised in a memorandum from the company president. After reviewing all the memoranda in his in-basket the night before the simulation began, Allen returned to this one and spent almost an hour thinking and making notes before going to bed. It became his all-consuming project throughout the simulation.

Allen heard about this responsiveness to superiors later during the debriefing. A plant manager for the simulation pointed out to him, "You were very much aware of the power difference. You were certainly interested in talking up to Carl [the division vice president] and to the president, but you didn't see me at all. It was very obvious."

3. Ambition to excel. Allen had quite a bit of ambition to be excellent, to make a mark, to leave something of Allen Bruce behind on the simulation. This led him frequently to make too much of small issues. The memorandum from the president that inspired his "game plan" for the entire simulation was a rather vague request that the directors of sales and marketing "plan for future problems and coordinate solutions." Allen blew this up into nearly a mandate to reorganize the sales and marketing function, even to reorganize the entire company.

4. Focused on his own ends. Allen had a single-mindedness of purpose, admirable in many ways, that left him little time for or interest in the concerns of others, particularly those persons he saw as unimportant to his ends. Subordinates and peers who did not fit into his scheme were not important to him. At one point one of the plant managers came to him with what she considered an important problem. She needed some help from the marketing end of the division, but Allen made no time for her. He exhibited impatience when she tried to talk to him. He agreed to get back to her, but never did. Ironically, if he had attempted to solve the problem she brought to him, he would have actually gotten some help in formulating his plan to coordinate solutions in sales and marketing. He was, however, so focused on his own ends that he could not see that helping her resolve her own problem might also help him with his own.

Allen recognized this later and at one point during the debriefing said,

> I focused on reorganization at the expense of virtually everything else. I tried to pursue some of the activities simply because I had a responsibility to do something there, but my overriding thought process was focused almost totally on how to accomplish this game that I got launched into of trying to turn the company around, to turn the organization structure around, and to end up—it wasn't clear where—but to end up in a position of more power than I started out with. That was the game that I was trying to play.

5. Complex of behaviors causing others to mistrust his motives. The other participants in the simulation, particularly those in his own division, felt that Allen was looking out entirely for "number one." By the end of the simulation, most of his fellow managers were looking askance at the things Allen was doing. Allen felt, and expressed during the debriefing, that he was looking out for the good of the organization as a whole, that he wanted to do something good for the organization. He admitted that he realized that making a big splash with the organization would make him look good, but maintained that his primary motive was to help the organization. In admitting that he was "playing a game," Allen showed that he was beginning to appreciate the meaning of his behavior, although the lesson was not necessarily easy for him to accept. He later said,

> It has occurred to me that the game I was playing was for my own potential gain at the expense of the organization. Yet the impact of what I was doing was potentially very large for the organization. I mean, if we had handled this slightly differently, we might have been able to pull off a reorganization.

He confessed to being bothered because he was "really doing nothing but playing a game."

6. Tendency to attribute his own motives to others. Near the end of the simulation, one of the other directors of sales and marketing submitted a plan that had the word "coordination" in it. Because of that word, Allen jumped to the conclusion that a plan was being submitted to rival his own, that this person had been maneuvering behind Allen's back to get that plan accepted by the management committee rather than Allen's. Actually the other director's plan was a modest proposal about transfer pricing. Allen realized at the end of the simulation that he had been accusing the other directors of sales and marketing of doing what he himself had done. He assumed they were maneuvering and manipulating as he had been. Allen considered the world a place in which nearly everyone was pursuing her or his own ends as vigorously as possible, and this was his justification for his behavior: "If I want to get done what I want to get done, I'm going to have to watch out for my own interests because that's what everyone else is doing."

During the debriefing, Allen heard much about his own behavior. The basic strength of his personality came through, enabling him to be surprisingly receptive to learning the effects of his behavior on others. He quite candidly admitted to having an overriding focus on his own agenda and a manipulative, "game-playing" attitude. None of this had been clear to Allen during the simulation itself. Only during the debriefing, as he began to describe his own actions and hear them described by others, did Allen begin to see what had happened to him. More important, he was able to recognize a pattern in what had happened that he had frequently repeated in his real work. For the first time in his working life, Allen understood why people saw him as threatening: because **he** saw **others** as threatening. He learned—quite powerfully—the need to trust others, to build relationships with peers and subordinates as well as superiors, and to invest more of himself in the concerns of others and the organization in general.

Benefits

Allen's case demonstrates the self-development that can occur through the combination of realistic, freely interacting simulation and postsimulation discussions. For Allen—and all who participate in some form of laboratory education—the most obvious and direct benefit is self-insight. To have a weakness—or strength—demonstrated clearly deepens one's understanding of oneself. Thus, one of the gains is informational. The participant is informed by the experience. There is also, however, a motivational gain. Most participants are inspired to **do** something about what they discover in themselves. This no doubt derives partly from the intimate relationship between knowledge and action. To know about a problem is often to create pressure to do something about it. During the simulation, problems often take the form of discrepancies between what participants intend to do and what, they discover later, they actually do.

A secondary gain is that managers taking part in a group-based debriefing become privy to what their fellow participants learn about themselves. If other participants are similar to oneself, they become mirrors for one's self. If they are different, they may become windows into a person one has difficulty understanding or dealing with. This gain applies both to simulation and to the broader category of laboratory education.

Another secondary gain is insight into the manager's job—into the amorphous process by which managers take action in organizations. Participants can learn about the tension between fighting fires and thinking strategically. They can learn about the setting agenda and the importance of choosing directions and doing so in conjunction with the persons around them. They can learn about the danger of spreading themselves too thin or of being focused on one thing to the exclusion of everything else. They can learn about how a team coalesces or fails to coalesce, and about the team leader's role in building a team. They can learn about the influence of peer upon peer. They can learn about work relationships up, down, and sideways inside one's unit and outside it—the formation and use of networks. They can learn about striking balances among many competing demands, such as the for getting work done versus building and maintaining relationships needed to do the work and the demands for taking quick action versus carefully laying the base to support action.

The motivation to change also comes from the experience's being participant centered. The insights participants gain are not something developed by experts and then handed over, as might be the case if the insights came only from what the trainers could observe the managers doing during the simulation. Such feedback, however accurate, may heighten a manager's cognitive awareness but leave her or him essentially cold and unmoved. Instead, the debriefing allows the participants to become heavily involved in creating an understanding of themselves and others. Just as managers more readily accept decisions they have helped make, so managers more readily accept insights they have helped form.

Costs

Notwithstanding the advantages, realistic behavioral simulation is not the "be-all and end-all." First, simulation is limited: It removes the participant from the context of her or his environment so that whatever is learned from the simulation must be placed in the context of the individual's (or team's) history and current circumstances. Second, simulation is powerful: It exposes participants to an intensity new to many of them, and therefore should be preceded in any development project by suitable preparation. Thus, simulation should be used with particular care and in conjunction with other methods.

Trainers thinking of using realistic simulation should know that it asks a lot. To achieve the fiction that the simulated organization is real, the trainers and their support staff must go to some trouble to put into place an office-like setting. Participants need desks and office supplies; a portable telephone system must be transported, set up, and later dismantled; a big stack of in-basket materials must be sent and distributed to each participant; and more. For the trainers to debrief participants in the simulation effectively, these trainers must be familiar with the detailed business information for the division for which they are responsible.

The simulation is a vital component, but just as vital is the structure built around the simulation to collect, assemble, and interpret data. Although data are collected during the simulation by having staff members record observations, a simulation of this kind generates behavior too complicated and scattered to rely totally on expert "raters," as assessment centers do. Instead, data are also collected from the participants themselves through a battery of questionnaires that tap perceptions of process and outcomes. In addition, data are collected in the series of discussions following Looking Glass, Inc., and these in effect reconstruct what happened during the simulation. Thus, the two simulations of this kind available at this time require that trainers have facilitative ability, familiarity with the simulation itself, and a knowledge of management.

Applications

The formats of behavioral simulations lend themselves to three types of applications, with all or most benefits accruing to each of the different applications. They can be used for individual development—the most common purpose—for team development, and for organizational diagnosis and development.

Individual development

When the exclusive purpose of the simulation is to assess individual development, participants typically come from different organizations—or, if they come from the same organization, they do not know each other or at least do not work together. The example of Allen Bruce illustrates the way in which individual development takes place in a realistic behavioral simulation.

Team development

When realistic simulation has the goal of team development, managers picked to go through the simulation are coworkers or members of the same management team. Putting an intact management team through an extended simulation-and-debriefing experience is, as are many forms of team building, a high-risk, high-gain proposition. This should only be undertaken if certain conditions are met. The team as a whole should understand what it is getting into and should be committed, or at least willing, to take part in this.

For a team to become informed and make a good decision is no small matter. The presimulation activities should include one or more diagnostic exercises to give the team a low-risk opportunity to sample learning from its own experience, to test its ability to benefit from this approach, and to give it a chance to work with the trainers and test **their** abilities.

Simulation for team development is as expensive as it is rewarding. A minimum of three days of the team's time is required to run the simulation and to debrief the team thoroughly afterward. Additional time is needed for "prework" and follow-through; in one project the time spent in preliminary activities rivaled that for the simulation itself. The simulation is also expensive with respect to staff time, requiring a staff-participant ratio of about one trainer to seven participants. The time demands on the team, the staff-intensive nature of the simulation, and the need to prepare carefully for the experience are directed toward capitalizing fully on the simulation and minimizing the risks entailed in putting coworkers through an intensive training experience.

The team that takes part in a simulation, however, gains a common experience, a rich empirical lode from which it can mine valuable insights. The simulation carries a double payload: The team can thus learn about its dynamics, and individual participants can learn about themselves. The data base for individual assessment draws on the dual sources of simulation and on-the-job experience. The team identifies its area for growth, with assessment of management culture thrown in in the bargain. Another advantage of team development is that the problem of transferring learning from the assessment setting to the organizational setting is lessened when persons who work together go through the simulation experience together.

Organizational diagnosis and development

Use of simulation for this end is rare in our experience, but holds enough promise to be worth discussing. As a form of organizational survey, or organizational diagnosis, the application is possible when participating managers are drawn from the same organization. They may or may not know one another, but as a rule they do not work together.

The chance to observe the management culture of an organization presents itself when a sample of an organization's management interacts for the better part of a day under the somewhat controlled conditions of a simulation. Just as individual managers tend to act characteristically in a simulation, so do groups of managers from the same organization tend to exhibit their characteristic cultural patterns. The simulation is not generally run to afford a glimpse of an organization's management culture—rather, it is run to assess the needs of individual managers—but since the managers come from the same organization, the opportunity arises to assess collective patterns as well.

For one organization's experience with Looking Glass, Inc., for example, an interesting managerial characteristic stood out. The managers as a group worked extremely hard to prepare for meetings, especially those with their superiors. This tendency meant that they were anything but sloppy and unprepared, but showed they were cautious and slow moving. In Looking Glass, Inc., as in real life, frequently one cannot understand a problem thoroughly unless one consults with other persons, including those at higher levels. Therefore, if you delay bringing up a problem with a higher-level person until you grasp it completely, you put yourself in a "Catch-22" situation: You cannot bring it up until you understand it, and you cannot understand it until you bring it up.

Assessing a management population's characteristics and needs is possible both by aggregating the assessments of individual managers—as assessment centers sometimes do (Bray, 1976)—and by looking at patterns of interaction for the sample of about 20 managers going through a given simulation. This opportunity for group-level, and even organization-level, analysis is a special property of an organizational simulation and is capable of providing valuable insights. The payoff is greater when the insights go beyond the observations of the staff and, again, are derived from the active participation of the managers themselves.

The less familiar the staff is with the organization, the more important it is to enlist the participation of the managers. Who can do a better job than the managers at recognizing the parallels between the patterns identified during the simulation and enduring patterns in their organizational experience? This analysis of management is accomplished by turning everyone's attention to the issue, preferably late in the after-simulation discussions, when the character of the group's behavior in the simulation has already been brought to light.

Participants in a realistic behavioral simulation examine their own behavior in much the same way that participants did in the T Groups of earlier days. Realistic simulation, however, reproduces a setting comparable to participants' back-home organizational experience. The debriefing following the simulation is structured and focused on the task in a way that T Groups are not. The lessons learned are less personal and emotional, and—to a greater or lesser degree— related to the manager's work environment. Although the content of what a participant learns is similar to what the participant might read in any good textbook on management, these otherwise banal lessons are rooted in the participant's own experience. This, of course, is also the genius of the T Group. The lessons learned are not simply guidance in **cognitive** form; they are strongly associated with vivid **images** from the participant's own experience.

REFERENCES

Bray, D. W. (1976). The assessment center method. In R. L. Craig (Ed.), *Training and development handbook* (2nd ed.). New York: McGraw-Hill.

Drath, W. H., & Kaplan, R. E. (1984). *The Looking Glass experience: A story of learning through action and reflection* (special report). Greensboro, NC: Center for Creative Leadership.

McCall, M. W., Jr., & Lombardo, M. M. (1979). *Looking Glass, Inc.: The first three years* (Technical Report No. 13). Greensboro, NC: Center for Creative Leadership.

McCall, M. W., Jr., & Lombardo, M. M. (1982). *Using simulation for leadership and management research: Through the Looking Glass,* Management Science, *28*(5), 533-549.

Developing Consultation Skills: A Simulation Approach

Ronald K. Boyer

Effective organizational consultants usually possess substantial skills of the following type:

- cognitive skills in such areas as organizational theory, design, and change, small group and interpersonal behavior, and individual behavior;
- interpersonal skills for developing and maintaining relationships with organizations and individuals with widely diverse backgrounds, values, and styles;
- personal skills needed to use one's "person" as an instrument of change.

For example, Schein (1978), in discussing matching individual and organizational needs, identifies three areas of competence: analytical competence, interpersonal competence, and emotional competence.

How do individuals become effective organizational consultants? Twenty-five years ago the answer seemed to be, "Grow older, go through a lot of trial and error, and learn from your experience." In 1960 the organization behavior program at Case Institute of Technology was started in the attempt to translate practice in organizational change from an "art form" to a more disciplinary base. During the past two decades, the field of organization development has matured. Experiments have been conducted and many books and articles written. Formal training in organizational consultation is offered in the curricula of many universities. A variety of organizations offer workshops and training programs for organizational clientele.

This article describes a simulation approach for developing consultation skills. This approach fits in the "niche" between courses and workshops providing primarily a cognitive emphasis and those emphasizing practice with "hands-on" experience and supervision. A simulation approach can be used toward the end of the cognitive offerings or at the beginning of practicum offerings. The advantage of simulation is that it permits some simultaneous training in cognitive, interpersonal, and personal competence without the time commitments and complications that may accompany a practicum approach.

©1987 NTL Institute. All rights reserved.

Cognitive approaches typically emphasize cognitive skills more than inter-personal and personal emotional skills. The advantages of cognitive approaches are that, relative to a practicum, they are easier to design, control, and implement. Practicum approaches are labor intensive for staff and participants. Arrangements with client systems are relatively difficult to develop and maintain, and client and participant schedules require considerable management.

Practica do, however, offer substantial opportunities for participants to develop interpersonal and personal competence and to integrate this with cognitive abilities, under supervision. Staff of such practica must ensure that participants have a minimal level of interpersonal and personal competence. For example, participants in the Consultation Skills program at NTL Institute must have participated in the Human Interaction Laboratory offered by NTL, or an equivalent. The simulation approach described below may serve as a transition between the cognitive and practicum approaches. It is less labor intensive, and thus easier to control and implement, yet permits simultaneous development of cognitive, interpersonal, and personal skills. Moreover, it can be used with less-experienced participants in the process of developing interpersonal and personal competence, or with those who have limited cognitive experience but are less clear about the content issues of organizational consultation and change. The simulation approach can also be used as a diagnostic step toward better deciding how to make pairings for consulting teams and matches with client organizations in later hands-on practicum experience.

Purpose of the simulation

The consultation simulation is designed to give individuals the opportunity to practice and develop their organizational consultation skills in a safe, supportive environment that encourages experimentation and risk taking, especially with respect to interpersonal and personal skills. The simulation design assumes that effective consultants need to balance the following skills:

- cognitive skills for understanding individual, group, and organization behavior and related theories for changing each;
- interpersonal skills for building and maintaining problem solving abilities and helping relationships with organizations and individuals with diverse values and styles;
- personal skills and knowledge about their values, reactions to stress, major modes of influence, how they manage their emotions when confronted with conflict, dependence, ambiguity, and so forth.

The simulation is usually undertaken after participants have been exposed to readings, discussions, and lectures on consultation process from such sources as Argyris (1970), Blake and Mouton (1983), French and Bell (1984), Lee and Freedman (1984), Schein (1969), and Walton (1969). A variety of experience-based exercises may also be employed. Although the major focus is on a process consultation strategy—with typical steps of entry, contracting, diagnosis, action planning, action taking, evaluation, and recycling—participants are encouraged to consider a rather eclectic orientation based on the notion of fitting the type of intervention to the needs of the client rather than to the preferences and personality of the consultant (Blake & Mouton, 1983). Presumably, during the simulation participants will have the opportunity to practice orchestrating the interrelationships among their cognitive, interpersonal, and personal skills.

Design of the simulation

Participants are formed into six-person teams: Two serve as clients, two serve as consultants, and two serve as observers. During three rounds of the simulation, each participant has the opportunity to practice being a client, consultant, and observer. Depending on the size of a class or workshop, several parallel teams of six persons may be formed.

The consultation simulation progresses through four phases. Phase I consists of "prework" done individually according to one's assigned role before the consultation with the client (this lasts one or two hours). Phase II consists of consultation with the client (lasting one hour). Phase III consists of prework done individually according to one's assigned role before a review of the consultation (lasting one or two hours). Phase IV consists of a review of the consultation by the entire consultation team, led by the observers of the consultation (lasting two hours). When several teams participate in the simulation, the coordinator may also choose to conduct an extended review session to compare and contrast experiences.

Table I (on the next page) shows the detailed tasks for each role and phase of the simulation. Each complete cycle of the consultation simulation takes at least six to eight hours, or two class sessions in the case of a three-hour seminar course meeting weekly. The simulation should be repeated three times to enable each participant to practice playing each role. A single cycle of the simulation, however, can be useful, as can more than three cycles.

Equipment and materials required

Typewritten handouts of material such as the tables with this article are given to all participants.

Each team of six participants will need a videotape recorder with recording and playback capacity, and a videotape that will record one hour's worth of material. Preferably, each should have a separate room (approximately 15 by 20 feet) with movable chairs; a table is optional.

Role of the simulation coordinator

The simulation coordinator should do the following:

- introduce the simulation and explain its purposes, design, and procedures,

- be available to consult with teams during Phase I (prework done individually according to assigned role before the client consultation),
- arrange the rooms and videotaping equipment for Phase II (the client consultation, schedule determined by team members),
- be available to consult with teams during Phase III (prework done individually according to assigned role before a review of the consultation),
- attend the sessions of Phase IV (review of consultation) as a consultant, doing so on a "round robin" basis if the simulation has more than one team,
- provide consultation and theory sessions for the teams following Phase IV.

Table 1
Consultation Simulation Design*

Phase	Client's role	Consultant's role	Observer's role
I	Prepare written case to be handed in (this is also to be prepared before Phase II).	Prepare for meeting with client(s).	Prepare observation schedule (what you will look for in the client-consultant meeting).
II	Meet with consultants for one hour (each team).	Meet with clients for one hour.	Observe client-consultant meeting and videotape the session.
III	Prepare written feed-back sheet for consultants noting your reaction as a client during the one-hour meeting (e.g., what they did or did not do, how you felt about the meeting). Prepare written review and critique of how you felt about being a client (e.g., what you would do differently, anything you did not or would not tell the consultants).	Prepare letter to client(s) indicating the next action step to be taken (to be given to client[s]). Prepare written report of supporting rationale for action step and report how you felt about being a consultant and what you would do differently the next time. Prepare written feed-back sheet for the client(s) with your reactions as a consultant during the one-hour meeting (Phase II).	Prepare written feed-back sheets for consultants and clients (e.g., on how they communicated, how they used one another's resources) and review videotape to identify highlights to share in Phase IV. Design the Phase IV session.
IV	This phase consists of a two- to three-hour meeting of those in all roles by teams to review and critique what happened during Phase II. Persons in all roles should have prepared written materials indicated above for Phase III, which are to be reviewed along with the videotape made in Phase II. The observer(s) are responsible for coordinating and facilitating the meeting for Phase IV.		

*Phase I consists of prework for Phase II, which is done individually according to one's assigned role. Phase II consists of a one-hour meeting of those in all roles, and is arranged when the consultants call the clients to establish the time and place. The observer(s) is responsible for setting up and operating videotape equipment during Phase II. Phase III consists of prework done individually according to role, and is prework for Phase IV.

Rationale for the design

The consultation simulation has many special features that facilitate learning. The use of videotape permits participants to hear and see themselves from a point of view beyond the limits of memory. This is especially refreshing if the schedule requires extended periods between consultation and review.

Serving as clients gives participants the opportunity to experience receiving consultation and understanding how clients might resist change. Co-consulting (two consultants working together) exposes participants to the dilemmas of collaboration, including differences in values, style, intervention theory, tolerance for ambiguity and conflict, and so forth.

Requiring the initial consultation meeting to be limited to one hour (Phase II) forces participants to manage their time and to experience taking action with data that is less than perfect or incomplete. This is helpful because beginning consultants tend to underestimate how much data they have and to resist committing themselves.

Having the participants step into the observer role and coordinate Phase IV (the review of the consultation process) provides them with the simulated practice of a client feedback session. Moreover, this requires them to design a learning experience for other team members.

Variations in simulation design

The consultation simulation can be done in its entirety with hypothetical cases generated by participants playing the client role. More experienced adult learners, however, frequently are in a position to be clients with "real" problems. Some participants may be consulting with "real" clients, and will wish to introduce these clients to the simulation process. Such additions should be encouraged—if time permits—because they add richness to the process. The teams must, however, be explicit about confidentiality and expectations for continued consultation beyond the simulation. The coordinator of the simulation should be confident that the consultants are sufficiently experienced and be prepared to provide necessary supervision.

The length and specifics of the consultation simulation can be varied, as indicated in Table 2 (on the next page). On the initial cycle of the simulation doing the complete cycle is helpful for practicing the basic procedural steps of consultation and for encouraging participants to identify and work with the many embedded assumptions they bring to the process. With experience in the simulation later cycles can be abbreviated.

Evaluation and limitations
of the simulation approach

This simulation approach requires high levels of commitment and involvement from the participants. It requires them to make their "persons" available for discussion. Although a basic structure is provided, much of the implementation

Table 2
Consultation Simulation Flow Chart*

Phase	Complete cycle (with written protocols)	Abbreviated cycle (without written protocols)
I (Prework before consultation with clients)	Individual role meetings lasting one-two hours	Individual role meetings lasting 30 minutes
II (Consultation with client)	Total team meeting lasting one hour	Total team meeting lasting 45 minutes
III (Prework before review of consultation)	Individual role meetings lasting one-two hours	Individual role meetings lasting 30 minutes
IV (Review of consultation)	Total team meeting lasting two-three hours	Total team meeting lasting one hour
Review of consultation issues across teams (if more than one team)	Multiple team meetings lasting one hour	Multiple team meetings lasting 30 minutes

*The consultation simulation can be repeated as many times as appropriate. Typically, class or workshop participants are divided into teams of six persons each, with each team consisting of two clients, two consultants, and two observers. When fewer than six participants are available, the simulation may use only one client or one observer. By cycling the consultation simulation three times, each team member plays each role once. Typically, the first cycle is a complete cycle with written protocols, and the next two are abbreviated.

is left to the participants. Participants typically learn much about the entry process, building relationships, contracting with clients, using diagnostic models, helping the client learn to use a consultant, selecting a depth for an initial intervention, setting realistic action goals, managing their own needs, and working with co-consultants. Learning can, however, be uneven. As frequently occurs in supervised practica, those participants with the most initial experience tend to learn the most.

The consultation simulation described in this article is an intermediate step or transition link between a cognitive approach and a practicum approach with "real" clients. Its relative advantages are the parsimonious design for raising the interpersonal and personal competence issues of organizational consultation and the relatively "safe" psychological consequences for both staff and participants. Miscues during a simulation are more easily forgiven.

The simulation necessarily focuses on the early and short-term aspects of an organizational consultation. Thus, participants are unable to experience the issues and changes taking place in a long-term organizational change project. This limitation also exists with many practica approaches. Long-term "learning" arrangements and adequate supervision can be difficult to arrange and expensive, however.

REFERENCES

Argyris, C. (1970). *Intervention: Theory and method.* Reading, MA: Addison-Wesley.
Blake, R. R., & Mouton, J. S. (1983). *Consultation.* Reading, MA: Addison-Wesley.

French, W. L., & Bell, C. H., Jr. (1984). *Organization development: Behavioral science interventions for organization improvement.* Englewood Cliffs, NJ: Prentice-Hall.

Lee, R. J., & Freedman, A. M. (Eds.). (1984). *Consultation Skills Readings.* Arlington, VA: NTL Institute.

Schein, E. (1969). *Process consultation: Its role in organization development.* Reading, MA: Addison-Wesley.

Schein, E. (1978). *Career dynamics: Matching individual and organizational needs.* Reading, MA: Addison-Wesley.

Walton, R. E. (1969). *Third party consultation and interpersonal peace making.* Reading, MA: Addison-Wesley.

Neurolinguistic Programming: Adding New Dimensions to Training

Judith H. Katz
Cresencio Torres

Neurolinguistic programming (NLP) is a revolutionary and exciting new technology for understanding and facilitating human behavior. First written about in 1975 (Bandler & Grinder), NLP has been found to be highly effective in both the communication process and the creation of change.

NLP's roots are in psychotherapeutic schools synthesizing knowledge from psychodynmaic, behavioral, and humanistic thought and practices. Only recently has NLP been applied to the context of business and organizations. Trainers are finding knowledge of NLP to be an invaluable resource for more effective facilitation. This article describes some of the basic assumptions and beliefs of NLP and identifies ways in which NLP can be integrated into training to create positive and dynamic learning outcomes.

NLP: An overview

NLP addresses the structure of experience. It synthesizes the three traditional schools of thought, leading to a dynamic new model of human behavior and communication. NLP was initially developed by Bandler and Grinder in the early 1970s as a way to find out what made "masters" such as Erickson, Satir, Rogers, and Perls so effective in their work (Cameron-Bandler, 1985). From their observations and research, Bandler and Grinder (1975, 1976) could identify core processes in the "master's" ability to establish rapport, collect information, and create positive outcomes via specific change. These process dimensions are highly useful in our work as trainers. Indeed, exceptional trainers unconsciously use the identified NLP patterns. The real challenge is to learn to identify the patterns and have more choices about how to use them in training.

©1987 NTL Institute. All rights reserved.

The following is a discussion of some of the specific assumptions and beliefs underlying NLP as a conceptual framework. After this, we present some of the specific patterns of NLP in establishing rapport and discuss the implications of using NLP skills and frameworks in training.

NLP assumptions and beliefs

NLP is oriented toward establishing positive outcomes as identified by the client with the aid of the facilitator—who is called the "programmer" in NLP terminology. This model focuses on the patterns and processes used by individuals rather than on the content. NLP has uncovered the process dimension of communication and change in much the same way the T Group has focused on the process of how individuals become a group. In applying NLP principles, the facilitator identifies patterns of behavior and understands underlying processes used by individuals and groups. Therefore, explicating sensory-based behavioral data is essential.

A belief exists that human experience is generated as a result of the interaction between one's external world, what our senses detect of it, and the meaning one makes of that information internally (Cameron-Bandler, 1985). According to the NLP model, behavior is thus seen as a manifestation of an internal response to both the external world and one's internal world. According to this view, language is a secondary representation in that it does not truly express what an individual undergoes at an experiential level. Therefore, behavior presents a more accurate, richer description. The congruency or lack thereof between the behavioral and linguistic dimension is an important source of data in NLP, as it is in training as we know it. Trainers using NLP pay attention to the patterns exhibited by an individual with respect to sensory-based behavioral data so that they may obtain higher-quality information about the person's experience in the world. Through understanding and explicating these patterns, change can occur. Therefore, for NLP the goal is to identify current patterns so as to create new patterns and new ways of thinking and feeling, and thus allow individuals to have more choices in their lives.

Identifying patterns and creating change are addressed at both conscious and unconscious levels. The unconscious is described in an Ericksonian sense— that is, as a positive force underlying the conscious level, which is a person's core. The unconcious is considered a repository of all one's past experiences and learning that act as a source of growth (Gunnison, 1985).

The facilitator's role in using NLP is to do the following:

- train others to expand their sensory awareness,
- identify patterns of behavior, and
- expand choices and motivation (Dilts, 1983).

NLP recognizes that we are cybernetic systems—that is, that the mind and body are deeply interconnected and interdependent. To occur, change must be made in ways that consider the individual within her or his environment.

Several core beliefs serve as the foundation for NLP trainers. A primary belief is that the "map is not the territory" (Conwell, 1983). As trainers, we must discover each person's own "map" of the world. NLP not only talks about the necessity of getting into someone's world and reality, but provides mechanisms by which a trainer can truly understand another person without applying one's own meaning and values to that individual.

Once patterns of behavior have been identified, the focus of NLP turns to creating change. NLP holds that change is possible and that clients have within them all the necessary skills and resources to achieve what they want. The task is then to determine how we can help elicit those resources within clients and help them reach their desired outcomes. Another NLP belief is that if something is possible for one person, it is possible for another as well—one merely must determine **how** to make it a part of one's experience (Cameron-Bandler, Gordon, & Lebeau, 1985). Part of the process of change is making individuals aware of the choices they have in their lives. Therefore, if one's present patterns are not working, one must try alternative behaviors. Choice is an important criteria for the model. The person who has the most choice and exhibits the most flexibility has the most control. For the NLP model, control means the ability to influence the quality of one's own experience and that of others with time.

Overall, NLP maintains a positive framework oriented toward outcomes and solutions, from which the consultant/facilitator operates. Problematic situations become challenges. Behaviors, attitudes, or perceptions that appear on the surface to be negative are believed to have an underlying positive intent. Therefore, one must find out what that positive intent is so as to preserve it and find better ways to meet that intent (Dilts, 1983). The facilitator's role is to help find ways to make individuals and systems more resourceful.

A goal of NLP is to create relationships and inteactions that are mutually fulfilling. Within this system, the most challenging belief for the facilitator is that "the meaning of one's communication is the response you elicit from the other person, regardless of intent" (Cameron-Bandler, 1985, p. 25). This view is consistent with our notions of feedback. For trainers, this belief has a profound impact, for it precludes the possibility of "resistant" clients. Accepting this makes the trainer responsible for attending closely to the response of any communication, as the response determines its meaning. The facilitator must then find flexible ways of stepping inside another's reality. From this perspective, resistance indicates inability by the facilitator, not the client. The trainer must learn to align the communication and intention by being creative and flexible enough to have the desired impact on others. For clients, this means helping persons develop the behavior, feelings, and ways of thinking that will systematically and consistently elicit desired outcomes.

Finally, NLP provides a frame of reference with a positive outlook. Within this frame, limitations are seen as opportunities, failure turns into feedback, problems become refocused into outcome, and "why" something is a problem is changed to "how can we create change?" This positive world of NLP enables trainers using these skills and processes to focus more on patterns and ways of creating change that will enable persons to be more of who they are—that is, to live up to their greater potential. We discuss below ways of identifying one of these core dimensions.

Establishing rapport

The key to being an effective trainer is the ability to communicate clearly with clients and participants. Establishing rapport thus becomes a primary goal of the training process.

Many models of communication identify content dimensions of interaction, including feedback skills, statements using the word "I", and "active listening" techniques. NLP addresses the patterns of interaction by examining the structure of how people communicate. This includes paying attention to establishing rapport on both a verbal and nonverbal level.

One basic premise of the NLP model is that we operate and make sense of our experiences through information received from our environment. We use five senses to make contact with the external world—seeing, hearing, smelling, feeling, and tasting. For the NLP model these sensory systems serve a more functional role than that attributed to them in more traditional models of communication, which regard them as passive "input" mechanisms.

Each basic component functions in three ways in forming experience:

> 1) as an input system through which we perceive our environment,   2) as an internal represntational/processing system we use to apply meaning to incoming data, as well as carry out such activities as thinking, making choices, learning, fantasizing, etc., and   3) as an output system used to externally manifest our behavioral response to the environment. (Cameron-Bandler, 1985, pp. 20-21)

We take in information through our senses, internalize meaning through them, and communicate to others using these systems in our language patterns. The NLP model refers to these systems as' language representational systems (LRS). LRS represent just one of the many patterns used in NLP to establish rapport and enhance the communicationn process.

Language representational systems

LRS are specific patterns of communication based on the internalization of sensory experience. We think in pictures, sounds, feelings, and words. We also communicate using these systems. The three major channels are the visual (seeing), kinesthetic (feeling), and auditory(hearing) language representational systems. The remaining senses of smell and taste (olfactory and gustatory, respectively) are seldom used in the verbal communicationn process (Torres & Katz, 1983). One must pay attention to the process level of communication— that is the language patterns used—to understand one's experience and to respond appropriately. The habitual use of one set of categories indicates one's primary system. A primary system is one that is more highly developed than the others and is used more fully.

LRS are identified by the "predicates" used in communication. Predicates are verbs, adjectives, and adverbs (Bandler & Grinder, 1975). The categories below identify sample predicates for each particular LRS.

- Auditory: loud, talk, sound, remark, speechless
- Visual: clear, see, appear, view, perspective
- Kinesthetic: feel, emotion, support, tension, handle.

The following sentences illustrate how predicates are used to identify LRS existing in everyday conversation.

"I see that your **perspective** on the training process is quite **clear**.

"**I feel** strongly about our not coming to **grips with the** situation."

"**Tell** me about their **discussion** regarding our previous **conversation**."

The first sentence contains visual predicates, the second kinesthetic predicates, and the third auditory predicates.

Another method of identifying LRS is to administer the Language System Diagnostic Test (Torres, in press). The test is designed to detemine one's primary system, used most when under stress and to solve problems; one's secondary system, used in everyday conversation in conjunction with the primary system; and tertiary system, which is used least often, mostly in one's unconscious. The diagnostic test is a useful training tool for helping persons become more aware of LRS and how they can be used to enchance communication.

Representational systems can be compared in many ways to the "interface" of computer languages. Just as computers must use identical language formats, so too must humans use compatible language systems to communicate effectively with one another (Andreas & Andreas, 1982). Mismatching language systems has an impact similar to that of trying to connect a computer using FORTRAN to another using Pascal, or of speaking to a person in French when that person speaks Spanish. When language systems are mismatched, this usually results in confusion, frustration, and—in extreme cases—conflict. For example, some trainers may find that although they are fully cognizant and confident about their work, certain participants do not really seem involved even if they initially had much interest, and appear to become lost during training. When this occurs, it often results from the trainers' inability to vary their own language patterns to include all three LRS. Using only one's primary system means one may reach only those persons sharing that communication system. An example of mismatched language systems is given below:

Trainer: "How do you **feel** about what's going on right now?"

Participant: "I'm **drawing** a **blank**. I just can't get the **picture**."

Trainer: "I know this may be **difficult** for you, but try to get in **touch** with what you're **feeling** right now."

As this example shows, the trainer is using a kinesthetic language system whereas the participant is using a visual one. The participant cannot get a picture of feelings, and therefore may become frustrated and confused and unable to respond to the trainer's request. This can create a feeling of failure in the individual. From an NLP perspective, this indicates that the individual's kinesthetic system is the least developed of the LRS. Therefore, the trainer may help the participant by using the primary visual system as a way to develop the kinesthetic dimension. By doing so, the trainer can effectively communicate with this person within the person's own system and help expand the modes used.

The ability to identify language representation systems and effectively match them has several implications. Doing so helps develop trust and the ability to establish rapport, whereas mismatched communication channels create confusion, misunderstanding, and conflict. By matching a person's LRS, communication will be more open, resulting in greater trust and rapport. Facilitators can play a significant role in groups or teams by serving as translator for different language modes and thus increasing understanding among group members. This greatly increases one's chances of being understood. Participants will **feel** more **involved** (kinesthetic), **see** things more **clearly** (visual), and **discuss** in more meaningful **language** (auditory) the training experiences they participate in. Through this process level, according to NLP, one can best establish rapport. Information and experience is easily shared and the learning process enhanced.

Implications of NLP for trainers

This article has presented a cursory overview of NLP's basic assumptions and one pattern found in NLP for establishing rapport—that is, language representational systems. As a system itself, NLP contains much more complex and in-depth structures and patterns for establishing rapport, gathering information, and creating change. NLP is such an exciting technology because it enables trainers to better understand how to create specific results that are not haphazard. By understanding the process level of interaction, and having a structure for not only gathering information but understanding what the information means, the targets and mechanisms for change become easier to create and replicate. NLP provides road maps of inteventions to use to create positive outcomes of specific change. Trainers can thus be more helpful in enabling clients to attain their goals.

This article cannot fully outline or discuss the vast array of NLP techniques, including mechanisms for identifying criteria and beliefs, using metaphors to work on the unconscious, the metamodel as a linguistic tool for gathering information, ways of identifying individual's patterns, changing strategies such as anchoring and reframing, and changing history. Each dimension has important applications for the training process. We hope that we can begin to use the rich resource NLP provodes for us as trainers. Neurolinguistic programming is one mechanism to take the "mystery" out of trainer effectiveness. By understanding NLP, trainers will get a better working knowledge of the structure of experience, not only for themselves but also for their clients and participants. Through learning about the structure of experience and the process dimensions of NLP for establishing rapport and gathering information, the change process becomes more concrete and predictable.

NLP is still in its genesis, having been developed in 1975. We are beginning to find new possibilities of what can exist in the world by determining the patterns of the masters and developing their strategies within ourselves. The belief that "if it's possible for others, it's possible for ourselves" gives us hope as trainers that we can be the best possible, learning from the masters and creating new models of trainer effectiveness. NLP has only recently branched beyond the realms of psychotherapy to business and sales. Our task as trainers is to take the patterns and processes of NLP and integrate them into our understanding of the training and change process. Now is the time for us as trainers to pay attention to programs of success and learn as much as we can to make quality and effectiveness more of a reality.

REFERENCES

Andreas, C., & Andreas, S. (1982). Neuro-linguistic programming: A new technology for training. *NSPI Journal, 5*, 37-39.

Bandler, R., & Grinder, J. (1975). *Structure of magic* (Vol. I). Palo Alto, CA: Science and Behavior Books.

Bandler, R., & Grinder, J. (1976). *Structure of magic* (Vol. II). Palo Alto, CA: Science and Behavior Books.

Cameron-Bandler, L. (1985). *Solutions: Practical and effective antidotes for sexual and relationship problems.* San Rafael, CA: Future Pace.

Cameron-Bandler, L., Gordon, D., & Lebeau, M. (1985). *Know how: Guided programs for inventing your own best future.* San Rafael, CA: Future Pace.

Conwell, L. (1983). *NLP training materials.* Tiburon, CA: NLP Center for Advanced Studies.

Dilts, R. (1983). *Roots of neurolinguistic programming.* Cupertino, CA: Meta Publications.

Gunnison, H. (1985). The uniqueness of similarities: Parallels of Milton H. Erickson and Carl Rogers. *Journal of Counseling and Development, 63*(9), 561-594.

Torres, C. (In press). Language System Diagnostic Test. In L. Goodstein & J. W. Pfeiffer (Eds.), *The 1986 annual—Developing human resources.* San Diego: University Associates.

Torres, C., & Katz, J. H. (1983). Neuro-linguistic programming: Developing effective communication in the classroom. *The Teacher Educator, 19*, 25-32.

The Myers-Briggs Type Indicator: The Revolutionary Human Development Tool for the 1980s[1]

Otto Kroeger

The Myers-Briggs Type Indicator (MBTI) has been called "revolutionary" because it makes easily comprehensible the seemingly random, often baffling behavioral patterns of ourselves and others that contribute to the success or failure of our daily interactions. Behaviors thus defined by the MBTI are approached and described in a positive, reinforcing way. Furthermore, by making the complex psychological theories of Carl G. Jung understandable to persons of widely varied backgrounds, the MBTI allows those with a deep interest in human personality to explore its limitless dimensions. This article introduces the reader to the Myers-Briggs Type Indicator and its theoretical foundation, and illustrates some of the MBTI's varied applications.

First developed in 1942 by Isabel Briggs Myers, with the help of her mother, Katharine Briggs, the MBTI entered this decade with a heritage of more than 35 years of research and study. At the time of her death in 1980, Isabel B. Myers was still actively conducting research and collecting data to ensure the ongoing validity and reliability of her work. The instrument's resultant high rates of validity and reliability have produced its widespread acceptance in disciplines focusing on people.

By design, the MBTI does not measure intelligence, pathologies, or deviations. It seeks instead to open the door to understanding one's own preferences as defined in the Jungian model and to provide a coherent, understandable framework within which to compare one's preferences to those of others. Creative, constructive use of differences emerges from this understanding, whereas a lack of understanding leads one to consider another's differences from oneself to be "flaws." The latter situation often results in negative reinforcement and name calling, causing many of us to unwittingly attempt to "shape up" other persons and make them just like ourselves. Understanding differences as just differences, however, without attaching value

©1987 NTL Institute. All rights reserved.

judgments, creates an atmosphere in which differences can complement rather than conflict with one another.

One's first exposure to the MBTI usually leaves an individual with much positive reinforcement, new insights into interpersonal differences, and a new perspective from which to understand those traits in oneself and others that have proven attractive or irritating in one's daily encounters. Even if one does nothing else with the MBTI, it has already led to a "win/win" situation. If, however, the excitement generated by this new awareness creates a desire to explore in more detail the intricacies of human personality, the instrument's theoretical foundations lend themselves to any depth of advanced study.

According to Jungian theory, one is born with a predisposition for certain personality preferences. These prenatal leanings reflect the genetic lines of both parents and anything else that is a part of the individual's birth experience. As life develops, the environment acts as a catalyst in determining the exact form the preference will take. If I am predisposed to prefer "Extraversion," unless the environment is utterly hostile to this I will become an Extravert, but I must still translate that preference within the context of my situation in life. Birth order, other family members, and other environmental factors are all part of life's forces that shape me. As I grow and develop, my Extraversion also develops and matures. During the years it takes on many different forms, and I may appear quite different from decade to decade. In reality, my preference will remain the same, but its strength or quality may give it a different "flavor" at different stages of life. One's basic personality is set in place fairly early in life, but one must modify daily some of one's behaviors if one is to survive and succeed.

A brief history of the MBTI

Isabel Briggs Myers and Katharine Briggs first obtained the copyright for the MBTI in 1942. Both members of this mother-daughter team had a profound interest in people and people's behavior, brilliant intellectual depth, and insatiable idealism. In 1956, after much hard work constructing and revising the early forms of the instrument, they saw it published by the Educational Testing Service in Princeton, New Jersey, and released with a restriction that it be used solely for research.

In 1962, Myers published the manual explaining her rationale for the MBTI's development, scoring, construction, and prediction validities. In 1975, following 13 more years of continued research and wider use within many different disciplines, Consulting Psychologist Press obtained the copyright for the instrument and released it for general use. Its increasing popularity and acceptance have been reflected in the steady growth of its use in a broad cross section of public arenas.

An overview of the instrument

The MBTI is a 166- or 126-question, forced-choice questionnaire. Persons frequently find the forced-choice format frustrating, but it is necessary if the instrument is to be consistent with Jung's theory that the various functions of personality are dichotomous. For example, his theory says that it is psychologically impossible to be both an Extravert and Introvert simultaneously. Therefore, any instrument that seeks to measure a preference for one attitude rather than the other must force one to choose between the two.

Developing an instrument to reflect a true preference was not easy, and the closer one's preference is to the dividing line between dichotomous choices, the more difficulty one may have discerning a preference according to that scale. Considering, however, that the purpose of the MBTI is to allow self-exploration and not confine or box anyone into a particular mold, even when scores are close, persons usually receive direction and a focus within a positive context that allows and encourages further exploration.

Reliability and validity

A varied set of dynamics affect measurement of the reliability of any psychometric instrument, so any figure cited should be viewed as a general idea rather than a concrete conclusion. Still, 80% of the persons who take the MBTI on two different occasions still show the same four preferences, with 20% changing one or two preferences. Only rarely—and then under extenuating circumstances—does an individual change all four preferences by the time the MBTI is retaken. Commonly, when one retakes the MBTI the strength of one's preferences may change along the scale between any two choices, but seldom does one actually cross the line indicating a switch to preferring the opposite choice.[2]

Validity is a much more complex issue, and one or two statistical quotations cannot reflect all the research on this issue. In light of this caveat, I can say with respect to construct validity that about 90% of the time Extraverts will make choices reflecting Extraversion, Introverts will make choices reflecting Introversion, and so forth—reflecting solid construct validity. Predictive validity is even more tricky to measure, but about 85% of the time one can make accurate career choice predictions, behavior style predictions, and the like based on MBTI scores. Empirically, the MBTI works, and therein lies the impulse for its overwhelming acceptance.

The bottom—and most important—line is that two women, neither of them psychologists, equipped with a deep knowledge of Jungian theory and a conviction that understanding differences would lead to more constructive use of human energy, designed an amazingly accurate, reliable, valid, insightful psychological tool.

How preferences work

Jung says that people constantly perform two conscious functions: Perceiving and Judging. That is, we gather data and then do something with respect to it. According to Jung, individuals collect and respond to data in different ways. These differences are what produce individual preferences, and the variations of those individual preferences produce the 16 different personality types.

The Perceiving function

The Perceiving function reflects how you obtain data. Some persons prefer to deal with incoming data in the here and now. They are factually oriented, realistically inclined, and practical. When Perceiving, they rely on the data exactly as it is transmitted by their five senses—that is, according to what they can taste, touch, smell, hear, and see. They prefer to accept, quite literally and without modification, what their senses tell them. The Myers-Briggs terminology refers to them as "Sensors," designated in the literature by the letter "S."

Others, however, when they perceive the same data, instantly relate them to other data and impart to them meanings not evident from the data themselves. Rather than generating data sequentially, they grasp unrelated pieces at random and instantly form hunches about what the data may reveal. These persons are called "iNtuitives," designated by the letter "N."

Sensors and iNtuitives learn in different ways. Sensors want to see the practical value of learning and prefer it to be "hands on" and useful; iNtuitives may prefer a more speculative arena in which to engage in the learning process. In timed intelligence tests, when Sensors were allowed three seconds more per question they quadrupled the number of correct responses obtained. Researchers found that the Sensors wished to read each question twice, not because they did not understand them the first time, but simply to assure themselves that they had captured every detail of what was asked.

The difference between S and N is crucial because most of our communication flows from our perceptions. Once, when Calvin Coolidge came out of church, he was asked what the preacher talked about. His literal answer, "About 20 minutes," was a classic "S" response. If the individuals communicating hold radically different perceptions, serious arguments follow because both parties firmly believe their perceptions to be right. For example, at work an S may ask, "What time is it?" an N answers, "It's late." The S tries again, "I asked what time it is!" The N replies, with a tinge of irritation, "It's time to go." The S, by now thoroughly frustrated, says with an unmistakable edge of sarcasm, "Read my lips! What time is it?" The N answers, "It's past three." "Close, but no cigar," replies the S.

Sensors frequently consider iNtuitives "airheads," and iNtuitives frequently consider Sensors "nitpickers." Yet they marry each other and work on staffs together, armed more often with bad names to call each other than with any true insight into the root of their differences.

Of the general U.S. population, about 75% are Sensors and 25% iNtuitives. Interestingly, about 70% of college faculties are iNtuitives, meaning that 25% make up the intelligence tests for 75%. This statistic reflects the fact that, each year, iNtuitive students win the National Merit Scholarship awards and, generally, the Rhodes Scholarships (Myers, 1984). To explain these data, I pose the thesis that iNtuitive faculty at intuitive institutions of higher learning create iNtuitive tests on which iNtuitive students in high school do well, with these tests labeled "National Merit Scholarship" examinations. In truth, such examinations may more likely reflect typological compatibility with the system that created them than "meritorious" scholarship.

The Judging function

As with perceptions, decisions are made according to preferences that are quite different from one another. Some persons prefer to translate the data they have collected into objective, nonpersonal, logical decisions that carefully weigh cause and effect, and consider carefully and impartially the consequences of each decisive step to the logical consequence of the total decision. This is called a "Thinking" decision. Others prefer to translate the data they have collected into subjective, interpersonal decisions that weigh carefully the impact of these decisions. This is called a "Feeling" decision. Again, this dichotomy is at the heart of many serious interpersonal issues.

Thinkers frequently consider Feelers "fuzzy headed," and feelers frequently consider Thinkers to be "ice-blooded." Neither is true. Thinkers feel and Feelers think. The MBTI terms refer only to the process by which one comes to a conclusion. Three words that may reflect a Thinking preference are clarity, justice, and confronting, whereas three words that may reflect a Feeling preference are harmony, mercy, and nurturing. The Thinking preference is designated by the letter "T," and the Feeling preference by the letter "F."

Thinkers and Feelers can both be decisive, or indecisive. The issue is the process. The Thinker prefers to remain objective and somewhat removed, whereas the Feeler becomes highly involved in the process. Both care, both have feelings, both think, but the process that brings each to the final conclusion is so different that those with one preference often do not understand those with the other, and both fall into the trap of name calling and putting others down personally.

Of the general U.S. population, about 50% are Thinkers and 50% feelers. This preference scale is unique in that it is the only one of the four showing a sex-based differential. Of the 50% in the U.S. who prefer the Thinking style, 65% are men, and of the 50% preferring a Feeling style, 65% are women. This poses staggering issues for the family, the work place, schools, and other areas of life. Given our societal "scripts" for men and women, when a "Thinking" woman behaves in ways for which a "Thinking" man would be lauded, she often gets called various bad names. When a "Feeling" man behaves in ways for which a "Feeling" woman would be lauded, he also often gets sharply criticized by those around him. Our society has some strong values related to behavioral patterns that are accepted as masculine or feminine, and it does not deal well with deviations, failing to recognize that they are actually grounded in the most elemental fabric of an individual's personality. In my own practice, this point has shed new insight into various "compensatory" patterns visible in the "super-macho" man or "ultrafeminine" woman.

Extraversion versus Introversion

Jung says that one's attitude about where one prefers to focus and process the results of the Perceiving and Judging functions is perhaps the most significant of all the differences. If you tend to move your perceptions and judgments to the outer world of people, things, and actions; if you are accused of opening your mouth first, then engaging your brain; if you have to hear what you are saying before you know what you are going to say; if you walk out of a meeting saying, "When will I ever learn to shut my mouth?"; if you frequently find yourself "eating crow"—chances are you prefer an Extraverted attitude. That is, you move your perceptions and judgments to the external world as a matter of testing, validation, and affirmation.

If, however, you take the same perceptions and judgments and massage them internally—asking "What do I think about that? What's going on?"—and then, **maybe**, share them with others; if you are articulate but first must write down or think about what you say, if you walk out of a meeting saying, "Why didn't I say. . ."—chances are you prefer an Introverted attitude. That is, you move your perceptions and judgments to the internal world as a matter of testing, validation, and affirmation.

Beware: This has nothing to do with how much you talk or enjoy others' company, but rather deals with the source of your energy. If your energy comes from outside yourself, you prefer the Extraverted attitude. If you need time alone each day to recharge and give yourself energy, if your confidence and trust start from within, you prefer the Introverted attitude. The Extraverted attitude is designated with the letter "E," and the Introverted attitude with the letter "I." Because this is a source of energy, and because—to state this somewhat dramatically—what energizes the E ultimately drains the I, and vice versa, this difference has great impact on all aspects of inter-personal relations.

As a nation, we are 75% Extraverts and 25% Introverts. Because of this statistical disparity, and because the Introvert must spend much time on "foreign" turf—the Extraverted or outer world—the Introvert is psychologically a much more complex individual. Introverts feel heavier pressures to socialize, verbalize, "hang out here"—all of which run counter to the basic disposition of their personalities. The words "one-third of your grade in this class will be based on your classroom participation" represent to an I one example of the pressure one faces in trying to survive daily in the outer world.

As a rule, Extraverts give ulcers and Introverts get ulcers. Merely telling an Introvert to "dump the extra baggage" and not take things so seriously or intensely is not the answer. Indeed, if the Introvert could so freely dispose of things kept inside, the Introvert would be an Extravert. At work, when one approaches an Introvert's desk and asks for an opinion, one generally expects a ready reply—but if the person indeed prefers Introversion, that person will first wish to "go inside" to "find" the opinion. The person who approached the Introvert, especially if he or she is an Extravert, may interpret the delayed response as a sign of lack of interest, incompetency, or even disapproval. The reverse sort of miscommunication may occur when an Extraverted person at work offers opinions without having read an action paper first, or just "shoots from the lip" without much regard for who may be listening or without taking seriously the comments made.

Extraverts need and give more "strokes." They think out loud and "talk their way back" to lost items. They tend to disclose more and can be invasive of an Introvert's territory. Introverts are more territorial, and—although they may enjoy getting strokes—are somewhat less free about giving them. Introverts work more effectively alone and prefer the final note on any issue to come from introspection.

The Extraverted attitude versus the Introverted attitude is an important source of discrimination in determining how one copes daily with the work place, and whether or not one gets to the end of the day feeling drained or high from it.

Judgers versus Perceivers

The first set of preferences Jung identified—Extraversion versus Introversion—suggests where one prefers to perform the basic functions: Perceiving (Sensing versus iNtuiting) and Judging (Thinking versus Feeling). The final set of preferences added to the typological theory represents an insightful extension of Jung's model by Briggs and Myers. This last set of preferences indicates through which of the functions—Sensing, iNtuiting, Thinking, or Feeling—one prefers to orient oneself to the outer world. If one prefers an outer world that is structured, scheduled, ordered, and organized; if one makes lists and uses them; if one prefers to plan one's work and work one's plan—then that person probably prefers to use the judging function to deal with the world, as does about 50% of the general U.S. population. This preference is designated with the letter "J."

The remaining 50% of the general population prefers an outer world that is spontaneous, responsive, adaptive, and flexible. This group makes lists and loses them. They would rather "wait and see" than decide too soon about an upcoming situation. They prefer to collect as much data as possible about any situation. Having decided, they know that the decision is always measured against subsequent data, because this group prefers to orient itself to the outer world through the Perceiving function. This preference is designated with the letter "P."

In my opinion, the preference for J or P causes the most interpersonal stress because it is the preference with the most direct impact on others we encounter as we follow life's daily routines. This preference is one's outer life. When one is ready to share either a perception or judgment, this is the preference that will be reflected interpersonally. A J shares judgments freely, an Extraverted J even somewhat obnoxiously. Frequently, Extraverted Judging types end up defending issues in which they do not even believe; in an Extraverted moment, one shared a judgment that now needs defending. Occasionally, a J—especially an Extraverted one—will answer a question that was not even asked. Extraverted Judging types can make great time going in the wrong direction, whereas Extraverted Perceptive types may never get anywhere because they keep getting diverted by new data. Both are necessary, can be helpful to each other, and—indeed—are attractive to each other. Without some understanding of type, though, the initial attraction gives way to increasing frustration.

Judging types delight in organizing life for themselves and anyone else within range. Indeed, Feeling Judging types can be hurt rather easily when someone rejects their plans or organization, and a Thinking Judging type simply does not understand why others do not appreciate and respond to "orders for the day."

Judging types can seem somewhat abrasive in their need for closure, whereas Perceptive types can appear more "laid back" than they really are. The former type is sure that nothing will come of such seeming laziness and lack of direction—surely idleness is the "Devil's playground"—whereas the latter does not understand the need for closure and wonders why all the fuss is being made over something that seems inconsequential. Hence, the "Judger" frequently tries to impose structure and compulsiveness on the "Perceiver," and the Perceiver simultaneously stretches or extends some deadline set by the Judger.

This interplay can be illustrated in a rather humorous and typical exchange between a J and a P. The J unconsciously moves through the house during the week to make certain that, in the multiple light switch sets frequently found at the ends of halls, the bottoms of stairs, or inside all entrance doors, all the switches are set in the same direction (for the "super J," up is on and down is off). Along comes a P who, with the flip of a switch, undoes a week of the J's organizational effort. The P is surprised at the forcefulness of the resulting blast from the J, considering it totally out of proportion to the event triggering it. Mystified, neither type understands that this fray was provoked simply by the Judging type's need for organization and the Perceiving type's immediate response to the need for light.

In countless ways, variations of this dynamic are acted out hourly, and relationships at work, home, and play are stressed, stretched, strengthened, or weakened. Judging types write the books on time management to beat Perceiving types over the head. Perceiving types are always buying executive organizers to "get it together," only to discover that the organizer winds up collecting dust in some corner of the office or home. A J is often frustrated by a P's adding new items to an agenda after it has been drawn up or just as a meeting is about to close. The P, however, does not understand why the J either seems so pushy for direction or has such high needs for control over what the P sees as all the wrong issues.

Js get frustrated with Ps who do not follow company rules and schedules at work, and who—in response to requests—respond with "Ask me later" when a definite "yes" or "no" would better satisfy the J's need for closure. In contrast, a P cannot understand the J's flat refusal when requests are made at the "11th hour" despite the lack of any apparent reason to deny the request.

In counseling, the difference between judging and perceiving types causes endless stress between counselor and client. The J client wants direction and lists of things to do between appointments that the P counselor fails to deliver. The counselor only helps the client define the issues and frequently fails to supply the additional closure the J wants. The J counselor reverses this, often bringing closure, definition, or direction too early to the situation, making the P client feel cramped or overly directed. Too much Judging is extreme rigidity, and too much

Perceiving is extreme "flakiness." For that matter, an extreme preference for any one of the personality dimensions discussed above provides an example of the old adage that one's strength maximized becomes one's liability.

The various combinations of the four preferences produce 16 possible types. The table below presents them in a way indicating how each type relates to the other.

Table 1
The MBTI Type Table

ISTJ	ISFJ	INFJ	INTJ
ISTP	ISFP	INFP	INTP
ESTP	ESFP	ENFP	ENTP
ESTJ	ESFJ	ENFJ	ENTJ

The significance of close scores

The MBTI is intended to help an individual discover a preference with respect to each of the four scales, and the relative strength of the preference. It does not measure the quality or degree of development of that preference, only its strength in relation to its opposite, or less preferred, choice. Therefore, even if the instrument indicates absolutely no preference for a dimension—whether this is E, I, S, N, T, F, J, or P—the individual still has and uses that dimension, but has a strong preference for its opposite. Furthermore, using the dimension that is not preferred requires more energy than would be the case if one's preference for the opposite dimension were not so pronounced.

In the case of weak preferences, a common problem is that of mixed signals. Persons whose preferences are less clearly defined frequently report feeling greater ease in using either dimension. They also, however, report getting feedback indicating they sometimes send confusing messages. For example, someone who reports a slight preference on the E/I scale may be able to switch back and forth between Extraversion and Introversion with much greater ease than someone reporting a strong preference for E or for I, but may not always know—or have much control over—when these "flip flops" occur. Those around this person may be confused by this ambiguity. This could be the case for any of the scales for which an ambiguous preference is reported.

In any case, the purpose of the MBTI is to open a nonjudgmental door to self-understanding. The insight thus provided is never an excuse for behavior, only an explanation. With increased understanding through insight, the way is opened for a variety of behavioral options.

Dominant and Auxiliary functions

Two additional, theoretical aspects of type need mention: the Dominant/Auxiliary functions and the "Keirsey Temperaments" (discussed further below).

The former concept has endless implications because it provides the key to understanding much of the complexity of human personality.

The theory suggests that early in life one of the functions—Perceiving (Sensing versus iNtuitive) or Judgment (Thinking or Feeling)—emerges as the favorite, most reliable, most dependable, most preferred function. It is called the Dominant function, or—in Myers' terms—the commanding general of the personality. It is the function that one comes to rely upon most and that one would rather use more than any other. It is the boss of the personality. The other function becomes the Auxiliary, and it serves as the support system to the dominant function—in Myers' terms, the loyal lieutenant. Thus, if the "general" prefers to collect data (Perceiving function), the "lieutenant" makes whatever decisions are necessary so that the general can do as it prefers. If, however, the general prefers to make decisions (Judging function), the lieutenant only gathers that data necessary to permit the general to perform its preferred task. Hence, according to this classification, people are either Dominant Perceivers (Sensors or iNtuitives) or Dominant Judgers (Thinkers or Feelers).

Various communication shortfalls happen when, for example, a Dominant Sensor thinks he or she shares a judgment, but the Dominant Judger heard it altogether differently. Or, for example, if a Dominant Feeler seeking data actually shares a judgment and wonders how the communication went aground. Thus various generals and lieutenants of our personalities attempt to deal with one another in the day-to-day patterns of social interaction.

The Dominant/Auxiliary dynamic becomes further complicated when considered within the context of an Introverted personality. With those who prefer Introversion, the Dominant function is habitually captive to the Introverted attitude. Hence, the most preferred, best developed, most reliable part of the Introvert stays Introverted, and the Introvert becomes oriented to the outer world (foreign turf) through the secondary, less preferred Auxiliary function. To state this dramatically, one does not meet the commanding general—the boss—of the Introvert's personality without an appointment, which is another word for trust. This phenomenon is one of the factors that accounts for the complexity of the Introvert mentioned above, and combined with the Introvert's minority status (introverts make up only 25% of the general U.S. population) causes Introverts to be "sociologically disadvantaged."

The implications of this are obvious, and the behavioral ramifications unending. In an ordinary day, in an ordinary office, home classroom, or other arena of human encounters, the Extravert comes at the Introvert through the Dominant (general) and is received by the Introvert's Auxiliary (lieutenant). With the Extravert, "what you see is what you get," whereas with the Introvert "what you see is only second best." The best remains inside the Introvert. The name calling starts as the Extravert experiences the Introvert as "closed" or "deceptive," even "uninterested," and the Introvert experiences the Extravert as "superficial," insecure," or "inappropriately disclosing." The outer world is considered necessary but tiring and draining turf to the Introvert, whereas it is an exciting and energy-charging arena for the Extravert. A real understanding of differences and careful contracting with one another is needed for these differences to be used creatively and dynamically.

Temperament theory

The Keirsey Temperament Classification is a departure from Jung's typology, but it affords behavioral descriptions that are insightful and helpful for understanding broad predictions about a person's style of teaching, leading, learning, counseling, entertaining, preaching, and other areas of human interaction. The Keirsey temperament theory is most beneficial for sorting through the impact of behavioral differences in daily living, working, and learning. If one's Perceiving preference is iNtuitive, then the Keirsey theory looks at how one evaluates or judges that iNtuitive perception as the second behavioral discriminator—that is, whether one is either an NT or an NF type. Although big differences occur between Extraverted and Introverted persons of either of these types, those differences are not as great as is the similarity of temperament among all NTs or all NFs.

If one's Perceiving preference is Sensing, the Keirsey Theory makes the next distinction that of how one uses the Sensing perception in the outer world—that is, whether one is an SJ or SP type. The differences between Thinking and Feeling will also manifest themselves for each type, but those differences will not be as great as the similarity of temperament among all SJs and SPs. The four temperaments include the following types:

- NT (ENTJ, INTJ, ENTP, INTP),
- NF (ENFJ, INFJ, ENFP, INFP),
- SJ (ESTJ, ISTJ, ESFJ, ISFJ),
- SP (ESTP, ISTP, ESFP, ISFP).

With the "quick study" grouping the temperaments permit, one knows that if one is dealing, say, with an NT, one is dealing with someone who looks at the world, perceives possibilities, and translates those possibilities analytically and impersonally. Therefore, such persons hunger to understand, control, predict, and explain the universe and its systems. Scratch an NT and you will discover a scientist. NTs learn, lead, manage, live, and grow by pushing against systems. In their need to understand, they are driven to ask "why," and the question can become more important than the answer.

The NF, in looking at the world, prefers to perceive possibilities and translates those perceptions subjectively and impersonally. In turn, such persons hunger to ask "who," and often have profound interpersonal skills. For the NF, most of life has to be translated through that person's ideals, which, in turn, are frequently related to people and issues affecting people. Scratch an NF and you will discover someone seeking to "become." NFs and NTs each make up about 12% of the general U.S. population.

The SJ perceives the world as it is, through the senses, and wants to structure, schedule, and order it. This is the temperament that eats, sleeps, and breathes organization. Committed to responsibitilies, duty, rules, and regulations, the SJ becomes the backbone of most of organizational life. Such persons readily accept positions of leadership throughout the community and readily develop procedures that oil the machinery of life. They make up about 38% of the general U.S. population. Scratch an SJ and you will discover duty personified.

The SP also perceives the world as it is, through the senses, and wants to stay open to receive more sensory data. This temperament thus eats, sleeps, and breathes "the moment." Action drives this temperament, and doing something is vastly preferred to thinking about it. Short attention spans and a low need for long-range planning mark this group, and—as you might imagine— such inclinations put them out of step with most of the remaining U.S. population, of which they make up 38%. SPs thrive on situations in which the outcome is unknown and they are free to test the limits. For this group, today must be enjoyed because tomorrow may never come. The crises of life were made for the SP, because crises provide the immediacy on which those of this temperament thrive. Scratch an SP and you will discover a firefighter.

At this point, applications of type and temperament theory are certainly obvious. Helping a family understand that member who is of a different type rather than pressure that member to conform can significantly affect the individual's contribution to the family system. Something as simple as an Introverted Judging parent imposing quiet, time alone, and reflection—in the name of good study habits—on an Extraverted Perceiving child, or an Extraverted parent always urging an Introverted child to be gregarious, can lead to poor grades, lack of interest in school, and an assortment of behaviors that are more counterproductive and productive. All of this is done, albeit with the best intentions, because one assumes one's own preferences should be the same for all unless one understands typology. After all, not only did the choices you made for yourself work, but all of life's situations have reinforced them—therefore, that is the way it should be. Hence people tend to impose their preferences on everyone else. Organized parents want organized children, and with an almost "hammer-and-chisel" intensity set out to make this happen.

The same dynamics are no less true in the work place, the school, or in any of life's other arenas. It is tragic that performance evaluations, grades, and other such rewards are meted out under the subtle influence of one's own personality. Therefore, just as the family "hammer-and-chisel" syndrome stays with one privately, one's personnel records accompany one forever, and do not so much provide a true reflection of competency, intelligence, or creative uniqueness as much as a reflection of how similar or different the "rater" and the "ratee" were.

I state above that a real understanding of differences and careful contracting are needed to make effective use of varied talents. The MBTI affords the user a most constructive frame of reference for both understanding and differences and contracting in light of behaviors affecting productivity. Furthermore, a brief examination of the distribution of types in any system allows one to see the "blind spots" and overly developed areas. Such insights open doors to various plans for solid action to confront issues within the organization.

The strength and significance of the MBTI lies in its positive, affirming approach to differences among people. The more one becomes aware of differences, the more one can constructively use them. Without this awareness, one can sometimes feel like a left-handed person totally surrounded by right-handed persons. Although we tend to say we like variety, overwhelming data for work and elsewhere (with the possible exception of marriage) indicate that "like begets like"— that we prefer others like ourselves. Organizations, circles of friends, and other such configurations appear more "alike" than not. To continue the analogy, when given a choice, "left-handers" pick left-handers, and right-handers pick right-handers. The result is both tunnel vision and an effort by those in power— supervisors, parents, teachers, coaches, and the like—to get persons to conform to the overall group. Such efforts stifle creativity, produce attribution, and give way to labels for behavior that haunt one for a lifetime, especially if one is of the type that is "different."

NOTE

1. This article is adapted from a forthcoming book by Otto Kroeger to be published by Delacort Publishers in May 1988.

2. The reliability/validity figures cited are based primarily on data I collected during an eight-year period of group and individual practice with the Myers-Briggs Type Indicator. For additional references on reliability and validity, see McCaulley and Carskadon (1983) and Myers (1962).

REFERENCES

Bates, M., & Keirsey, D.W. (1984). *Please understand me* (4th ed.). California: Gnosology Books.

Campbell, J. (Ed.). (1971). *The portable Jung.* New York: Viking.

Center for Applications of Psychological type. (1975). *Bibliography: The Meyers-Briggs Type Indicator.* Gainesville, FL: Center for Applications of Psychological Type.

Jung, C. G. (1923). *Psychological Types.* New York: Harcourt, Brace.

Jung, C. G. (1961). (A. Jaffe, Ed.). *Memories, dreams and reflections.* New York: Random House.

Kroeger, O., & Associates (1985). *TYPEWATCHING tape series: The entertaining and easy way to understand the sixteen different personality types of the Myers-Briggs Type Indicator.* Arlington, VA: Otto Kroeger Associates.

Lawrence, G. (1979). *People types and tiger stripes.* Gainesville, FL: Center for Applications of Psychological Type.

McCaulley, M. H. (1981). *Jung's theory of psychological types and the Myers-Briggs Type Indicator.* Gainesville, FL: Center for Applications of Psychological Type.

McCaulley, M. H., & Carskadon, T. G. (1983). Test-retest reliabilities of scales and subscales of the Myers-Briggs Type Indicator and of criteria for clinical interpretive hypotheses involving them. *Research in Psychological Type, 6: Applications of Psychological Type.*

Myers, I. B. (1962). *The Myers-Briggs Type Indicator.* Palo Alto, CA: Consulting Psychologist Press.

Myers, I. B. (1980). *Gifts differing.* Palo Alto, CA: Consulting Psychologist Press.

Sanford, J. A. (1980). *The invisible partners.* Ramsey, NJ: Paulist Press.

Schemel, G. J., & Borbely, J. A. (1982). *Facing your type.* Wernersville, PA: Typrofile Press.

Role Analysis Group: Integrating and Applying Workshop Learning

William H. Barber

Introduction

This article presents a training method that enables learners to apply their workshop experience to back-home issues—and to do so as a central part of their training.

The theory behind experience-based learning—such as that of Kolb, Rubin, and McIntyre (1974), Johnson (1974), and Schein and Bennis (1965)—identifies the following steps needed for this type of learning to occur.

1. experience,
2. analysis,
3. conceptualization, and
4. application.

Often the fourth step, application of workshop learning, is given only brief, pro forma attention. This means not only that a key step in the education sequence is treated inadequately, but that a rich opportunity to strengthen the work of a total training session is missed. In response to this situation, this article offers a method for enhancing the application and personal integration segments of training programs.

The role analysis group[1] has been used with a wide range of clients, including corporate managers learning leadership skills, internal corporate management consultants learning advanced organizational consulting concepts, doctors and nurses learning to become more interpersonally effective with patients and staff, church bishops framing policy statements, and Native American Indian tribal chiefs learning systems and communication theory. This group method has also been used in conjunction with seminars on special topics such as adult development, authority and responsibility, and stress management.

©1987 NTL Institute. All rights reserved.

External boundaries

The role analysis group has the following formal characteristics:

Composition. A group consists of 6-10 members and one or two staff consultants. Members preferably come from different organizations, and persons with similar positions in their organizations—such as financial officers or line managers—may be assigned to the same group.

Task. The task is precisely stated, often in writing, as the following: The group is to (1) explore unresolved workshop issues and (2) relate workshop learning to back-home issues, problems, and questions.

Time. Approximately one-fourth of the total time for the workshop is devoted to role analysis group work. This time may be allocated to part of each day—such as the evening session or the first session each morning—or consolidated toward the end of the workshop, depending on the training objectives.

Role. Members are each asked to present specific back-home issues for application or unresolved workshop issues. Staff members are to provide consultation linking the training experience to the individual member's back-home situation.

Internal boundaries

What material for discussion will enable group members to integrate various parts of the training—including unsettled or incomplete aspects—and begin relating what they learn during the workshop to the organizational and/or personal issues facing them back home?

Group consultants set the expectation that each group member will take at least one turn presenting a particular back-home problem or unresolved workshop issue for analysis and consultation. The group avoids general discussions or "debriefing," and consultants state that group members are expected to examine specific problems. Some groups initially resist this focus, but comply if the consultant is precise and, if necessary, firm about the best way to accomplish the task of the role analysis group.

A group member speaking about her or his back-home situation describes the facts, such as the formal organizational structure, reward systems, internal politics, environmental demands, and especially her or his own history, "personal agenda," and personal conflicts. This discussion can address the questions "What is the problem for you?" and "How is that a problem for you?"

The consultant may summarize the situation by using a visual display of facts and reporting lines, including open-systems diagrams (Rice, 1969). As the situation a person experiences back home becomes more elaborate, the consultant invites attention to the training workshop, and may ask, "What is your experience in this workshop that relates to this back-home problem?" Often the back-home problem is reenacted in such a way that it can be examined with here-and-now information from the subject and other group members. A "bridging" question is, "Are there ways in which what you are learning in this workshop offers you ideas for understanding the problem?

An alternative to presenting the problem is to invite the person to describe a back-home role he or she wishes to discuss. This could relate to a work role or to one with another organization, such as a church, club, or committee. Again, data about the organization's structure, history, politics, rewards, and motivations is elicited, with the group member's own role always remaining in the forefront.

As the back-home situation is described, the group member is invited to examine her or his particular workshop experience. While this experience is being described, ways of relating that experience to the member's back-home situation may be examined. As the image of this situation becomes more complete, the focus can move toward problems for which the member seeks consultation, or to ways of relating the training workshop experience to the member's back-home situation. Constraints, conflicts, and dilemmas quickly become apparent, and the linkage to application of the training workshop then becomes the consultation task.

The consultant may invite the group to consider the type of problem involved. Is it one of structure, relationships, technology, environmental demands? Who and what are involved in the problem? What person or object is referred to but underestimated or taken for granted? What is the goal or direction toward which the person is moving or needs to move? The consultant resists offering solutions and remedies and instead encourages the group members to consider "the problem" from a new position.

It could be said that individual consultation is occurring in a group setting. Although other members are not excluded, the primary exchange takes place between two persons—the member and the group consultant. Freud's "observing ego" comes into play for the observing members, who listen and watch as their colleague engages in this "role consultation" (Freud, 1921). Observing members report identifying greatly with the "protagonist," and they feel much involved in the discussion. Their comments are invited after the protagonist and consultant have begun analyzing the material presented.

Case study

The following role analysis group work occurred toward the end of a six-day workshop on leadership, which was attended by 60 scientific, technical, and management specialists from different organizations. The format of this workshop was heavily experiential, using simulations, exercises, and unstructured small groups without formal leaders.

John Smith was a senior-level scientific specialist with a large, international business machine corporation. He began reporting his back-home problem by saying that he felt "disconnected" from junior coworkers in his company. His role called for much contact with younger members of the organization, and he reported being chronically dissatisfied with the lack of a strong working relationship between himself and his junior colleagues. When he had asked a friend and colleague in the company for advice, this friend commented that he had observed that younger scientists were always conscious of the difference between their own level of experience and expertise and John Smith's high level of competence, and noted, "I think they are always mindful of the gap between you and them."

As part of its mission, John's company had an explicit policy and commitment toward developing technical and scientific professional personnel. This was the part of his work role in which John felt himself deficient. He reported various examples of projects he had initiated to remedy this situation, which—for various reasons—had been terminated earlier than he had wished.

The consultant asked John how he was feeling about his work while in the training workshop. "It's great," John replied. "I'm learning a lot." He went on to note that he had been the focus of complaints from some members of the workshop, who said he was blocking the completion of group projects, and that, although he was friendly with a small group of "personal friends" he had made during the workshop, he was not "mixing, being a part of things" and was not responding to requests for his help with group tasks. These requests, it was discovered, were from training workshop members younger and less knowledgeable and experienced than John with the technical material on which the groups were working.

When asked about his own personal and professional development, John said,

Oh, I'm overtrained and overprepared. Along with all the academic degrees, I've had several years of specialized extra training and a number of advanced professional certificates. Much of this isn't essential to my work, but it was something I wanted to do to be able to feel I had gotten as much training as possible so I could be well prepared.

The consultant asked how John related his present workshop experience to the back-home problem for which he was requesting consultation. At first John failed to see a connection, but quickly began to explore the considerable similarity between the two situations. His behavior in the workshop in relating to younger colleagues was almost identical to his behavior with junior coworkers in his company.

Among the theoretical concepts presented in the training workshop were notions of authority relationships and boundaries, and how roles are assumed and work delegated to persons in various roles. The concept of "person," as distinguished from "role," includes one's personal history, experience, strengths, and vulnerabilities. When asked why he pursued so much extra education and training beyond that needed for his professional role, John reported that he had always felt inadequately trained and qualified for his profession, and that he found his "extra training" helped compensate for his feelings of professional inadequacy. As a person, John did not feel adequate, despite his efforts to be trained for his role.

The consultant suggested that perhaps John's treatment of junior colleagues reflected his unacknowledged sensitivity toward their professional development needs and professional inadequacies, and that his ineffectiveness in working with them was related to John's own professional development issues—a pattern repeated in the training workshop.

The consultant suggested a direction for moving out of this pattern, based on the concepts of authority and boundaries: "It is as if you avoid expressing your vulnerability and uncertainty [i.e., your own 'person'] at the boundary of authority."

John was quiet for some time; he said he was both "touched" and "upset" by the consultant's last comment. "It felt right on target," he said, for understanding his problems with his junior colleagues. Other group members also reported making "useful connections" with this analysis.

Outcomes

Postworkshop evaluation instruments invariably rate the role analysis group as being among the more significant parts of the training. The following statements illustrate the special flavor of the role analysis group:

> "It became more important to me each day."
>
> "It was hard work, but I learned useful ideas from each member."
>
> "I found a solution to a complex problem."
>
> "This part of the seminar snuck up on me; at first I thought it was a rap session, but I learned differently."
>
> "I find myself studying my notes from the role analysis group."
>
> "The presentations during the week were interesting, but the role analysis group is of continuing practical help for me."

A valuable side effect is that training staff members to assume the role of group consultant in itself offers a staff training benefit, aids team building among the staff during the workshop, and—most important—provides a mechanism for workshop management and leadership. Brief, prepared reports from group consultants at staff meetings after each role analysis group session provide a conduit for knowing about the trainees' experience in the workshop, a mechanism for supervising staff, and a method for combining the various parts of the training into an integrated whole.

Summary

The role analysis group is a procedure for specifically applying workshop learning to back-home material. Members' anxiety that often accompanies experiential learning can be managed and channeled into the relevant study of the kinds of problems related to why they came to the workshop. In addition, the role analysis group provides a way to supervise and integrate the work of training staff members with different theoretical orientations and different levels of training and experience.

NOTE

1. The term "organizational role analysis" was used in 1971 in group relations conferences supported by the Center for Applied Social Research and by the Tavistock Institute in London. The terms was used to describe one-to-one consultation with managers attending the conferences (Reed, 1976).

REFERENCES

Freud, S. (1921). *Group psychology and the analysis of the ego*. New York: International University Press.

Johnson, D. W., & Johnson, F. P. (1975). *Joining together: Group theory and group skills*. Englewood Cliffs, NJ: Prentice-Hall.

Kolb, D. A., Rubin, I. M., & McIntyre, J. M. (1974). *Learning and problem solving in organizational psychology: An experiential approach*. Englewood Cliffs, NJ: Prentice-Hall.

Reed, B. D. (1976). Organizational role analysis. In C. L. Cooper (Ed.), *Developing social skills in managers*. London: Macmillan.

Rice, A. K. (1969). Individual group and intergroup processes. *Human Relations, 22*(6), 565-584.

Schein, E. H., & Bennis, W. G. (1965). *A general overview of our learning theory in personal and organizational change through group methods: The laboratory approach*. New York: Wiley.

Assessment of Small Group Dynamics: The SYMLOG System[1]

Michael A. Ichiyama
W. Brendan Reddy

Obtaining a useful conceptualization of interpersonal and group processes is a central concern of trainers and practitioners in the human relations arena. Consultants and trainers work with a wide variety of groups, and often focus their efforts on imparting knowledge to their audiences about the dynamics underlying relationships with others in the hope of promoting personal growth or change. Practitioners who are involved with work groups, committees, or teams—in which task efficiency rather than self-enhancement is the primary goal—depend upon their skills of observation and group process diagnosis to guide their interventions. Whether for educative or application uses, these professionals rely on their comprehension and evaluation of group dynamics in much of their work.

At the heart of small group dynamics lie social interaction processes. Many theorists highlight social interaction in their definitions of a group (Bales, 1950; Cartwright & Zander, 1968; Hare, 1976; Homans, 1950; Shaw, 1981). By examining the larger pattern of social interactions among members of a group, important aspects of group structure such as roles, norms, coalitions, and subgroupings can be uncovered. To capture the complexity of interpersonal relations among individuals— and the emergent group structure—within a manageable framework suitable for application use would seem a formidable accomplishment. For the trainer and practitioner alike, such a tool for educative and diagnostic purposes would be invaluable for working with small groups.

This article presents such a framework in the form of a condensed version of SYMLOG (an acronym standing for the "systematic multiple-level observation of groups"). SYMLOG is a theory and set of methods for the study of group dynamics (Bales & Cohen, 1979), and is the product of more than 30 years of theorizing and research by Bales on social interaction as observed in self-analytic groups. In its entirety, SYMLOG is a large and complex system, but one of its virtues is its flexibility. Even in its most basic form, SYMLOG has value for applications, as the

©1987 NTL Institute. All rights reserved.

data obtained can be computed and analyzed by hand and yet still be meaningfully related to a working body of theory and research findings. An additional advantage of SYMLOG is its generality. SYMLOG can be used appropriately across multiple levels of analysis—that is, it is equally appropriate for individuals, dyads, and groups across levels of observed behavior, conversational imagery, and expressed values.

This article is aimed primarily at those readers who have little or no familiarity with the SYMLOG system. Even those readers who are familiar with SYMLOG, however, should find our fundamental exposition interesting, as we have incorporated into our presentation citations from recent articles and papers on SYMLOG that have been printed following publication of the SYMLOG text, and a summary of some current advances in SYMLOG research and application. As we can only present the most basic tenets in the space provided, readers who wish to employ SYMLOG in their own work should consult the following publications: *Personality and Interpersonal Behavior* (Bales, 1970); *SYMLOG* (Bales & Cohen, 1979); and the *SYMLOG Case Study Kit* (Bales, 1980). The purpose of this article is to provide the reader with an introductory synopsis of the system.

Historical and theoretical overview

An overarching concern in the illustrious academic career of Robert F. Bales was the measurement of social interaction (Bales, 1984, p. 98). Bales tackled a formidable beast in attempting to synthesize and measure the essence of social interaction in all its complexity. Decades of study in social psychology concerned with this fundamental problem resulted in many isolated and microlevel theories and lines of research with no encompassing frame of reference to integrate them. This state of fragmentation within social psychology contributed to the "crisis" in the field (Boutillier, Roed, & Svendson, 1980; House, 1977; McMahon, 1984). Bale's quest was to provide a system of measurement and body of theory that would place the pertinent elements of interpersonal behavior (and group dynamics) into a meaningful framework.

The early efforts of Bales focused on the direct observation of interpersonal behavior within the context of small groups. The product of his early work is *Interaction Process Analysis* (IPA) (Bales, 1950), which supplies an observational method for the study of small groups, containing an ordered set of categories through which observers may classify interpersonal behaviors as they occur. While IPA became widely used and highly regarded, Bales came to realize that the creation of a comprehensive theory and an adequate formulation of empirical generalizations addressing the study of social interaction and group dynamics must necessarily include the perceptions and characteristics of the individuals being observed—that is, the group members themselves.

This shift in emphasis from observer to participant-observer resulted in Bale's second major book, entitled *Personality and Interpersonal Behavior* (Bales, 1970). During this period Bales discovered, through factor-analytic methods, the three-dimensional structure that became the organizing framework of SYMLOG. A major portion of *Personality and Interpersonal Behavior* is devoted to describing personality types as manifested in interpersonal behavior corresponding the locations in the three-dimensional spatial model. In making his assumptions about the concepts of the general nature of personality in this work, Bales was strongly influenced by Freud and psychoanalytic theory. From a sociological perspective, the influence of Mead (1934) and symbolic interaction theory appears evident in the book's emphasis on the importance of interaction processes, self-image, and the individual definition of the social situation. *Personality and Interpersonal Behavior* was a large step within an extensive program of research, which culminated in SYMLOG.

In summary, Bale's early work concentrated on interaction processes in small groups. In 1970, he incorporated personality as an important variable in the study of small groups. The publication of SYMLOG represented his thorough integration of interaction processes and personality into a new perspective for the study of small group dynamics. SYMLOG, with its graphic representation of group dynamics through the use of field diagrams, resurrected field theory—albeit in a new form (Bales, 1985). Recently, Hare (1985a) has suggested that the SYMLOG system could be used to bring a much-needed consistent frame of reference to existing texts in group dynamics and social psychology.

This article can only touch upon the substantial history and theoretical network underlying SYMLOG. Elaborations of the development of SYMLOG and its numerous theoretical connections may be found in the SYMLOG text (Bales & Cohen, 1979) and subsequent works (Bales, 1984, 1985; Polley & Bales, 1985). We now turn to a description of the basic organizing framework that lies at the heart of SYMLOG theory and method.

The SYMLOG three-dimensional space

The SYMLOG spatial model is based on the assumption that one can describe the quality of behavior, or any action of interpersonal behavior, by reference to three dimensions. These three dimensions, in systematic relation to one another, constitute the basic conceptual structure of the SYMLOG space. Obtaining this fundamental structure provided a means of capturing the complex, global process of interpersonal and group dynamics into an orderly and manageable framework (Bales, 1984).

A recent textbook on group dynamics describes the SYMLOG spatial model as "rather imposing" (Forsyth, 1983, p. 116), and it may appear so to many people. The model may be difficult to grasp not so much because of its complexity as much as because it is a *different* conceptual scheme from what is typically encountered. The SYMLOG model is cubic, unlike the more common linear categorical schemes, and this may make it appear more foreboding than it actually is. Some argue that the three-dimensional model should be readily conceptualized by the average person, as it is consistent with the way we perceive objects in our physical reality. The remainder of this section describes the SYMLOG spatial model, our goal being to do so in a way that provides clarity and ease of conceptualization. The reader unfamiliar with SYMLOG is encouraged to visualize the model as an actual physical space that spatially

188

represents an internal perceptual structure that appears to be shared across individuals and groups (Bales & Cohen, 1970; Isenberg & Ennis, 1981).

Conceptualizing the SYMLOG space

The three basic dimensions underlying the spatial model emerged from multiple and repeated factor analyses conducted using many types of measurement, including personality test data, value statements, ratings of self and other perceptions, and thousands of hours of coded observations in groups (Bales, 1970). Bales (1985) considered the salience of these dimensions (1985) not to be something new, emphasizing that they "have been discovered again and again, but have not been seen in their full generality. . ." (p. 2). They are closely related to dimensions found by others studying different domains.

Bales plotted the three dimensions in geometric relation to one another so as to form a "space" within which the perceptual domain of interpersonal behavior could be captured. The bipolar dimensions are named for physical space: upward-downward (U-D), positive-negative (P-N), and forward-backward (F-B) (see Figure 1). Corresponding to the poles of the physical dimensions in Figure 1 are accompanying descriptive adjectives, which are used as mnemonics with the meanings that seem natural to most persons. The first dimension, upward-downward (U-D), refers to the relative dominance (U) or submissiveness (D) of persons, as people tend to associate dominance with being "up" and submissiveness with being "down." Similarly, the second dimension, positive-negative (P-N), represents a continuum from friendly (P) to unfriendly (N) orientations. The third, forward-backward (F-B), corresponds to task-oriented, instrumental behavior (F) on one end of a continuum to emotionally expressive behavior (B) on the other. The dimensions of the conceptual space are independent of one another, so that movement along one dimension does not necessitate corresponding movement along the other dimensions.

The complete SYMLOG space in Figure 1 is represented as a cube made up of smaller cubes. The smaller cubes represent various locations in the space within which persons or images are placed. The cubic model was obtained through a "trichotomization" of each of the basic three dimensions of the space into its two poles and a neutral middle area. For example, one may be perceived along the U-D dimension as exhibiting behaviors that are dominant, submissive, or neither. The procedure results in 3^3—27—different combinations of the trichotomized dimensions. The SYMLOG types are based upon the 26 possible directions emanating from the neutral center of the space. The center location in the space represents the combination of the three neutral parts of each dimension.

At the poles of each dimension in Figure 1 are corresponding descriptions of physical direction (e.g., upward, downward, positive, negative, forward, backward), and their behavioral meanings. Below the diagram are descriptive adjectives for behaviors corresponding to each of 26 directions (or locations). These directions are made up of various combinations of the main directions— U, D, P, N, F, and B—and are represented by the letters on the smaller cubes (e.g., UP, UPB, DNB). Each adjective set describes behaviors associated with their respective locations in the SYMLOG space. Figure 1 graphically represents the inclusive categorical scheme within which persons may be located and classified on the basis of behaviors, values, or imagery (Bales, 1970; Bales & Cohen, 1979). A few hypothetical examples may help elucidate the logic of the space.

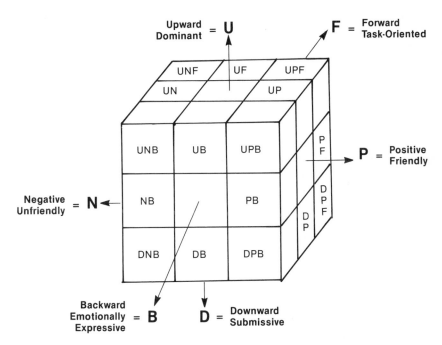

U	.... active, dominant, talks a lot	N	.... unfriendly, negativistic
UP	.. extroverted, outgoing, positive	NB	.. irritable, cynical, won't cooperate
UPF	. a purposeful democratic task leader	B	.... shows feelings and emotions
UF	.. an assertive business-like manager	PB	.. affectionate, likeable, fun to be with
UNF	. authoritarian, controlling, disapproving	DP	.. looks up to others, appreciative, trustful
UN	.. domineering, tough-minded, powerful	DPF	. gentle, willing to accept responsibility
UNB	. provocative, egocentric, shows off	DF	.. obedient, works submissively
UB	.. jokes around, expressive, dramatic	DNF	. self-punishing, works too hard
UPB	. entertaining, sociable, smiling, warm	DN	.. depressed, sad, resentful, rejecting
P	.... friendly, equalitarian	DNB	. alienated, quits, withdraws
PF	... works cooperatively with others	DB	.. afraid to try, doubts own ability
F	.... analytical, task-oriented, problem-solving	DPB	. quietly happy just to be with others
NF	.. legalistic, has to be right	D	.... passive, introverted, says little

Figure 1. The SYMLOG cube diagram with adjective behavior descriptions. (Bales & Cohen [1979], reprinted with permission)

Imagine a newly-hired office worker in initial face-to-face interaction with an autocratic manager. The manager addresses the worker in an aggressive manner with an unsmiling face, riveted eye contact, and expansive posturing and movements. The manager makes no attempt to be sociable or accommodating, but is strictly businesslike, giving orders and reminders of production quotas and office policies. The verbal and nonverbal behaviors exhibited by the manager remain consistent over time and create, from the worker's perspective, an image of the manager as having an authoritarian-type personality. In SYMLOG terms, the manager was perceived as someone who seemed dominant (U), unfriendly (N), and task-oriented (F), and would thus be located in the **UNF** area of the SYMLOG space. Contrast the autocratic manager with a friendly, collaborative, and conscientious coworker. This person is perceived as someone who is neither dominating nor passive, but pleasant to work with, or **PF** in SYMLOG language. A third example may be the resentful and alienated employee who feels disillusioned and unappreciated in the work environment. This employee has become sullen and withdrawn and tends to react to authority through passive-aggressive gestures. He or she may be perceived as occupying **DNB** in the SYMLOG space.

The above hypothetical examples offer concrete instances of how persons may be located in the SYMLOG scheme. A total of 26 types or locations exist in the model. Detailed definitions of each SYMLOG type in terms of personality descriptions, behaviors, values, and content images may be found in *Personality and Interpersonal Behavior* (Bales, 1970) and Appendix A of the SYMLOG text. With respect to small groups, once each group member is located within the SYMLOG space, a total "group picture" or spatial representation of the group structure is created. From this "group space" an analysis of the perceived dynamics of the group can occur. The interpretation of the SYMLOG field diagram is addressed further below.

Before leaving our basic sketch of the SYMLOG three- dimensional space, we mention a few considerations about the nature of the space. First, the reader must be aware that persons located in the space are rated according to their relative locations along the **continuum** of each of the three basic dimensions. Hence, subtle differences may be observed among persons who appear to occupy the same general location in the space. The categorical scheme of SYMLOG is employed for clarity of interpretation, whereas actual measurement is accomplished by treating the dimensions as continuous variables, providing a more precise evaluation. Second, the particular constellation of images of persons in a group is unique to the perceiver (Bales & Cohen, 1979). Thus, a particular group member's individual field or perception of the group may differ substantially from other members' views of the groups or from the aggravated group field. The SYMLOG system accounts for individual differences through its "eye of the beholder" perspective. Third, Ennis (1982) has noted that close proximity in the SYMLOG space reflects the common behavioral styles of two persons, rather than any close relations that may or may not exist between them (p. 201), thus defining a property space rather than a relational space. This assertion has been qualified somewhat by Parke and Houben (1985, p. 133). Similarly, Polley and Bales (1985) emphasize the nonuniform nature of the space. This means that conflicting or complementary relations cannot be directly inferred by simple considerations of distance or proximity between persons in the SYMLOG space; their relative locations to each other must also be considered. Finally, Bales's contention that the SYMLOG space is ubiquitous and generalizable across individuals has received some empirical support (Breiger & Ennis, 1979; Isenberg & Ennis, 1981).

This section seeks to provide the reader with a basic understanding of the SYMLOG space. From this central framework the diagnosis and assessment of group dynamics can be accomplished through the analysis of SYMLOG field diagrams, which are two-dimensional representations of the SYMLOG space. The next section discusses obtaining the data required to construct the field diagrams.

Obtaining the data

The SYMLOG system employs two primary data collection techniques: the interaction scoring and adjective rating methods. The decision to employ either or both methods depends upon one's overall purpose for data collection and on considerations of time and resource expenditures.

The interaction scoring method is the most detailed and, in some respects, the "purest" technique, and the unit of analysis is the single act of the single individual. Interaction scoring is an observational technique in which detailed descriptions of acts, one by one, are made in the course of actual interaction at the time each act occurs. Interaction scoring requires one to write down observations while watching and listening to the interactions of group members. The scoring method requires training observers and, although it has the advantage of richness of detail, it also requires a relatively large amount of time and effort compared to the rating method. It is a somewhat more obtrusive technique than the rating method, and is also restricted to an external-observer focus.

Because it has practical advantages and is most appropriate for applied purposes, the remainder of this section addresses the SYMLOG adjective rating method. Ideally, both methods—scoring and rating—could be used together to gather supplemental information that would be otherwise unobtainable by either method alone. A detailed treatment of the interaction scoring method appears in the SYMLOG text. With either method, the results can be used to locate individuals in the SYMLOG space.

The SYMLOG adjective rating method

Bales and his colleagues developed and refined the adjective rating form as a means to provide a more compact rating method than the reading of the full descriptions of the various locations and levels as found in Appendix A of the SYMLOG text. A simplified rating method is especially essential when group members have no familiarity with SYMLOG at all, which is usually the case in most application settings. The adjective rating form is the product of more than 15 years of refinement. The factor structure and reliability studies underlying its development may be found in the SYMLOG text.

The SYMLOG rating method is used to help obtain a **retrospective** account of the characteristic behaviors of any group of individuals one has seen in interaction with one another. It provides a recapturing from memory of the global perceptions that group members have of one another. It can be completely unobtrusive, as ratings are made outside of the actual group interaction period, and it may be used to obtain observer or participant-observer perspectives. The participant-observer, or "eye-of-the-beholder," perspective considers the subjective views of the actual group members, emphasizing each member's unique "definition of the situation." The rating technique has the advantage of greater representativeness if the group under scrutiny has a long and varied history together, as compared to the interaction scoring of a small and perhaps unrepresentative slice of the group's interaction scoring (Bales & Cohen, 1979).

Figure 2 presents examples of SYMLOG general behavior and value descriptions adjective rating forms. The behavior form has been more thoroughly researched and employed in numerous validation studies; still, the values form is a reliable measure and may be more appropriate for certain purposes. The two forms are parallel or cognate in that a value description is often a more generalized extension of an evaluation originally made on the more specific behavior form. The cognate relationship between behavior and values in the SYMLOG system illustrates two levels in the "multiple level" scheme of SYMLOG. This article cannot elaborate on the numerous levels, but the SYMLOG text provides detailed descriptions of each of them. That the behavior and value forms are parallel does not suggest that the ratings of the two different levels will yield identical results. Obtaining both types of ratings, however, can provide illuminating comparative data. For group self-analysis, Bales (1980) recommends gathering both behavior and value ratings so one may consider, for example, the gap between one's espoused values and actual behavior. Often persons believe their values are misunderstood, and they frequently behave in ways that are incongruent with the values they profess.

A recently developed SYMLOG rating form was created for use in organizational contexts. The Individual and Organizational Values Form was designed to tap a level midway between the behavior and values forms (Bales, 1983). For application use, this form reduces the complication of separate behavior and value ratings. This copyrighted instrument is available in Scantron form from the SYMLOG Consulting Group, Woodland Hills, California. Polley (1987) has completed a large sample validation of this form.

Close inspection of the rating forms in Figure 2 shows that each set of adjective items represents each possible combination of the three factors (U-D, P-N, F-B), as denoted by the "dimensional letters" to the left of each item. The dimensional letters correspond to the locations in the SYMLOG space (see Figure 1). The rating form was constructed in such a way that 6 items measure 1 dimension only, 12 items measure all combinations of dimensions taken 2 at a time, and 8 items measure all combinations of dimensions taken 3 at a time, resulting in 26 items. Therefore, some of the items measure more than

SYMLOG

Your name _____ Group _____

Name of person described _____ Circle the best choice for each item:

General Behavior Descriptions

		(0)	(1)	(2)
U	...active, dominant, talks a lot	not often	....sometimes	... often
UP	..extroverted, outgoing, positive	not often	....sometimes	... often
UPF	.a purposeful democratic task leader	not often	....sometimes	... often
UF	..an assertive business-like manager	not often	....sometimes	... often
UNF	.authoritarian, controlling, disapproving	not often	....sometimes	... often
UN	..domineering, tough-minded, powerful	not often	....sometimes	... often
UNB	.provocative, egocentric, shows off	not often	....sometimes	... often
UB	..jokes around, expressive, dramatic	not often	....sometimes	... often
UPB	.entertaining, sociable, smiling, warm	not often	....sometimes	... often
P	...friendly, equalitarian	not often	....sometimes	... often
PF	..works cooperatively with others	not often	....sometimes	... often
F	...analytical, task-oriented, problem-solving	not often	....sometimes	... often
NF	..legalistic, has to be right	not often	....sometimes	... often
N	...unfriendly, negativistic	not often	....sometimes	... often
NB	..irritable, cynical, won't cooperate	not often	....sometimes	... often
B	...shows feelings and emotions	not often	....sometimes	... often
PB	..affectionate, likeable, fun to be with	not often	....sometimes	... often
DP	..looks up to others, appreciate, trustful	not often	....sometimes	... often
DPF	.gentle, willing to accept responsibility	not often	....sometimes	... often
DF	..obedient, works submissively	not often	....sometimes	... often
DNF	.self-punishing, works too hard	not often	....sometimes	... often
DN	..depressed, sad, resentful, rejecting	not often	....sometimes	... often
DNB	alienated, quits, withdraws	not often	....sometimes	... often
DB	..afraid to try, doubts own ability	not often	....sometimes	... often
DPB	.quietly happy just to be with others	not often	....sometimes	... often
D	...passive, introverted, says little	not often	....sometimes	... often

Value Descriptions

U	...material success and power	not often	....sometimes	... often
UP	..popularity and social success	not often	....sometimes	... often
UPF	.social solidarity and progress	not often	....sometimes	... often
UF	..efficiency, strong effective management	not often	....sometimes	... often
UNF	.a powerful authority, law and order	not often	....sometimes	... often
UN	..tough-minded assertiveness	not often	....sometimes	... often
UNB	.rugged individualism, self-gratification	not often	....sometimes	... often
UB	..having a good time, self-expression	not often	....sometimes	... often
UPB	.making others feel happy	not often	....sometimes	... often
P	...equalitarianism, democratic participation	not often	....sometimes	... often
PF	..altruism, idealism, cooperation	not often	....sometimes	... often
F	...established social beliefs and values	not often	....sometimes	... often
NF	..value-determined restraint of desires	not often	....sometimes	... often
N	...individual dissent, self-sufficiency	not often	....sometimes	... often
NB	..social nonconformity	not often	....sometimes	... often
B	...unconventional beliefs and values	not often	....sometimes	... often
PB	..friendship, liberalism, sharing	not often	....sometimes	... often
DP	..trust in the goodness of others	not often	....sometimes	... often
DPF	.love, faithfulness, loyalty	not often	....sometimes	... often
DF	..hard work, self-knowledge, subjectivity	not often	....sometimes	... often
DNF	.suffering	not often	....sometimes	... often
DN	..rejection of popularity	not often	....sometimes	... often
DNB	admission of failure, withdrawal	not often	....sometimes	... often
DB	..noncooperation with authority	not often	....sometimes	... often
DPB	.quiet contentment, taking it easy	not often	....sometimes	... often
D	...giving up all selfish desires	not often	....sometimes	... often

Figure 2. SYMLOG General Behavior and Value Descriptions Adjective Rating Forms (Reproduced from Bales [1980] with permission from The Free Press).

one dimension simultaneously, which accounts for the seemingly inconsistent sets of adjectives within some of the items.

Administration of the rating forms

The SYMLOG rating method is very flexible, hence considerations of data collection must be tailored to meet your own needs and those of your target group. Although the best results come from obtaining ratings from all members in the group being assessed, as well as ratings from an external observer (yourself as a consultant, for example)—in many instances of application this is not feasible. When assessing a work group for team building, for example, one may find it too obtrusive, time consuming, or threatening to the group members to obtain their individual ratings. For most applications, the group will have no knowledge of the system, hence requiring time for orientation and/or education relevant to the system. The group may be experiencing intragroup conflicts of such severity that one might consider the in-depth processing afforded by SYMLOG assessment to be unduly stressful as an early intervention.

Fortunately, the SYMLOG system offers alternative means of collecting useful assessment data. One may observe the group for a given time period and make the ratings from the perspective of an external consultant. Such a method would be inobtrusive and yet provide meaningful data for evaluation that may or may not be shared with the group. Ratings from a cooperative group leader could be quite useful, as that leader would typically have greater experience with the group and hence provide a more representative evaluation. In some instances, perhaps some, but not all, of the group members will provide ratings.

Although the single set of ratings from a consultant with only short-term experience with the group is least preferred, if the consultant can gain some temporal experience with the group through several sessions, the use of "imagined other" ratings may be helpful (Bales & Cohen, 1979). With this alternative, the consultant makes ratings from the perspective of each group member as the consultant "imagines" each group member would make her or his ratings. This technique has the advantage of providing individual field diagrams and the group average diagram, which gives useful comparative data. In all of the instances described above, sufficient data can be obtained for group evaluation purposes.

For a SYMLOG group self-study, Bales (1980) has suggested that each member provide the following types of ratings:

a) behavior ratings of each member of the group, including a self-rating;

b) behavior ratings of how you wish you were able to act;

c) behavior ratings of acts you consciously try to **avoid**;

d) value ratings of the kinds of values you think you to hold;

e) value ratings of the kinds of values you think you actually (**actual**) show in your behavior; and

f) value ratings of the kinds of values you consciously try to **reject**.

Of course, these ratings can only be obtained with cooperation from all group members. They are generally suggested types of ratings and are not all required for an adequate group dynamics assessment. You may wish to employ only behavior ratings in your assessment, or you may pick and choose the types of ratings that suit your purposes. An additional type of rating that often yields interesting data is that of how you might **expect** others to rate you. Analyzing the relative discrepancies between how you see yourself, how you think others see you, and how others actually see you can be illuminating food for thought. Recently, Fassheber and Terjung (1985) found the "expect" image to have higher predictive power than either "self," "actual," or other images in determining behavioral characteristics outside of the group situation. In any event, it is recommended that ratings of self, other members, and "wish" be obtained at a minimum for group analysis when such data is available.

One of the most important considerations when obtaining SYMLOG rating data is the instructional set, or the specific directions given for completing the ratings. Sloppily worded instructions could result in data that is inconsistent across raters and unrepresentative of the perspectives desired. For example, are the ratings to be confined to interaction in the group only, or are they to include interactions outside of the group? Are the ratings to consider behavior in general or to be specific in reference to certain individual(s)? Considerations of the situational context of the instructions are essential to obtaining consistent and representative ratings.

In addition to the situational context, the time frame must also be specified. For example, are the ratings to be made in reference to a single group session, more than several weeks of sessions, or several months? Bales and Cohen (1979) suggest that ratings be made at several time periods in the group's life to trace changes over time. Following the first ratings, the second ratings would refer to the time period between the first and second ratings, the third ratings to the time period between the second and third ratings, and so on. We emphasize that one must clearly specify the time period for the ratings in the instructions to the group members.

Our final instructional consideration deals with the multiple descriptive adjectives within each item. Often, persons will have difficulty rating a particular item because they do not find all of the adjectives within an item to apply for them. We have found it useful in the instructions to our raters to point this out, stating clearly that most of the items have two or more descriptions within each item, and that even if only one description seems to apply for a person, one should use it as a guide in making one's ratings.

As a final note for this section, we ask the reader to be aware that the ratings can be obtained either on the rating forms directly (by circling the desired choice) or by numbering the choices on the Directional Profile Form. The Directional Profile Form is made up of columns for each rating that correspond to the 26 rating form items. It is an intermediary form used to summarize the ratings for manual calculation in constructing the field diagrams. The Directional Profile Form and accompanying instructions may be found in the SYMLOG text and case study kit. We will not describe in detail the summarization procedure for computing the rating data, as this involves simple arithmetic calculations and is fully described elsewhere.

We briefly describe in this section the SYMLOG adjective rating method. Once the desired rating data have been obtained, the results can then be used to construct the SYMLOG field diagrams, the modus operandi for group dynamics assessment.

The SYMLOG field diagram

The concept of a field. Before delving directly into the structure of the SYMLOG field diagram, we briefly discuss the underlying concept. As noted above, overt behavior and expressed values represent only two conceptual levels of analysis within the totality of multiple-level processes that occur when two or more persons interact. In any given interpersonal transaction, an individual acts within the multilevel context of one's thoughts, feelings, attitudes, values, beliefs, and fantasied desires. The emitted social act consists of nonverbal, overt, and verbal behaviors that are perceived, processed, and reacted to by another individual in a similarly multilevel way. The continuous interaction of internal processes and external acts as communicated among individuals creates a rapid and dynamic feedback system. This interactive system of interpersonal and psychological processes has been defined as a social-psychological "field" (Bales, 1985).

Bales identified two types of fields. The "individual field" includes the set of images in the mind of an individual group member. One may view this as the social interaction field as seen by an individual member, but in reality it is only a part of the more inclusive social interaction field. The "social interaction field" was hypothesized to consist of all the individual fields in a group **and** all the communicated acts observed by members interacting with one another. The SYMLOG method provides spatial representation of both types of fields through an individual field diagram and a group average field diagram (Bales & Cohen, 1979).

The field diagram. The SYMLOG field diagram (Bales & Cohen, 1979) serves as "a graphic summary of information about the members of the group and their locations, as seen from the point of view of some individual rater, or, alternatively, some number of raters added together and averaged" (p. 31). Figure 3 is an example of a field diagram with four images, represented by circles of varying sizes, plotted onto the diagram. Upon inspection one sees that the field is a spatial analog of the SYMLOG cube model.

To make the spatial transition (from the three-dimensional model to the two-dimensional diagram), the reader is encouraged to imagine the field diagram (Figure 3) as if one were viewing the SYMLOG cube (see Figure 1) **from the top of the model downward**. From this perspective, one would be viewing the model directly along the U-D dimension, with the U pole closest and the D pole farthest

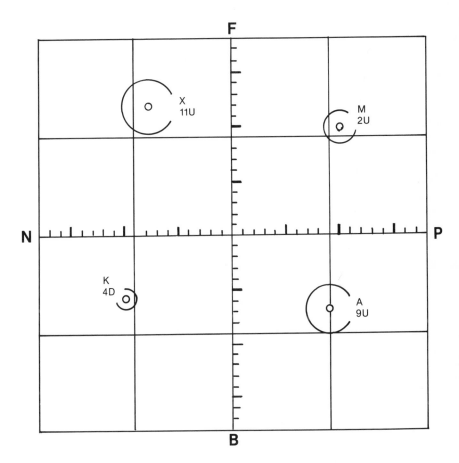

Figure 3. SYMLOG Field Diagram with four images inscribed (Adapted from Bales [1980] with permission from The Free Press).

away from view. The two remaining orthogonal dimensions (P-N and F-B) make up the plane of the field diagram, with the dimensional letters representing their corresponding bipolar directions on the diagram, which is how they would appear from the top-down perspective.

Notice that the field diagram is gradated in 18 equal units from the central point of the diagram along each of four vectors corresponding to the bipolar directions (P-N and F-B). These are the measurement units used to locate individuals based upon their summarized ratings with respect to these dimensions. The images obtained from ratings are represented by circles of varying sizes. The sizes of the circles correspond to their position relative to the U-D dimension and are also gradated in 18 proportional units of smaller or larger circle sizes to remain consistent with the P-N and F-B measurement units.

The *SYMLOG Case Study Kit* (Bales, 1980) contains a template entitled "Scale of U-D Circle," which consists of a scale of circles of ascending size from 18D (smallest) to 00 (neutral) to 18U (largest). Circles that are smaller than the 00 circle represent submissive (D) behavior, with large D scores represented by smaller circles. Circles larger than 00 represent dominant (U) behavior, with larger U scores represented by correspondingly larger circles. The reader should note that although the use of size gradients for U-D placement is structurally different from that of the linear gradients of the P-N and F-B dimensions, it is also spatially consistent with the top-down perspective. Viewed from the top of the cube, the closer an image is to the viewer, the larger it would appear. Hence, an image of 1OU would appear as a larger circle than an image of 5D, as the 1OU circle is closest to the top (or U direction) of the cube.

Each completed and summarized SYMLOG rating form that you obtain will result in three dimensional scores (U-D, P-N, F-B), which are then used to plot the resultant image on the field diagram. To illustrate, four images have been plotted in Figure 3 as obtained from four SYMLOG adjective ratings. The resultant dimensional scores are shown in Table 1.

Table 1
Dimensional Scores for Figure 3 Images

	Dimensional score		
Member	*U-D*	*P-N*	*F-B*
A	9U	9P	7B
X	11U	8N	12F
M	2U	10P	10F
K	4D	10N	6B

For example, A's image would be plotted by locating the corresponding points along the P-N (9P) and F-B (7B) scales—with points of increasing value emanating from the neutral center (00) of the diagram—and plotting the intersecting location with a small "core circle" (Bales, 1980). Hence A's image is located in the PB quadrant of the diagram. The image is then completed by drawing the appropriate size circle around the core circle (using the U-D template) and then labeling the circle with identifying letters (A) and the number indicating the location of the point along the U-D dimension (9U). The same procedure was used to plot the images for X, M, and K in the Figure 3 field diagram. The four images are placed in various locations in the field and represent hypothetically different behavioral styles and personality characteristics. Readers should note that an "image" in the SYMLOG field diagram may denote the observed behavior of actual persons rated or other types of ratings, such as "wish" or "avoid." In addition to behavior ratings, images from value ratings may also be plotted onto the field diagram using the same procedure described above.

Each field diagram should include the pertinent identifying information as requested at the top of Figure 3. Identification of perceptual context, time frame, and measurement method are important considerations when analyzing a field diagram. In addition, space in the top portion of Figure 3 is labeled "expansion multiplier." Because of a mathematical regression that occurs when averaging across individuals, the group average diagram will often appear constricted, and will need to be expanded before it can easily be analyzed or compared to the individual field diagrams (Bales & Cohen, 1979). The expansion multiplier is a formula used to expand the diagram and bring the most "far out" image (the image furthest from the neutral center of the diagram) to the edge of the diagram. The description and formula for the multiplier may be found in Appendix K of the SYMLOG text.

Interpreting the field diagram

Based on the information presented thus far, we can make some summary observations about the four images in Figure 3. For example, member X was seen as the most dominant (11U) and task-oriented (12F) individual in the diagram and was also viewed as somewhat negative (8N). X portrays an image in the UNF direction of the SYMLOG space, and may be described as someone who values an active reinforcement of authority, rules, and regulations and who tries to control what the group should consider right or wrong. X presents an image of an authoritarian personality who tends to give commands and show disapproval from a rigid, dogmatic, and self-righteous position of moral superiority. In contrast, member A was viewed as relatively dominant (9U), friendly (9P), and emotionally expressive (7B), or in the UPB direction of the SYMLOG space. A may be described as valuing sociability and emotional support. A presents an image of someone with a nurturing personality type who tends to protect the less able members and provide reassurance and acceptance without regard to task performance. The descriptions of members X and A were based on their SYMLOG directional definitions as found in Appendix A of the SYMLOG text, using the cutoff points suggested by Bales and Cohen (1979, p. 425). Similarly, member K (DNB) may be described as behaving in a withdrawn, alienated, and dejected manner, whereas member M (PF) was viewed as cooperative, responsible, optimistic, and idealistic.

Although the brief descriptions above provide interesting data about the characteristics of each person on an individual level, they say little or nothing about the interpersonal dynamics that may exist among them. Understanding personality differences is a necessary but not sufficient requirement for adequate analysis at the group level. Group dynamics assessment must take into account the interactions of the particular constellation of personalities in the group as well as the particular group situation and setting, which include its purpose, history, and cultural context. The field diagram provides the framework for analyzing group level phenomena such as coalition formation, polarization, subgroup structure, and group roles and norms. An important model of subgroup formation has been devised by Bales and Cohen (1979).

The polarization-unification overlay

One of the most important aspects of intragroup functioning addresses the relative degree of cohesion or conflict that exists among group members. The polarization-unification overlay provides a convenient means to analyze and describe the pattern of images represented in a field (Bales & Cohen, 1979). The polarization-purification template is presented in Figure 4. The overlay is a transparency of the Figure 4 inscription, which can be superimposed upon the field diagram and manually adjusted for analysis. The overlay consists of two adjacent circles, each 18 field diagram units in diameter. The solid line running through the center points of the circles is the "line of polarization." At each pole of the line of polarization are the letter inscriptions R and O. The reference direction (R) and opposite direction (O) are used for placing the overlay for individual field diagrams with the reference circle, capturing image that are consistent with the individual's desired behaviors and espoused value. The image found in the opposite circle would constitute an opposing subgroup. The long dashed line running between the circles is referred to as the line of balance. The letters at each end of the line of balance, M or S, stand for "mediator direction" and "scapegoat direction," respectively. The area between the short dashed lines within each circle is referred to as the "swing area."

Polley (1985a) recently described the SYMLOG polarization- unification overlay as a model of subgroup formation that is based on a few simple assumptions. It was first assumed that the area of one field diagram quadrant (18 units square) represents the approximate limits of diversity allowable for a cohesive subgroup. If the overlay can be adjusted so that all the group members fit within one circle (18 units in diameter), the group is assumed to be unified. If they cannot all be captured by one circle, then the overlay is adjusted in an attempt to fit all members into two circles. If this can be done, the group would be described as polarized. If a member is located on or near the line of balance to the negative (N) side, he or she would be identified as a potential scapegoat. A member on or near the line of balance to the positive (P) side is referred to as a potential mediator. The specific guidelines for overlay placement can be found in the SYMLOG text and case study kit. For our purposes, the presented general description will suffice. We now illustrate a basic application of this interpretive model on the field diagram of a hypothetical work group.

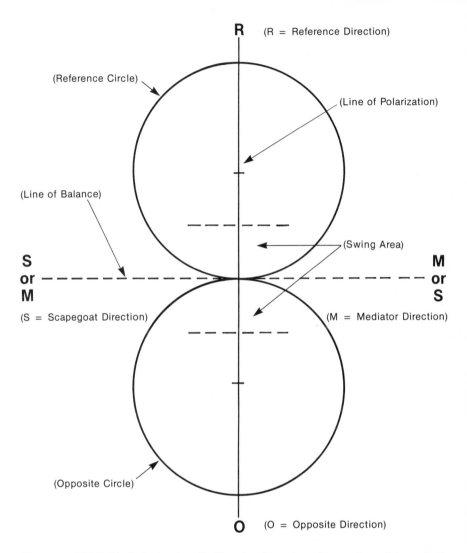

Figure 4. SYMLOG Polarization-Unification Template (Reproduced from Bales [1980] with permission from The Free Press).

Analyzing a field

In the interest of space, clarity, and simplicity, we have limited our discussion to the individual field diagram of a single hypothetical group member. Figure 5 is an individual field diagram as constructed from the ratings of member A.

From the perspective of member A, the group appears to be fragmented and polarized between conflicting subgroups across the NF and PB directions in the space. A identifies himself or herself as a subgroup leader in coalition with member B, who appears to share similar values with A, but is less active in the group, as suggested by B's neutral U-D rating. B tends to favor and identify with the warmth and supportiveness of A, but is not active enough in the group to assume a leadership role. As such, B is in a poor position for reducing conflict or polarity in the group.

In the opposite direction of the PB subgroup composed of the coalition of members A and B is the NF subgroup, composed of members X and Y. A views X as a dominant and authoritarian figure (UNF) in coalition with member Y. Although Y is less active in the group than X, their expressed values appear to be shared. Y may be seen as an agent of authoritarian X.

Perhaps the most troubled individual in the group is member P. P is located in the swing area of the group, and appears not to be firmly committed to either subgroup and to be caught in the middle of the value conflict between the NF and PB subgroups. P's submission U-D rating (8D) suggests that P may be experiencing feelings of prolonged frustration in the group, and has become inhibited and withdrawn in response. P is a likely candidate to leave the group, given the appropriate circumstances.

Note that A's "wish" image is captured within the PB subgroup circle. A apparently wishes to behave in an outgoing, socially extroverted, and somewhat expansive manner (UP), but perhaps feels the need to protect the group in opposition to a perceived threat from authoritarian member X. A's "avoid" image is located in the opposite subgroup circle along with X and Y. A consciously tries to avoid behaviors that are unfriendly, disagreeing, and guarded. The "ought" image is located on the periphery of A's subgroup in the PF direction from A's self-image. The disparity between A's self-image, in terms of exhibited behaviors (UPB) and the values A feels he or she ought to hold (UPF), is an example of a discrepancy between behavior and values. Although A would apparently like to focus more on task concerns, the behavioral emphasis is on protecting the emotional cohesion of the group (UPB), perhaps because of A's perception of autocratic X as a clear and present danger to the group's survival.

The prevailing group norms appear to be split between values of autocratic, task-oriented leadership (NF subgroup) and the preservation of socioemotional stability (PB subgroup). This group appears fragmented and full of value conflicts, and would constitute a poorly functioning work group. How can the conflicts and polarization of this group be reduced?

As one means to effectively reduce conflict and polarization in a group, Bales (1983) suggested that it is best to try to activate values in the mediator direction. As previously mentioned, the mediator position is located on the positive side of the line of balance (the dashed line at right angles to the line of polarization). In Figure 5, member M appears to occupy the mediator position.

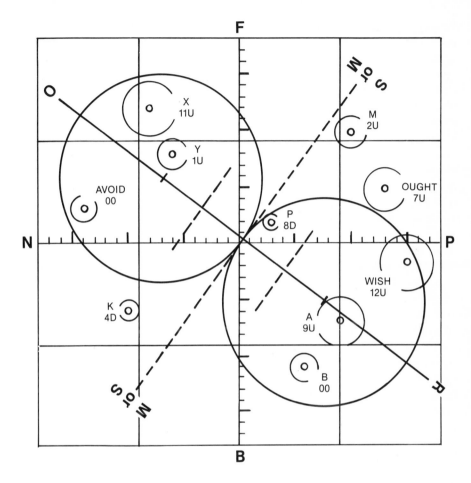

Figure 5. A's Field Diagram with overlay placement.

M is not associated with either subgroup, but does share the task-oriented values of X and the friendly values of A. Members in the mediator position can help neutralize or reduce polarization if highly activated (Bales & Cohen, 1979). For example, M may help reduce subgroup conflict by encouraging the conflicting members to move toward collaboration and cooperative ventures. In the current situation, M would have to increase her or his level of activity and participation so as to stimulate constructive movement in the group.

On the opposite or negative side of the line of balance is the scapegoat position. Member K appears to be in danger of being made a potential scapegoat for the group. The scapegoat can help reduce polarization temporarily by becoming a common object of rejection and displaced hostility for the conflicting subgroups. This is a less-than-ideal way to neutralize polarization, as it provides an unstable and at best temporary solution (Bales, 1980). K is in potential danger of being simultaneously rejected by members of both subgroups, which may serve to increase K's alienation from the group and activate her or his eventual departure.

As a closing observation to our example of field diagram analysis, the reader should be aware that the hypothetical polarization in Figure 5 is an example of poorly functioning work group (Bales, 1983). Polley (1979) has described the NF-PB polarization as one of maximum solidarity with the degree of polarization decreasing with counterclockwise rotation in the space. Thus, the picture of an "ideal" work group may look something like the field diagram in Figure 6. This hypothetical group appears relatively unified in expressed values and behavior, with the average member falling in the PF quadrant. Notice that the variation in dominance between members, although not equal, is also not severely discrepant. Also note that the group, although relatively unified, shows a healthy variation within the subgroup. An overly cohesive subgroup would probably not have the necessary flexibility to deal with unexpected events. Kelly and Duran (1985) recently presented evidence in support of this "ideal" work group configuration.

Even a most skeletal SYMLOG field diagram analysis, as we have presented, yields an impressive amount of information about the dynamics of the group. Our example analysis provides descriptive data on group members, including personality characteristics, behavior styles, and expressed values. At the group level, the analysis illustrated subgroup structure, member roles (including leader, mediator, and scapegoat), coalition formation, and group norms. The analysis also identified members who are in conflict or alliance and members who may be experiencing stress and/or feelings of alienation from the group.

Current advances in SYMLOG

Research. SYMLOG is far from being a static system. A substantial number of developments in theory and research have occurred since the publication of the SYMLOG text. In recognition of his contributions to the field, Bales received the 1983 Cooley-Mead Award from the American Sociological Association. His recipient address for this award discussed the integration of social psychology (Bales, 1984). A subsequent theoretical article (Bales, 1985), based upon an invited address to the American Psychological Association in 1984, elaborated upon the integration theme and proposed the three-dimensional model as the ubiquitous framework for a new field theory and a potential basis for the integration of social psychology. Polley & Bales (1985) built upon the new field theory and described the nonuniform nature of the SYMLOG space and its network of connections to numerous concepts and theories in social psychology.

A significant development in SYMLOG theory and method is the refinement by Polley (1985a) of a general theory of polarization and unification

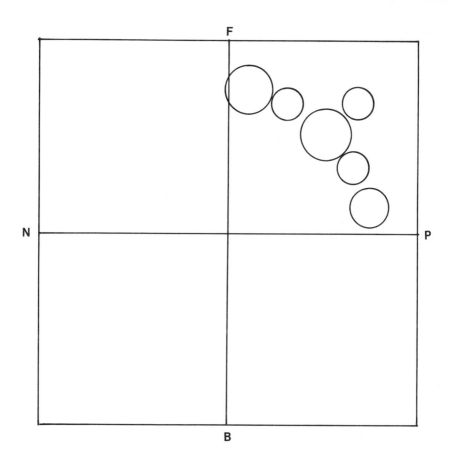

Figure 6. Field Diagram of a hypothetical "ideal" work group (Adapted from Polley [in press] with permission from the author).

and a computer-based model for identifying subgroup structure and determining the severity of polarizations. This objective and mathematically derived model improved upon the subjective and mechanical method of the polarization-unification overlay (Bales & Cohen, 1979). Subsequent testing of the general model has been undertaken on management groups (Polley, in press) and work teams (Polley, 1985b).

A methodological study by Isenberg and Ennis (1981) compared the imposed and derived structures of a small group through SYMLOG and multidimensional scaling techniques. The substantial overlap found between the two methods supported the psychological salience of the SYMLOG model. The SYMLOG method and "blockmodeling" techniques were found to mutually reinforce one another (Breiger & Ennis, 1979; Ennis, 1982), suggesting a possible juncture between personality and social role.

Additional developments in SYMLOG research include leadership theory and assessment (Bales & Isenberg, 1982; Jesuino, 1985), the adoption of the SYMLOG adjective rating form for use with children (Parke, 1985), and the illustration of a proactive model of consultant intervention based on the analysis of shared myth and fantasy (Polley, 1984). Based on negotiation records, Hare (1985b) assessed creative and conforming behaviors in third-party negotiations between Egypt and Israel using the SYMLOG categories. Analyzing a sample of grade school and junior high school classroom groups, Parke and Houben (1985) found three main group types—unified, polarized, and fragmented—and four intermediate group types. A paper by Hare (1985a) addressed the general significance of SYMLOG to the study of small group dynamics.

The establishment of an international network of small group researchers has recently culminated in the creation of the *International Journal of Small Group Research* (whose editors are R. B. Polley and J. Schneider), which publishes articles using SYMLOG and other theories and methods for the systematic study of small groups. The topics covered in a recent international conference on SYMLOG and group interaction have been summarized by Fisch (1985). Finally, an edition of SYMLOG research articles and papers with an applied emphasis will soon be available in book form (Polley, Hare, & Stone, in press).

Application. Advances in research on SYMLOG have been accompanied by developments in the arena of applications. Robert J. Koenigs and Margaret Cowen head the SYMLOG Consulting Group based in Woodland Hills, California. They have developed a consulting service for practitioners who work with small groups in a wide variety of settings, particularly in the areas of organization development, assessment, and team building. The consulting service includes computerized analysis and interpretation tailored to meet particular needs. In this way they have addressed the increasing demand for technological development in the analysis of group behavior. The success of the SYMLOG Consulting Group has resulted in the establishment of international franchises in Europe.

Finally, SYMLOG workshops have been held throughout this country and abroad. Most recently, NTL Institute and the SYMLOG Consulting Group cosponsored the first SYMLOG certification workshop in Bethel, Maine, an additional indication of its appreciation and growth in the applied arena.

NOTES

1. The authors wish to express their appreciation to Richard B. Polley, Robert F. Bales, and The Free Press for their cooperation with this article.

REFERENCES

Bales, R. F. (1950). *Interaction process analysis.* Cambridge, MA: Addison-Wesley.

Bales, R. F. (1970). *Personality and interpersonal behavior.* New York: Holt, Rinehard & Winston.

Bales, R. F. (1980). *SYMLOG case study kit.* New York: The Free Press.

Bales, R. F. (1983). *Hints for building teamwork.* Weston, MA: SYMLOG Consultants.

Bales, R. F. (1984). The integration of social psychology. *Social Psychology Quarterly, 47*(1), 95-101.

Bales, R. F. (1985). The new field theory in social psychology. *International Journal of Small Group Research, 1*(1), 1-18.

Bales, R. F., & Cohen, S. P. (1979). *SYMLOG: A system for the multiple level observation of groups.* New York: The Free Press.

Bales, R. F., & Isenberg, D. J. (1982). SYMLOG and leadership theory. In J. G. Hunt, U. Sekaran, & C. A. Schriesheim (Eds.), *Leadership: Beyond establishment views.* Carbondale, IL: Southern Illinois University Press.

Boutilier, R. G., Roed, J. D., & Svendsen, A. C. (1980). Crises in the two social psychologies: A critical comparison. *Social Psychology Quarterly, 43*(1), 5-17.

Breiger, R. L. & Ennis, J. G. (1979). Personae and social roles: The network structure of personality types in small groups. *Social Psychology Quarterly, 42*(3), 262-270.

Cartwright, D., & Zander, A. (1968). *Group dynamics: Research and theory* (3rd ed.). New York: Harper & Row.

Ennis, J. G. (1982). Blockmodels and spatial representations of group structure: Some comparisons. In H. C. Hudson (Ed.), *Classifying social data.* San Francisco: Jossey-Bass.

Fassheber, P., & Terjung, B. (1985). SYMLOG rating data and their relationship to performance and behavior beyond the group situation. *International Journal of Small Group Research, 1*(2), 97-108.

Fisch, R. (1985). Report on the second European workshop "SYMLOG and Interaction in Groups," July 16-20, 1984, at the University of Konstanz (West Germany). *International Journal of Small Group Research, 1*(2), 173-175.

Forsyth, D. R. (1983). *An introduction to group dynamics.* Monterey, CA: Brooks/Cole

Hare, A. P. (1976). *Handbook of small group research (2nd ed.).* New York: The Free Press.

Hare, A. P. (1985a). The significance of SYMLOG in the study of group dynamics. *International Journal of Small Group Research, 1*(1), 38-50.

Hare, A. P. (1985b). Creativity and conformity during Egypt-Israel negotiations. *International Journal of Small Group Research, 1*(2), 122-130.

Homans, G. C. (1950). *The human group.* New York: Harcourt, Brace, & World.

House, J. S. (1977). The three faces of social psychology. *Sociometry, 40*(2), 161-177.

Isenberg, D. J., & Ennis, J. G. (1981). Perceiving group members: A comparison of derived and imposed dimensions. *Journal of Personality and Social Psychology*, 41(2), 293-305.

Jesuino, J. C. (1985). The assessment of leaders by SYMLOG. *International Journal of Small Group Research, 1*(1), 87-88.

Kelly, L., & Duran, R. L. (1985). Interaction and performance in small groups: A descriptive report. *International Journal of Small Group Research, 1*(2), 182-192.

Lewin, K. (1951). *Field theory in social science.* New York: Harper.

McMahon, A.M. (1984). The two social psychologies: Postcrises directions. *Annual Review of Sociology, 10,* 121-140.

Mead, G. H. (1934). *Mind, self, and society.* Chicago: University of Chicago Press.

Parke, B. K. (1985). A field adaptation of the SYMLOG adjective rating form suitable for children. *International Journal of Small Group Research, 1*(1), 89-95.

Parke, B. K., & Houben, H. C. (1985). An objective analysis of group types. *International Journal of Small Group Research, 1*(2), 131-149.

Polley, R. B. (1979). *Both sides of the mirror: Subjectivity in small groups*. Unpublished doctoral dissertation, Harvard University.

Polley, R. B. (1984). The consultant as shaper of legend. *Proceedings of the Academy of Management*, 157-161.

Polley, R. B. (1985a). A general theory of polarization and unification. *International Journal of Small Group Research*, *1*(2), 150-161.

Polley, R. B. (1985b). *The diagnosis of intact work groups*. Paper presented at the Academy of Management (Div. 7), 44th Annual National Meeting.

Polley, R. B. (1987). The dimensions of social interaction: A method for improving ratings scales. *Social Psychology Quarterly*, *50*(1), 72-82.

Polley, R. B. (In press). Exploring polarization in organizational groups. *Group & Organizational Studies*.

Polley, R. B., & Bales, R. F. (1985). *The topology of social psychological space*. Unpublished manuscript.

Polley, R. B., Hare, A. P., & Stone, P. J. (in press). *The SYMLOG practitioner: Applications for small group research*. New York: Praeger.

Shaw, M. E. (1981). *Group dynamics: The psychology of small group behavior* (3rd ed.). New York: McGraw-Hill.

Straight Talk:
A Norm-Changing Intervention

Kaleel Jamison

Over the past few years, it has become increasingly clear to us that one of the most helpful interventions we can make in an organization is to change its norms of communication to **straight talk**. We introduce the concept of straight talk as a normative foundation during the contracting phase and we describe our rationales, assumptions, and values.

Straight talk as we use it is directed at **spoken** communication. Written communications are a topic by themselves.

Straight talk is the practice of speaking clearly, directly and honestly. This is done without rudeness or humiliation. The foundations include the following:

- respecting others enough to be honest with them;
- passing information in a way that produces an effective organizational environment for efficiency, the development of individuals, and to utilize differences.

It also presumes that conflicting views, values, cultures, and styles are best addressed openly and that those differences— properly resolved—will enhance rather than detract from the organization.

Early in the process of team building, management development, and other such training events we present the concept and guidelines of straight talk. We ask participants to agree to experiment with straight talk to enhance the group's work and the individual's interactions. In long-term interventions, we can achieve additional modification of organizational norms and culture through multiple interventions. However we structure the interventions, straight talk is the underlying norm that we begin with, and we weave it into all communications as other interventions progress. The concept's impact is dramatic and the results are powerful.

©1982 Kaleel Jamison. All rights reserved.

The theory

What, after all, remains to be said about communication? "Lack of communication" has come to be a cliché, a bore. What new ideas can be advanced? What new techniques have not been looked at? Yet "poor communication" continues to be the reason most often given for why events, situations, tasks, political organizations, management strategies, relationship, governments—you name it—so often go awry. Because of bad communications—never mind the cliché—we continue to fail to reach our desired goals. There is little doubt: In spite of research, techniques, theories, papers, and hand-wringing, individuals and organizations continue to communicate in ways that leave much to be desired.

Misunderstood or misleading communication is the problem, and restructuring people's language is a major part of the solution. Language is a tool of power. Politicians have always known that. Anybody who doubts it has only to have described the process of biting into a lemon to know that the words can cause the salivary glands to flow. Language is a causative agent.

In organizations of all kinds, we depend on human interactions to operate—on directions given, instructions received, discussions of problems to reach solutions, compromises when circumstances are less than ideal. Efficient communication is essential to efficient operation—to the coordination and performance of the group. Language is the essential tool.

In practice, because human beings are complicated, and because they often lose sight of what they are trying to do, and because they fall habitually into the traditional norms of their groups, clear communications get clouded—by all sorts of things.

Few people **or** organizations practice straight talk—clean, clear, straight, crisp communication. Yet straight talk is the foundation for real systems change. Not the result—the precondition. Straight talk has the added advantage of enabling individuals within an organization to grow. That individual growth makes the organization richer, because it fosters the kind of healthy conflict that produces innovative solutions. Straight talk is the best basis for effectiveness. Straight talk challenges the norms of the organization and makes change a reality.

It must be clear at the outset that straight talk is not a license for rudeness, a brutal response, or boorishness. It should not be used to embarrass or humiliate. It does not make a case for public rebuke of someone who reports to you or the verbal "assassination." It is not a "hit-and-run" process.

When the goal is organizational effectiveness and straight talk is the mechanism, the process is essentially reciprocal and feeds on itself. Figure 1 shows how the mechanism operates.

Organizational Efficiency

When people in an organization learn to talk straight, they **enhance the organization's efficiency**. Straight information is communicated clearly, both vertically and horizontally in the organization, without second guessing, without hidden agenda. The result of this straight, uncluttered information flow is that work is accomplished in a timely fashion. With crisp communication, and without political innuendoes, game playing becomes a thing of the past. Information is given in clear, crisp terms. The information is shared sufficiently to be effective. Real messages are communicated.

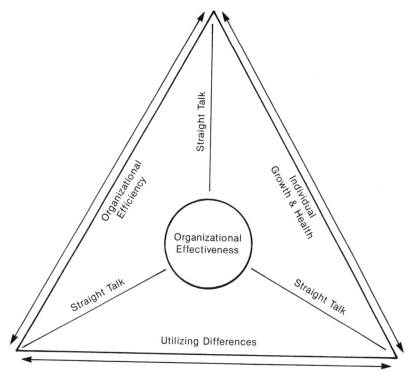

Figure 1. Straight talk process model

The crispness and candor lead to **individual health and growth**. People feel free to verbalize in order to reduce stress, to offer and to accept clear and critical feedback about performance, to have their ideas and contributions considered and valued and used. Considerable research has been done on the negative impact of health to holding in, not saying it all, not saying what is central. Stress can build when people have to deal with ambiguity and tension because of a lack of clear communication, particularly on issues that involve conflict. Personal development is enhanced when people at all levels in organizations are able to give and receive straight feedback—both positive and critical. Straight talk—clear, candid, straightforward communication—is the foundation for worthwhile feedback.

The result of the more direct language interchange is a **richer system**—one that permits conflict because contained within are the language skills needed to resolve conflict productively and to use what it has produced. Through straight talk disparate individuals are invited to contribute. Different viewpoints, different perceptions, different cultures, different genders, different colors, different learning styles, different temperaments—all are encouraged to surface. The outcome broadens the collective experience of the organization. By hearing and using different points of view from different cultures and backgrounds and from different levels and complexes of skill, an organization develops into a **productive multicultural system**—rather than an organization that contains many cultures whose suspicions and prejudices of each other create unresolved conflict and constant friction. Skill is required to foster, value—even respect—differences in others. Divergent cultures can only form a productive multicultural environment when straight talk is a day-to-day norm that is valued in the organization.

The whole cyclic process is stimulated to continue; if no one has a hidden agenda or a stake in masking the real message, the communications stay straight and effective. Political maneuvering, with all the energy it dissipates, becomes pointless. If you can get done what you hope to get done with straight talk and healthy conflict resolution, no political maneuvering is necessary.

Straight talk runs counter to most organizational norms, which are traditionally built on the communication systems of white men. White men have long been dominant members of organizations and they have been quintessential game players from their earliest societal conditioning. White men's communication norms, which have become traditional in organizations, may be subtle, not clear, not straight—based instead on "keeping cool," "admitting nothing about a weakness," "never revealing your hand," "keeping your opponent (note the adversarial concept) off balance," and couched in the "board room whisper."

Connecting Language

Straight talk, on the other hand, is **not** neutral or hidden in its messages. Straight talk is direct, plain, honest, pulls no punches, is crisp and causes a communicating **connection**. It takes full account of the "co" in communication, a syllable that carries with it the idea of interchange between two parties of equal status.

For instance, the comment "that's interesting" is noncommittal. It says nothing. **"It's interesting"** may be saying, **"It's interesting; I don't agree with it."** Or, **"It is of interest to me."** Or **"It's interesting; but it won't work."** Or, **"It's interesting; I wonder if we'll come up with something worthwhile if we explore that."** Or some other variation of an "effective/ineffective" evaluation.

The person who has offered the idea is likely to go away thinking that the response has been any one of these, or indeed any one of innumerable other responses.

Nonconnecting words leave the impression that the speaker has either not taken the trouble to evaluate the idea or that the speaker is trying to be tactful about a stupid idea. Words like **interesting, fascinating, remarkable, intriguing, surprising,** and **curious** sound as though they are a response, but they are not.

All these situations may also convey subtle message of lack of respect and consideration for the idea, or a wish to shield somebody who is perceived as weaker or not as competent as the commentator. Because "that's interesting" does not connect the commentator with the idea or with the person who has offered it, it fails to qualify as a communication. It is at best inefficient, at worst patronizing.

Connecting language is **evaluative: "I like," "I dislike"**; "That's **effective,**" "That's **ineffective**"; "That's a good idea," "I do not agree, but let's generate some other alternatives."

But straight talk is **respectful** of the partner in the process. Straight talk is not rudeness or sarcasm. Some people think that straight talk implies bluntness—the unvarnished and hurtful remark, the dumping of one's own emotional frustration on another person, or the "hit-and-run" remark that wounds and permits no response—all in the name of "telling it like it is."

This is not what straight talk is all about. Communications in straight talk must always be made with underlying respect for the listener, and a response must always be—at least implicitly—invited. Respect is at the very core of the process. It makes the difference whether the entire process will be successful. It says that the partner in the communication is considered strong enough to deal with another point of view.

Nonconnecting language often turns up when full respect is missing. Much of what is perceived in organizations as racism and sexism has an elusive quality of noncommunication about it. Whites in organizations often soft-pedal their responses to blacks, fail to counter the ideas of blacks, back away from productive conflicts, do not give straight critical feedback about performance. Blacks, who notice such things and feel left out of the communication process, often fail to tell whites when they do this. Similarly, women are often "protected" from critical feedback.

Style

Lack of connection also may come from differences in style—in both perception and communication. There are, for instance, important differences between men's and women's styles of communication, and there are important differences between how women and people of color communicate in an organization and how those in the majority (white men) communicate by the traditional norms.

A man, for instance, reports Problem A, followed succinctly by Solution Z. The man's communication norms are for the briefest report. He thinks this shows that the problem has been met and solved. A woman will mistrust a terse statement of solution without reference to the process. She will report Problem A, then explain process steps B, C, D, and so forth to show how she arrived at Solution Z. A man will perceive this as excessively detailed and may even view the exposure of the process as an exposure of weakness. He will be annoyed that the woman has taken time to show how she arrived at the solution—even though her data may be pertinent. He will also read this approach as a lack of confidence on the part of the woman manager, and his confidence in her will be impaired. Then he may decide that he needs to "help" her to be "more efficient." Understanding the difference in style, and straight talk, can help women and men to arrive at conclusions comfortable for both. This will happen **only**, however, if they can talk straight about their communication uneasiness.

Conflict

Conflict makes most people uneasy. It has a bad reputation, and the socialization norms most people learn traditionally have called for an avoidance of conflict. Women and people of color, particularly, have learned to go along to get along.

The loss of conflict, however, causes another loss that is serious. **Excellence** in any group or organization process **depends** on conflict. Only conflict can raise the different points of view, surface innovations, hone ideas that may be initially rough, tap all the resources of all the participants.

Conflict is not often seen as productive. Most people avoid it and in the process they avoid clarity and progress. Learning to use conflict productively, without hurt to the people in the organization, involves communication skills. They can be learned, and they must be learned.

The skills necessary to conflict are rooted in communication. They involve listening to yourself and to the other person, clarifying what the other person is saying, then staying with your own point of view and with the conflict in a respectful way that says you regard your partner as a worthy opponent. It is all right to say, sometimes, "I need to think that through," and withdraw temporarily. Do not use the need to think over another point of view as an excuse to retire from the field and the conflict. Come back, and work for solution, resolution, collaboration, or compromise (one view or the other or a modified version). If you have to go with one view or the other, then work for understanding why the other person thinks or feels as he or she does. If time permits, you can hold off on a final solution until there is more data, or some further enlightenment comes. For yourself, be authentic. Do not hasten to agree to something you feel uneasy about just to close out the conflict. If you handle your position with sufficient respect for the other person's viewpoint, and try hard both to listen to that and to communicate your own, you will see finally how productive and rewarding conflict can be. Working the process all the way through produces satisfaction and depth in the solution achievable in no other way. The process itself produces a closeness, a connectedness, and a new working relationship that are invaluable.

Some people see conflict—especially if it is protracted—as a side-tracking interaction that takes time and interferes with "getting on" with the task at hand. It must be admitted that a repeated conflict **can** be time consuming—especially if it is carried on with a highly inexperienced person or with a person who has other interpersonal problems or favorite axes to grind. In such cases, of course, limits must be put on the amount of time the conflict can be permitted to take. If those boundaries can be put on with respect, and accompanied by an invitation to work the conflict out when there is more time, the value of the conflict will not be lost.

Language as a top-down intervention

How the person in authority communicates affects and reflects the management style of the organization. When the manager's position is high enough, that style

affects the entire organization. If he or she is open and straight, the whole organization will move toward an open, straight style of management and communication. The process starts at the very top of the organization. When a consultant
goes into an organization, interventions will be most effective if they begin with
the top management group.

The best approach is to work on team development at this level, building
in norms for straight talk from the top down. Talking straight in an organization
in which that is not the norm takes courage, even for top managers or a CEO.
Top managers are typically protected from **too much** information. What "too
much" turns out to be, all too often, is information badly needed by the manager.
It may be bad news, or it may be problems with process. Good managers should
value straight talk, but often they are so overloaded with information, with input
from those who report to them, that they have little choice but to take partial or
imperfect or skewed information. Thus, their ability to manage on the basis of
sound data may suffer.

Middle managers also have to make difficult decisions about what and how
to report to their top management. Because traditional management norms are
as they are—for always looking as though the manager is on top of the situation—
middle managers inevitably select and slant information. They know that if they
look as though they are **not** on top of things they will be "helped" by other aggressive managers or by supervisors; and such "help" often means that a piece
of their territory will be annexed. Managers often know it is risky to discuss a
problem in a straight way with a top manager. That is unfortunate, but if for some
reason the top manager has signaled that straight talk is not welcome, then there
is trouble brewing. For as each communication becomes just a little less accurate,
accuracy and precision are less and less available, and soon decisions for correct-
ing course are off themselves. If straight talk is not welcomed at the top level, that
signals that productive conflict is not wanted, and that shuts off the flow of ideas
and stops dead the inclination to risk that produces truly inspired management.

The **management style** in an organization also affects communications. The
only way some managers know how to manage is by giving direct orders: Do it
my way, because that is the "right" way. It is as though the manager were saying:
"If I can replicate myself, I will have succeeded in creating a competent person
who will function correctly."

This method differs radically, however, from the quite usual technique of
modeling. In modeling, the manager behaves in an effective way to demonstrate
a behavior that can be adopted by the manager's direct subordinates and will contribute to their development. For instance, if a manager models "straight talk,"
the aim is for the direct subordinate to see the behavior in use, but **not** to mimic
or second guess the manager or try to be the manager's clone.

There are times—no doubt about it—when political considerations are just
too strong to be ignored and when a manager makes the conscious decision not
to talk straight. No manager should make a decision to waffle, however, without
an awareness of what the lack of a straight communication may do. Just as straight

talk has many ramifications, just as that produces a kind of "ripple effect," so too does a miscommunication—which is what a political communication is. To the extent the communication is off target, actions, reactions, decisions, and outcomes can be affected. When you have to delay a straight communication or give a neutral one, the important thing to keep in mind is that such a response does the organization no good. So before you decide on such a response, assess the cost.

Straight talk

If we agree that it is important to talk straight, then it is necessary to make a beginning. There are two schools of thought on how to bring about change within organizations. One holds that change must come from inside the individual, that change must take place in values and attitudes before change can occur in the organization. Another view holds that change happens from outside in—that by asking people to behave "as if" causes attitudes and values to change and effects the deeper change wanted. "Dress for success" would be one oversimplified example of this kind of change.

Language forms are another outside/in-kind intervention. We can begin useful change by **practicing** the language behaviors that lead to the insights that change other behaviors. We **must** pay attention first to the language **forms** we use. They matter.

What straight talk is not

As we pointed out earlier, straight talk is not dumping. It does not have to be a clout with a two-by-four. Straight talk should be candid, spoken with respect. Connecting language does just that: It says a thing straight, and it accords respect in the saying. For instance, this is a dump:

> You're being tedious, and boring. (This message can also be delivered silently, by yawning or looking away.)

Much better is to give some input about the impact of the communication on the listener:

> I'm having a hard time giving this conversation my full attention, and I would like us to discuss the central issue in the matter.

Sugar coating

Sugar-coated language is a way to protect myself—though it looks like a way to protect you. If I fail to give hard information to you, if I fail to talk straight, I treat you as though you were too fragile to receive my information. Sugar coating keeps the communicator "one up." It also distances the message and the communicator by avoiding the need for engaging in conflict. Part of learning to talk straight is learning to deal with the productive conflict that provokes.

Diction

On the simplest level, the **words** used are significant. We can diminish not only ourselves but others with the diction we choose. Abuses are common, traditional, often thought of as of no importance, but they are. For instance, the word **boss** implies a person who says, "do this, do that." the word **manager** is broader and indicates someone who can perform many functions and help others to be more productive. **Boss** is also a word with male connotations, while **manager** connotes both genders. The organization that would like to be both multicultural and fully "bi-gender" does well to use these non-sexist forms.

Words also connote rank and can diminish respect. I substitute the work **principal** for the word **subordinate** when I talk about ranks. Business organizations are hierarchical: That is, one efficient form of operation. Hierarchy need not damage the respect necessary to keep each individual organization member fully empowered and contributing.

Syntax—the one-up question

Questions are often used instead of statements—to obscure straight-out opinion. Typically, such forms avoid responsibility, but win the action.

Sentences that begin with **"Don't you think that"** or **"Isn't it true that"** have a hidden statement or opinion underneath the question. For example, with **"Don't you think this meeting would go better if people said what they had on their mind?"** what's being said is, **"This meeting would go better if people said what they had on their minds."** An adult can take responsibility for that statement. No manipulation needs to take place.

An alternative way to ask a true question and state an opinion forthrightly is simply to make the assertion: **"This meeting would go better if everyone said what they had on their mind."** Then ask, verbally or nonverbally, "What do you think?" A nonverbal way to ask can be through silence and eye contact, allowing space for the other person to answer. Then the other person's opinion can be given without my having to ask. This way we both can make a connecting statement and avoid the one-up, one-down situation.

Eye contact

Eye contact is the single most important piece of body language to reinforce a verbal message. When you deliver a message, the most powerful way to do it is to make eye contact first. Volumes have been written about eye contact or its lack and how people read the hidden messages in this kind of behavior. Learn to use it for straight, honest communication.

Talking about someone

Yet another subtle behavioral pattern is talking **about** someone in a group who should be talked **to**. Doctors sometimes do this—talk to someone else in the family **about** the patient, though the patient is sitting there, and is certainly the person who needs to receive the direct communication. If a person is present, it is respectful—and straight and efficient—to talk to the person, not **about** the person. For example, **"That was a good idea that Pat had"** is less preferable than **"That was a good idea you had, Pat."**

Tentatives and Qualifiers

Most of us also use **tentatives** and **qualifiers**. This, too, we do without thinking. We pick up the habit of using words like **sometimes, perhaps, maybe,** and **just.** Often, by the end of a sentence, passion, authority, meaning, and precision have been undercut. Remember that nothing you say is likely to be considered absolute. Most people are skeptics; you **will** be questioned. It is not impolite or inappropriate to make an assertion. When it **is** necessary to be tentative, or to qualify what you are saying, the tone of your voice can indicate that feeling. The nature of tentatives and qualifiers is to mitigate the force of an assertion, so they are not good for making a firm, powerful statement. Use them sparingly.

Extra words, preambles, and garbage language

Extraneous words are misleading as well as weakening. They cause the **listener** to be distracted, to "lighten up" and to lose concentration as **you** waste time and fill space. Be selective about extra words if you must use them.

The following preambles also cloud meaning and damage direct communication:

- what I want to do next is . . .
- what I want to say is . . .
- you know. . .

These are extraneous and detract from the statement. **"Oh"** and **"um"** and **"well"** fill silence while we think. The world can bear a moment of silence. Learn to be silent for the time it takes to formulate a precise answer. You will simply be credited with being a thoughtful respondent.

Another reason given for using **"uh"** and **"um"** is that they serve as a device for "holding the floor." A better way to keep the floor, however, is simply to say, **"I'm not finished."**

Intensifiers

Intensifiers are words like **very, really,** and **so.** Research at the University of Minnesota (Carson, 1976) has shown that these words are used most frequently by people who see themselves as oppressed. Women use more intensifiers that men. Emphasis is usually placed on the intensifier rather than on the word it is meant to intensify.

- "I **very** much like your blouse."

- "I **really** like your blouse."
- "I'm **so** upset."

Intensifiers weaken the communication. As a language habit, they are overstatement, and the speaker is not taken seriously. Because they are characteristic of the language norms of women, children, and those not dominant in society, they do not signal power. A more powerful way to communicate is to say in a firm voice: **"I am upset."**

Some words intensify by their meaning. **Love** for **like** is such a usage: **"I love that shirt."** I do not **love** the shirt, I **like** it. Words like **disastrous, fantastic, super, marvelous** are also escalators that, overused, make meaningless overstatements. If I always make a heavier case than is necessary, my language will become debased coinage, and when I need to have my intensity taken seriously, that communication will automatically be discounted.

Diminishing language

There are two kinds of diminishing language—self-diminishing language and language that diminishes others. I can, for instance, diminish myself if I say the following:

- **"You may not agree with this, but. . ."**
- **"This is probably not right, but. . ."**

My audience is already thinking, **"Well, if she does not think it's right, I am not going to think it's right."** I have made it harder for my idea to be considered. Should I feel oppressed when it is not taken seriously?

I also diminish myself if I say at the end of a sentence **"okay?"** or **"is that right?"** or, **"I guess."** These forms imply that I need permission and approval to go on to the next sentence. I suggest that I do not have the power or the strength or the judgment to move on until you and your approval and tell me that I **may** go on.

As we pointed out earlier, we can also diminish others with our language forms. We often do that, even when we do not intend to. The earlier example of using the word **subordinate** is an example of how language can diminish another person. **Principal** is an empowering form. Another common way to diminish others is to use the word **girl** instead of **woman**. (This usage also diminishes the person who uses it, however, characterizing that person as someone what is not aware.) **Woman** evokes a powerful response. A **girl** is an immature female, a child. If I refer to a person past age sixteen as a **girl**, I am using diminishing language. The same is true for the terms **boy** and **man**. I do **not** call a **man** a **boy**.

Few language patterns cause more confusion than the terms for man and woman. That is because the language norms of our sexist society have imbued gender-related language with all sorts of connotations. I have stopped using **female/male** in my designations, because these terms are mere biological designations and do not carry with them either power for myself or affirmation of power for the other person. We need badly to attach new connotations to the words that we use to effect change in sexist language patters. **Ladies/gentlemen** also carry behavioral expectations, expectations that for women are restrictive. These terms carry stereotypes and norms of protectiveness for women and of a power inequity between women and men. Because they do, such terms only perpetuate what needs to be done away with. I use **woman/man**, and I put woman first to wrench the language out of its accustomed pattern and underline the power that is—and ought to be—there.

Women further diminish themselves when they allow people to refer to a group of women as **guys**. I am not a **guy**. Nor do I recognize a generic masculine form.

Similarly, **minority** is no longer the best way to denote people of color. It is not accurate, and it sets up a "one-down," "less-than" implication. Specific terms for groups such as blacks, Asian-Americans or Hispanics are still proper usage, but spoken of collectively, "people of color" is preferred.

Names

Names—especially in business—are notations of personal power (Carson, 1976). When children are in school, they are Susie and Bobby. When he arrives in the business world, he will be Robert L. Jones, or R. L. Jones. She is likely still to be Susie or Sue. The diminutive diminishes one in the business world. Make no mistake about it. Until she becomes Susan, she will be treated like Susie—as not quite capable of assuming her full power.

A notable exception to the rule that nicknames diminish power is the use of a male diminutive. Bobby, or a nickname such as Skip, denotes inclusion in and acceptance by an old-boy network that validates power. Women and black men, who are not in any case included in such networks, **cannot** afford the diminutives and the nicknames because for them these connote stereotypes that cause them not to be taken seriously.

One subtle form of discrimination experienced by Hispanics and Asian Americans, as well as by those from other cultures, is that people shorten their names, as though the speaker's difficulty with pronunciation of a foreign name were an excuse to diminish its bearer. For example, one woman I know whose name is Evangelina is called Vangie, though she prefers her full name.

The language context

Language has another peculiar property. It exists both in space—its context— and time. The problem is that **all** the time and **all** the experience of **all** the communicators is brought to bear on a given single utterance, spoken in a specific context, with a specific intent.

A turn of phrase, a word choice, simply an association, or the timbre of a voice can cause the simple thing I have said in one context to associate itself with something from another context that creates a reaction or response never intended. Communications are like chemical compounds: They react, sometimes violently, in the presence of other substances. Human beings are complicated, and even the clearest communications can get clouded. Some communications are made clouded or coded on purpose—as ways to manipulate other people and so gain or secure more power. Some misunderstandings happen because people who talk to one another have picked up careless language habits. Some happen because people are unskilled.

Person: I or You

If you could choose to make only one change in your language, the most important one would be to change the use of the term **you** to the term **I** when you are speaking of yourself. The use of **I** when you are talking about the self is the single most powerful, clear, and direct behavior you can choose. Reserve **you** for referring to **others**. "When you stand up in front of a new group, you feel tense" is actually a way of saying: "When **I** stand up in front of a new group, **I** feel tense."

The second statement is undeniably authentic. I **know** how I feel. It also invites **you** to respond, because I have not spoken for you. So **I** empowers—and takes note of—the speaker's view and distinguishes it from others' statements in a way that the universal **you** does not.

Language can distance me not only from other people but from myself as well. If I use "ownership language," that usage can help me to understand myself better, be more integrated, and thus communicate with **you** more clearly. For instance, **"I"** connects me with myself. **"You"** distances.

Not	*Rather*
That feels good	I feel good.
It hurts.	I hurt.
You hurt me.	I hurt.

This injunction to pay attention to the **person** is a warning for spoken language. It is intended to encourage assuming responsibility for a statement. Language conventions have their place, however, and **written** language, which lacks the reinforcing signs of body language and instant response, may use the person as a means to clarify or make its style more direct or colloquial. The written use of "we" is a useful means of including the reader or signaling standard behavior. In verbal communication **"we"** makes the assumption that **"I"** can speak for other people and may cut off dialogue and interfere with communication.

Avoiding saying "no"

People **mean** "no" far more often than they like to admit. There is the habit in this society of saying something else. Saying something else when "no" is what is meant is especially normative in business organizations. **No** is often a necessary communication, and no is frequently misunderstood because it is so fuzzily communicated. We fear, apparently, that if we say **no**, the listener will no longer like or respect us. The relationship will be broken, will be endangered, will be lost or will become uncomfortable. **No** might invite conflict. Some people feel angry that they have been asked a question for which the response will have to be **no**. That anger, unexpressed, comes out in other ways and may skew other communications or interactions. Avoiding **no** is another pattern based on assessing the other person as fragile. It does the other person an injustice to assume that he or she cannot find an alternative. We protect. We also fail to talk straight when we waffle about saying **no**. Sometimes people have to say **no** to others, because they have to say **yes** to themselves. That is a legitimate need. Learning to say **no** respectfully but straight out is one of the most useful of the communication skills. It is straight and clear. It is time saving. It is efficient.

Sloppy language and sloppy communication waste time. They also deprive people of the power and self-confidence they need to be effective. They send projects reeling off in directions never intended. They foment unnecessary and unneeded political intrigue. They cause abuse of rank and the hierarchical structure of organizations.

Bad language habits can be changed. Even deliberate misuses of language can be changed when they are identified and when it is made clear to their users that there are appropriate ways to enhance personal power and influence without

It is only fair to acknowledge the difficulty of changing language patterns. I find daily that there are parts of my language that need work. To change requires commitment and an effort to change, and these additional efforts often feel like a burden in busy schedules. If we do not examine our habits, we will use energies anyway in a communications process that is less than efficient and certainly less than effective. Precision (or its lack), choice of words, sensitivity to connotation and language norms, accretions of social history around words—all affect the kind of communication we practice. We should pay attention to everything we say and work to improve those habits that require change. There used to be a truism that "you are what you eat." To some extent, you are what you **say**, and you create a climate and empower yourself by what you say and how you say it.

Describing the ideal communication process is not easy, because once it has begun to percolate, it goes through the organization, both up and down, and it causes all sorts of reactions and interactions that feed on and enhance one another.

In the final analysis, organizational effectivess is the aim, but in order for an organization to be efficient, its individuals must be functioning at an optimum level. The respect that straight talk fosters for the individual makes individual growth take place and then makes that competence fully available to an organization that values it. Such respect leads to a fully multicultural organization, because all of the talents and skills of all its people are being used. The richness of the multiculturalism leads to a stronger, more diversified organization, with a wider range of views and skills to draw upon. The whole process explodes, and all of the offshoots produce benefits in and of themselves.

REFERENCE

Carson, J. (1976). *The Rumplestiltskin syndrome: Sexism in American naming traditions.* Paper delivered at the Pioneers for Century III Bicentennial meeting, University of Cincinnati, OH.

Designing and Running Training Events: Rules of Thumb for Trainers

Barbara Benedict Bunker
Thomas Nochajski
Neil McGillicuddy
Debbie Bennett

How do people learn to design and run training events? What knowledge do they have that guides their practice? How do they learn what to do?

In the l950s, when the field of experiential learning was just developing, most people learned by the apprentice method. The lore of what works was handed down by more-experienced practitioners to their juniors. In the late l960s and 1970s, manuals began to be published that discussed both old and newly created training exercises and theory (e.g., Pfeiffer & Jones, 1970-1986). Yet even these new materials did not seem to do justice to all that is known by excellent trainers.

In 1980, the senior author of this article (Bunker) expressed interest in the rules of thumb that guide the practice of experienced trainers. She studied a number of training events in order to explicate these rules.

In this article, we look at recently published guides for trainers who design and run workshops and other experiential training events, doing so to determine the extent of agreement about "how to's" for trainers. Specifically, our discussion falls into three parts: We begin by comparing instructions for preparing for a training event, then we deal with rules of thumb for designing, and we conclude by examining the actual running (intervention) of training events.

We reviewed a considerable body of published material—three books and 20 chapters or articles on training—looking for "rules of thumb." By this we mean rather specific prescriptions about what one should do in particular situations, such as the following: "If participants are logy after lunch, plan some activity that will get them active and engaged." This is the type of information that trainers find useful, especially when they are inexperienced. We distinguish our rules of thumb from more general prescriptions that, unfortunately, fill the literature and are so general and sometimes value laden that they do not provide specific guidance.

©1987 NTL Institute. All rights reserved.

Examples of these general prescriptions include the following: "Trainers should always try to know who the participants are," or "Shared decision making is good." Below, we examine the rules of thumb currently described in the literature and the agreement or disagreement among authors about these rules of thumb.

Predesign considerations

All the major authors[1] considered some type of needs assessment an important step before beginning to design. Beyond this, individual authors suggested that assessments done by outsiders be checked by insiders (Lippitt & Schindler-Rainman, 1975), that several methods produce better data (Davis, 1974), and that involving participants in this process can convert frustrations into problems to be solved (Miles, 1981).

All the authors who wrote about the topic found setting objectives to be important. Some preferred behavioral objectives (Davis, 1974), others simply emphasized specificity of the objectives as most useful. The major authors and Lippitt and Schindler-Rainman (1975) emphasized being clear about the different types of learning objectives, such as skill training and awareness training, among others. Setting priorities for objectives was thought to provide a good guide for deciding how much can be accomplished in any training event (Davis, 1974).

Books on training usually devote sections to staff selection, training facility selection and preparation, and how the staff should conduct itself while planning. Although much is said about these topics, we did not find many rules of thumb for them. One exception is the maxim that using check lists is crucial for trainers (Davis, 1974). The assumption is that the many aspects of designing and operating a training event are too complex to keep in one's memory, and therefore—without some systematic method of review (the check list)—trainers are apt to overlook actions that they know are important. Davis (1974) goes furthest with this point by providing check lists for 12 different operations, including materials, facilities, and participants. Two other authors support the use of check lists (Lippitt & Schindler-Rainman, 1975; Miles, 1981.)

Finally, some rules of thumb about staffing are proposed. If the training program is large in size or long in duration, Miles (1981) suggests that different people conduct the training from those who conduct the administration. The assumption is that too much administrative complexity (which occurs with some large workshops) or too much time spent carrying a dual role may erode staff energy and be detrimental to the program. Similarly, in a training design with some depth of participant involvement, a ratio of one staff member for every 10 participants is considered best for maximum learning (Davis, 1974).

Designing

Bunker's (1980) categories of important principles of design (see Table 1) were used to organize our search for rules of thumb for the designing process. We thus organize our presentation of results under those categories, with two additions.

Table 1
Categories for Important Principles of Design*

---

1. Initial activities
2. Establishing a collaborative relationship between staff and participants, and among participants
3. Levels of participation
4. Maintaining energy
5. Maximizing sources of positive psychic income and minimizing resistance
6. Factors that increase the probability of design effectiveness:
   a. size of groups
   b. who is grouped with whom
   c. flow (e.g., self-disclosure, what follows what)
   d. conceptual "input"
   e. transfer of training and action taking
   f. giving instructions
7. Time allotted to meeting design objectives
8. Debriefing structured experiences

---

*Adapted from Bunker (1980), p. 125. Reprinted with permission from John Wiley and Sons.

Initial activities. Many practitioners have theories about the importance of the opening activities of an experiential learning event. Participants' needs for orientation were emphasized by two major authors, who view adults as needing to know the schedule, the rules of the game, and who the staff and other participants are.

Staffs must know whether participants attend voluntarily or are required to attend, and what participants are expecting that can lead to fruitful early activities in which the staff shares its goals and participants share their needs and expectations. These activities are also seen as setting the climate for the entire workshop, as they establish the staff's interest in participant needs, its willingness to listen and be influenced, and its license to help. Miles says, "Remember that learning is unlikely unless people come to believe that the program will be of help" (1981). What happens in the first session is often considered a bellwether for the rest of the workshop.

Establishing a collaborative participant-staff relationship. Three authors share the notion that the way the staff relates to clients has effects on the psychological state of their readiness to learn. They emphasize that adults must be responsible for their own learning (Davis, 1974; Miles, 1981; Pfeiffer & Jones, 1973). Thus, good designs have built-in periods of feedback and negotiation with the staff (Cooper & Harrison, 1976; Lippitt & Schindler-Rainman, 1975; Miles, 1981). Davis (1974) warns trainers not to ask clients for their opinions if the trainers are not willing to change the design. Moreover, staff are urged to put themselves empathetically in the participants' roles when designing a training event (Cooper & Heenan, 1980; Miles, 1981).

Levels of activity and participation. These are issues closely related to the staff-participant relationship discussed above. An underlying assumption is that involvement and shared leadership increase commitment, which in turn increases learning (according to the major authors).

Miles (1981) and Cooper and Heenan (1980) also emphasize the different parts of the self that may be involved in learning, such as the intellectual, emotional, physical, and spiritual self, and the importance of varying learning activities to deal with the many ways people learn.

Maintaining energy in the workshop system. This is a central design concern of many who write about these processes. The rule of thumb expressed by three authors is to vary the activity type, length, and intensity so that participants do not get bored. Building in time for breaks and paying attention to the needs for coffee or juices are also considered important to boosting energy (according to the major authors). The leaders' energy and activity levels are often felt by participants as energizing (Cooper & Heenan, 1980; Davis, 1974). Therefore, staff needs must also be taken seriously so that staff energy is maintained.

Motivating participants by positive psychic income and reducing resistance. Lippitt and Schindler-Rainman (1975) and Davis (1974) discuss reinforcement of participant behavior and successful experiences as important to maintaining motivation. Similarly, two authors deal with resistance as a normal part of any change process, but one that must be carefully understood. Miles (1981), however, reminds trainers that not all negative comments signal resistance, and Davis (1974) indicates that a climate of safety, mutual commitment, and choice is apt to help people deal constructively with their resistance.

Increasing the probability of design effectiveness. In this section we look concretely at the lore of what works in specific designs. For example, what size groups are best for certain types of activities? Our reading found two recommendations: Davis (1974) says that interaction groups should be no larger than 7-12 members, and that the design using an expanding panel with an empty chair becomes unmanageable with more than 20 persons involved.

Group composition is considered by Pfeiffer and Jones (1973) to be most sound if the group is heterogeneous. This is limited by the need for an individual to be able to identify with at least one other person in the group. Sometimes, for persons with a great deal of experience, an advanced group is preferable to division based on other criteria.

A key aspect of any design is what often is referred to as **flow.** Flow describes the sequence of events and was the subject of much attention in all the writings we examined (28 different items).

The major authors and Pfeiffer and Jones (1973) made general statements about the sequence of activities. They seemed to consider a logical order flowing from objectives to be important, whereas Miles (1981) emphasized the psychological, learner-centered sequence rather than a purely logical order. Davis (1974) expressed concern that the pace be set so that all participants could keep up and experience success. The major authors and Pfeiffer and Jones (1973) agreed that specific progressions should move from the less difficult to the more difficult, from the less risky to the more risky, and from easier concepts to harder ones. Similarly, they argued that skills should be demonstrated before they are practiced, and practiced before they are used in exercises. The major authors also have rules about the need for variety and balance; for example they called for not too much cognitive material being provided at one time, general sessions interspersed with small groups, and tense sessions followed by more relaxed experiences.

Other rules of thumb concerning flow include the argument that as the program progresses the trainer should gather data on how it is affecting the participants. This allows the trainer to change the flow if necessary to maximize learning (Miles, 1981; Pfeiffer & Jones, 1973). Also, Lippitt and Schindler-Rainman (1975) discuss the value of a longer design that allows an interim period between workshop sessions, a period in which participants can digest, practice, and increase their learning.

Specific methods within the design flow and their usefulness were discussed by three authors. Davis (1974) recommends discussions, reading, and drama as the main ways to communicate knowledge. When gaining knowledge is the objective, tables for taking notes may be useful and make participants feel less self-conscious.

For skills training, several specific rules of thumb were provided. Demonstrations model, but do not teach, skills. To be effective, skills training requires practice according to criteria, followed by performance feedback (Cooper & Heenan, 1980; Miles, 1981). When a new skill is learned, a small group may be a safe place to try it out (Miles, 1981).

When a trainer is **giving instruction** to the group, its members must use judgment about when to share decision making and when to be more authoritarian. Specifically, when time is limited or when establishing group rules, more authoritarian behavior may be called for (Cooper & Heenan, 1980).

Davis (1974) gives two rules of thumb regarding the instruction process. When written materials are passed out, one should do this at the moment one wants persons to look at them. This avoids paper shuffling and a lack of attention. When assigning discussion topics to a group, the discussion quality depends on the clarity and the depth of the question assigned.

Three authors agree that an important maxim is to **keep the design simple.** "Less is more" in this situation (Cooper & Heenan, 1980; Middleman & Goldberg, 1972; Miles, 1981).

Davis (1974) gives more attention to the use of **aids** in training than do any of the other authors. Thus, we have organized his rules of thumb as "do"s and "don't"s. **Do** use name tags; provide a hole punch if you are using notebooks; always carry magic markers, masking tape, and flip charts; use videotapes rather than movies, as videotapes are more flexible; use visual supports with lectures; distribute pencils rather than pens if a sharpener is available; have a copying machine nearby. **Don't** use microphones or lecterns that produce distance, or use tape recorders if they make persons nervous.

The transfer of training from the workshop setting to the back-home work setting is a concern shared by many authors. How can the design be tailored to enhance this transfer? Here we found some differences of opinion among our authors. Lippitt and Schindler-Rainman (1975) believe that application to back-home activities is most effective if it occurs throughout the design, not only toward the end. Miles (1981), however, indicates that bridging activities only work well after people have had a chance to reexamine their own behavior and develop new frames of reference. Then, he finds, they can diagnose their own job situations and make specific action plans for back home, including what to do when new behaviors meet resistance. He believes that bridging activities are more effective if they occur during the last third of the design. This apparent contradiction among authors may be a real difference, or each of these rules may apply to a particular type of training situation.

Lippitt and Schindler-Rainman (1975) and Pfeiffer and Jones (1973) emphasize the importance of continuity of support in the transfer process. This can be facilitated by telephone calls following training, or by asking people who are known to be supportive at work to help with the transfer. Some staffs have participants write contracts for back-home application, with planned follow-up built into the contract. Consultation with other participants in action planning also helps make back-home transfer issues real. Generally, trainers help the transfer if they use many work-related examples when presenting conceptual material.

Miles (1981) points out that attitude change as a workshop product has different transfer problems than does skills training. He believes that the appropriate training method for attitude change is the use of small, diverse groups that have sustained interaction and that ask members for commitment in the form of actions or decisions congruent with the desired attitude. Attitude change is less apt to decay when learners have made personal commitments to new attitudes, when the new attitudes are well linked with old ones, and when they have had an opportunity to explore counterarguments.

The environment created by room arrangement has a great impact on the training design (Davis, 1974). Two issues are focal: The type of learning situation, and the power relations desired among the workshop group members.

Knowledge learning can occur in large group arrangements. If no writing is necessary by participants, the circle-within-a-circle chair arrangement is good because it distributes power and promotes interaction (Davis, 1974).

Skill acquisition learning must have flexible seating. The fishbowl structure is appropriate for skill practice. If tables are needed for practice, an open, triangular shape is effective (Davis, 1974).

For attitude learning, tables—perhaps even chairs—are a hindrance. Informal circular arrangements in which persons sit on the floor work best. For attitude learning, everyone should be free to select her or his own space and position (Davis, 1974).

When using tables and chairs, arrange them to create the power structure you consider most desirable. Wider tables will create more distance between individuals and more formal interaction. Those occupying positions at the ends of tables gain more power and control. Often, tables can be formed into squares or triangles to equalize power (Davis, 1974).

Time allotted. Several theories were presented on the relationship of ending events to the learning process. Some trainers (Cooper & Heenan, 1980) believe that learning requires summary and closure; other believe a more open-ended finish will lead to more learning after the workshop itself is over (Rice, 1965). The authors we evaluated were from the school that prefers to tie things together and acknowledge the ending. Some (the major authors) suggested that the central objectives of the workshop be reviewed and that the workshop not be permitted just to run out, but instead be clearly ended.

Evaluations of the workshop should occur at its end. Staff are advised to conduct their evaluations immediately after the workshop to ensure recall and the capturing of salient suggestions (Davis, 1974). Feedback from participants can take many forms, but should be planned as part of the design (Cooper & Heenan, 1980; Miles, 1981). Miles (1981) also believes that the evaluation should assess outcomes compared to the workshop objectives. Participants' views of what they found useful and not useful are emphasized by Cooper and Heenan (1980).

Intervention

In this section we investigate the theory of practice with respect to running training events. What can the trainer do to help the design work and to reduce problems that may interfere with learning? Some rules of thumb call for working in face-to-face groups to help them learn. Others address helping individuals or the staff. We begin by discussing intervention at the group level, and then the consideration of other levels.

Group-level interventions. Writers differ as to what they consider the proper trainer role in relation to group norms. Cooper and Heenan (1980) state clearly that the trainer should not force persons to conform to group norms. Davis (1974), however, believes the trainer should gently stop certain participant behaviors that inhibit learning, such as putting others down, displaying sarcastic humor, and taking credit for others' ideas. For Davis, the trainer is a "norm sender," and this requires intervention at the group level. The establishment of norms that create a good climate for learning is supported by the trainer through many types of interventions. For example, ensuring that everyone has a chance to speak both helps individuals and establishes a norm that individuals will each get a hearing in the group.

Some interventions at the group level seek to help the group stay focused on its task and not get sidetracked. For example, Mill (1980) suggests that if the group switches topics suddenly, this can be called to its attention through descriptive rather than interpretive comment, or the trainer might suggest the group decide if it wishes to change topics rather than just go along with the shift; similarly, if the group moves away from a sensitive but energizing topic, this behavior of the whole group can be pointed out. Pfeiffer and Pfeiffer (1975) suggest that a trainer can get a group to deal with issues that are suppressed by asking everyone to imagine herself or himself walking away from the group and asking group members if they regret not having said something. Sometimes two real issues develop in a group at the same time, and in this case the rule of thumb is to call this to the group's attention and ask it to choose the order which it will deal with these issues (Mill, 1980).

Group-level interventions also provide useful ways to deal with individuals in the group. For example, the group may have selected an individual to deal with a particular issue when the issue is really the shared concern of several members. A group-level intervention will clarify this situation and enable all those who are involved to engage in the issue (Cooper & Heenan, 1980). Sometimes a group will prematurely focus on an individual and try to deal with emotional or personal issues. If this occurs, the trainer can move the focus off the individual by making a group-level comment (Cohen & Smith, 1976). If, however, an individual is not on the group's "wave length" and is distracting, the trainer may support the individual's interest in what is important to that person but redirect the conversation back to the main group topic (Cooper & Heenan, 1980). In this role, the trainer acts as a traffic cop to maintain the flow.

Sometimes when a trainer intervenes, a participant will use this as an occasion to argue with the trainer. The dilemma here is that the group can then get focused on the trainer. If the trainer does not consider this desirable, the trainer can make a group-level comment about the interaction and question whether the group wants this to go on; this often changes the direction of the group's attention (Mill, 1980).

Sometimes the climate of a group is not conducive to learning. When that occurs, Davis (1974) suggests the following interventions to change the mood. For cold groups, do warm-up activities; for sleepy groups, increase active participation; for hostile, dense, or "off-the-subject" groups, ask them why they are in this mood or state; for "fun-and-games" groups—that is, groups in flight—remind them of the objective(s) and, if that fails, join in the fun.

The relationship of the trainer to the group is important and discussed in a similar way by seven authors. The general theme is that participants must feel responsible for their own learning and not depend on the trainer (Boone, 1975). Thus, trainers should not allow themselves to be trapped into answering a long series of questions for participants, but rather should challenge them to figure out the answers for themselves (Cooper & Heenan, 1980). Clarifying the trainer role and the client-trainer contract will help this process (Lippitt & Schindler-Rainman, 1975). Miles (1981) puts it well by saying that trainers should work themselves out of a job—that is, they should not do for participants what they can do for themselves (Freedman, 1978). This means you should keep quiet so the participants can speak, turn questions to you back to the group, point out successes, and encourage the group to make plans without the trainer (Cooper & Heenan, 1980; Miles, 1981). Of course, at times the trainer will move in and supply a missing function, but then the group should do this itself in the future (Gustafson & Cooper, 1978).

Over time, participants may even move into the trainer role by facilitating, organizing, and the like. This is to be encouraged, though the group may resent this behavior from a member if it occurs too early in its development (Davis, 1974; Mill, 1980).

Individual-level interventions. Some people are not aware of their feelings or behavior and need help to increase their awareness. Feedback is helpful, as is asking these persons to describe their physical feelings; even listing a number of "feeling words" may help (Mill, 1980). Other interventions include using imaginary roles, nonverbal mimicry, and sentence completions (Pfeiffer & Pfeiffer, 1975).

When persons feel blocked but want to go further in self-learning, trainers may find it useful to ask them what the worst and best things are that could happen if they moved on (Pfeiffer & Pfeiffer, 1975). Then perhaps they can rehearse what they are about to say.

Reluctant members pose special problems for groups. If too much attention is focused on them, blockage can occur. Mill (1980) suggests that trainers should recognize when the group puts too much pressure on such a member and the amount of group energy directed toward that person, and intervene to shift focus if necessary. Reluctant members often generate hostility in others, which can be brought to their awareness. When the reluctant member joins the work of the group, this behavior should be recognized and reinforced. If, however, this occurs at the end of the group's work, the trainer may find it necessary to suggest that such persons deal with their issues outside of the group.

People who continually put themselves down or apologize create discomfort in others. The following are suggested strategies for changing these behaviors: have the "self-downgrader" tell each member why that member should appreciate her or him, and have the "apologizer" make assertive statements to others (Cooper & Heenan, 1980; Pfeiffer & Pfeiffer, 1975).

Blocking, dominating, and monopolizing behaviors require trainer intervention, unless the group acts itself. Early in the group's life, such behaviors may be ignored (Davis, 1974); later, the group may be strong enough to cope with them. If not, a strong group-level norm about "hearing from everyone, or those who haven't had much chance to speak" is in order (Davis, 1974). If that fails, an individual intervention that suggests active listening rather than a directive to stop talking is more effective (Cooper & Heenan, 1980).

Participants who speak for others in the group instead of only for themselves should be encouraged to make "I" statements and thus assume "ownership" of their views (Miller, Nunnally & Wackman, 1976). When participants attribute their views to others, an intervention that checks whether this is really accurate can also be useful (Cooper & Heenan, 1980).

The general posture that trainers take toward group members can be important for the members' learning. Providing support, being alert for signs of stress, allowing members to work at their own pace, and encouraging self-diagnosis provide the background for a productive relationship (Cohen & Smith, 1976; Davis 1974; Golembiewski; 1979; Miles, 1981). Golembiewski believes that the transfer of learning is directly correlated with the degree of autonomy participants feel. In this context, the trainer may need to question ideas or behavior, but not persons. Effective modeling at this point can provide members with an example for dealing with difficult persons. For example, for a "fighter" you can support knowledge and creative thinking, but not the hostile part of the behavior; when persons play "dumb" you can challenge them to make up an answer or choice and reinforce that behavior; when persons are overly verbal and intellectualizing you can suggest they express their ideas in one sentence; when persons complain you can support them and work to make them more comfortable (Cooper & Heenan, 1980). All of these individual-level behaviors can become irritating to the group. Trainers are advised to ignore them initially, but to call attention to them when group irritation is sensed (Cooper & Heenan, 1980). These are individual issues and must be dealt with at the individual level.

Some interventions create problems and should be avoided; thus, rules of thumb are offered as to what not to do. Generally, these address things that get trainers in trouble or do not forward the group's progress. For example, trainers should not "take head trips"—that is, move the group to intellectualizing through trainer modeling (Mill, 1980; Pfeiffer & Pfeiffer, 1975); nor should they "pull rank" on participants, which violates norms of collaborative working together (Miles, 1981).

Trainers should not do for people what people can do for themselves (Freedman, 1978), and should also avoid giving too much support—that is, support at every sign of tension (Miles, 1981).

Problems develop if the group becomes too highly focused on the trainer (Mill, 1980). Some interventions have this effect and should be avoided, such as comments that couple the trainer with one group member. As a model, trainers should avoid making "us" or "we" statements and should not infer that issues are difficult to deal with.

At the group level, Mill (1980) states it is best to avoid interventions of the "either/or" variety and to avoid interventions that require a group consensus. When starting meetings, avoid structures that focus too much on only one dimension. For example, if a group experiences conflict but the meeting starts with a positive relaxation exercise, this may make it difficult for the group to deal with the negative issues.

Finally, trainers are admonished not to start what they cannot finish and to avoid activities they have not previously experienced or observed (Miles, 1981).

We turn next to advice to trainers about what works—about what they should do. Many of these address the trainer's own style, as well as the focus of the training.

Use the participant's language. Do not use social science jargon, but adjust your language and use clear, precise terms (Golembiewski, 1979; Freedman, 1978; Mill, 1980).

Keep the focus on the here and now by role modeling, especially when giving feedback (Banet, 1974; Golembiewski, 1979; Miles, 1981; Pfeiffer & Pfeiffer, 1975).

The trainer's behavior should model the norms the group espouses. Try new behavior, make inquiries be open, and the like. (Banet, 1974; Gustafson & Cooper, 1978; Miles, 1981; Mill, 1980).

Confrontation needs trainer support, because without this no growth will occur. Trainers need to support confrontation because it gets issues out in the open where the group can deal with them. The trainer may even be a role model for this (Davis, 1974; Golembiewski, 1979).

Trainers also act as role models for group members when they **share feelings.** Feelings often provide the data the group needs to do work. Trainer modeling is a way of encouraging expression of feelings by all members (Cooper & Heeman, 1980; Miles, 1981; Mill, 1980).

All sorts of general prescriptions suggest what effective trainers should do. Trainers must look at the whole group, not just at whoever is speaking, and should read both nonverbal and verbal behavior (Mill, 1980). Trainers must consider what they might do before they do it (Davis, 1974). Pfeiffer and Jones (1975) say that interventions should be located—that is, the trainer must know what he or she is responding to, what the intervention is designed to do, and how this fits in with the general needs of the group. At the same time, trainers are urged to go with the flow, to trust the process. This advice seems contradictory, unless one understands that the intention is for the trainer to think conceptually while at the same time feeling intensely what is going on in the group. When one can do both, one's resources for intervention are enlarged. Because the facilitator is not responsible for the group in the usual sense of leadership, it is better to err on the side of too few interventions than to control too much through overactivity (Cooper & Heenan, 1980; Mill, 1980).

How should trainers use their "persons"? How much can they be themselves? Certainly, they should not attempt to copy anyone else's style (although they may borrow aspects of another's style) (Cooper & Heenan, 1980). They should be open and direct with the participants (Cooper & Heenan, 1980; Golembiewski, 1979). The trainer's role is to open up possibilities for people, not to direct them (Gustafson & Cooper, 1978). Early in the group's life, it is inappropriate for the trainer to take a participant role. This may occasionally happen with a fully coalesced group, but even then the trainer does not fully give up the trainer role (Mill, 1980). The trainer is free to experiment with interventions, to reword them if they do not get a response, but must also be ready to drop them if they do not work (Pfeiffer & Pfeiffer, 1975).

How to give feedback is treated by two authors (Chin, 1975; Golembiewski, 1979). We wish readers to note that, although this material fits our definition of rules of thumb, these rules have become well-known, widely published rules of the interpersonal communication literature. Briefly, these prescriptions for effective feedback are the following:

1. feedback should be descriptive of words and behavior,
2. feedback should not make inferences, attributions, or evaluations,
3. feedback should only be given for behaviors that can be altered,
4. feedback should include the impact of that behavior on the giver,
5. feedback should be requested by the recipient, thus increasing the feeling of safety.

Golembiewski's advice (1979) to trainers about the situation in which feedback occurs recommends a group setting, because this allows information to be verified or rejected by others. Groups create feelings of trust and support that contribute to the individual's ability to hear feedback. The purpose of feedback is to help the recipient effectively solve problems, not to create new problems. Thus, feedback should be considered in that light before it is given. The trainer can strengthen the emphasis on facilitating change by suggesting alternative or new behaviors and by reinforcing any attempts at new behavior. If individuals seem resistant to the feedback they receive, the trainer may find it useful to ask them to state in their own words what they have heard.

Trainer awareness. Before trainers can intervene, they must become aware of the individual and group behaviors that provide the data base for the interventions. Rules of thumb suggesting which areas and issues are especially fruitful for understanding group behavior point to the following as especially useful: inclusion issues in the group, developing norms, participation rates, who fills task and maintenance roles, who is influential and how, verbal and nonverbal behavior, the treatment of silent members, decision-making processes, and group atmosphere (Hanson, 1972).

Other group patterns that trainers should be aware of are those of establishing scapegoats and dominance (Golembiewski, 1979). Humor can dictate the dominance hierarchy if the trainer notices who makes jokes and who laughs at the jokes (Rossell, 1981).

Self-awareness is the essential base of competent training. Trainers' needs, even their prejudices, can be managed if they recognize when an intervention is being considered (Davis, 1974; Golembiewski, 1979).

Awareness of participants is also essential. For example, some participants who are apt to become defensive when receiving feedback may need extra support from the trainer (Gibb, 1961).

Golembiewski (1979) gives an interesting example of the rules of thumb about individual behavior when he discusses the implications of different patterns of self-disclosure. Disclosure that expects no reactions or repercussions suggests a low-level commitment to the group process. Anonymous disclosure implies a weak learning link. Disclosure with risks only for others does not encourage risk at the group level. Disclosure that is to remain confidential may not improve the interaction system. These rules of thumb suggest interventions to trainers based on the assumptions they contain.

Codesigning and cotraining require some special behaviors that facilitate the effectiveness of the staff team. Design teams need to process their work together, paying special attention to how differences of orientation are being handled (Mill, 1980; Pfeiffer & Jones, 1975). Being open with one another about reactions and being open about one's energy level with regard to the task help the group be more effective (Cooper & Heenan, 1980). When leading a workshop with another person, it is best to design it together. If that is not possible, however, a thorough understanding of its overall purpose and the method is essential (Cooper & Heenan, 1980). Cotrainers must decide ahead of time how leadership of the workshop will be shared and how much freedom each trainer has to make changes in the design, time schedule, and the like (Cooper & Heenan, 1980).

Rules of thumb for the relationships of staff members to one another during the workshop include the following. "Criticize off-stage, support on-stage and invite mutual coaching" (Davis, 1974, p. 236). In small groups, it is best if both trainers use the same pace of intervention. If one person intervenes a great deal, this may not leave room for the other to do so and thus lead to imbalance. Cotrainers should not speak directly after each other (Mill, 1980).

Two trainers should never work with the same participant. Cotrainers need to divide the work when a display of heightened affect occurs. One should work with the affected person, while the other helps the other group members deal with and understand their reactions to the situation (Pfeiffer & Jones, 1975).

Review and discussion

In this article we present the rules of thumb for trainers that we found in books and articles on conducting training. We organize our discussion into three sections: preworkshop rules of thumb, designing rules of thumb, and rules of thumb for intervening during the workshop.

In our presentation, we indicate those areas for which most authors seem to agree, or at least consider an issue of enough importance to discuss. What stands out is the number of prescriptions mentioned by only one author. We do not feel this indicates controversy in the field. Rather, so many of these dicta seem to exist that no one author can cover more than a sampling. Thus the student must read everything to know the broad range of knowledge available. We hope that this summary will serve as an organizing guide for those trying to gather these bits of theory of practice.

In Bunker's (1980) article, she notes that one of the authors gathered rules of thumb in field settings in which two different types of workshop were being run. We have reviewed that work to compare what is recorded in the literature and what trainers say when they are at work. When we compare the design sections of both articles, the two seem to cover similar ground. The differences are in terms of specificity. In the field setting, rules of thumb are more specific, and more rules exist for categories such as time allotted and maintaining psychic income. The training literature, in contrast, devotes more material to transfer processes and design flows. We found predesign rules of thumb in the literature, but not in the field. This is probably because the researcher was not involved in the predesign phase of the field workshop setting.

We have chosen to organize our discussion of intervention strategies substantively with regard to the intervention target—that is, the group or individual level—and also according to topics of trainer awareness and cotraining relationships. In the field data collection (Bunker, 1980), intervention rules of thumb were organized according to different trainer roles. Intervention is a rich and complex area, and new attempts to structure it are continually needed in the field. Cohen and Smith (1976), for example, propose an intervention cube as a basis for trainer decision making about interventions. Their model, however, applies primarily to groups focused on individual development rather than on a broad range of training settings. Despite differences in the organization of data from the field and the literature, much overlap occurred for the rules of thumb. Because some of our material also came from writing about experimental groups, rules of thumb about group-level interventions were much in evidence. In the observed workshops, the group structures used were of a shorter duration and managed more by task instruction than those of self-directed groups with trainer facilitation. Even so, rules of thumb for discussing the trainer as a process intervener (Bunker, 1980) are similar to those for group-level material.

At the individual level, we located a variety of interesting and new prescriptions for working with people. These add to the richness of our knowledge of how to work with individuals. The section on trainer awareness is paralleled in the field data collection, but the section on cotraining is not, even though each intervention observed in the field was led by pairs of staff. Perhaps this resulted from the author's failure to ask questions of the field staff as to how they managed their relationships.

We can see how rich the possibilities are for developing a theory of practice of training, and how situation specific many of the prescriptions for trainer behavior are. This helps us understand the desire of new trainers to work with as many experienced people as they can. In each new situation with each new person, they are apt to learn many new rules of thumb.

We still consider it important to have written works that describe practice in the training field, even if it is difficult to reflect the diversity of situations in written material. Our intention with this article is to contribute to this work and to provide an organizing framework to facilitate progress toward a real theory of practice.

NOTE

1. The term "major authors" designates those who wrote the three books that are entirely about training (Cooper & Heenan, 1980; Davis, 1974; Miles, 1981).

REFERENCES

Banet, A. G. (1974). Therapeutic intervention and the perception of process. In J. W. Pfeiffer & J. E. Jones (Eds.), *The 1974 annual handbook for group facilitators.* La Jolla, CA: University Associates.

Boone, T. A. (1975). Therapy or personal growth. In J. E. Jones & J. W. Pfeiffer (Eds.), *The 1975 annual handbook for group facilitators.* La Jolla, CA: University Associates.

Bunker, B. B. (1980). Developing a theory of practice for experiential learning. In C. P. Alderfer & C. L. Cooper (Eds.), *Advances in experiential social processes* (Vol. 2). New York: John Wiley and Sons.

Chin, R. (1975). Evaluation research and documentation in programs using laboratory method. In K. D. Benne, L. P. Bradford, J. R.   Gibb, & R. O. Lippitt (Eds.), *The laboratory method of changing and learning: Theory and application.* Palo Alto, CA: Science and Behavior Books.

Cohen, A. M., & Smith, R. D. (1976). *The critical incident in growth groups: Theory and technique.* La Jolla, CA: University Associates.

Cooper, C. L., & Harrison, K. (1976). Designing and facilitating experiential group activities: Variables and issues. In J. W. Pfeiffer & J. E. Jones (Eds.), *The 1976 annual handbook for group facilitators,* La Jolla, CA: University Associates.

Cooper, S. & Heenan, C. (1980). *Preparing, designing and leading workshops: A humanistic approach.* Boston: CBI Publishing.

Davis, L. N. (1974). *Planning, conducting, and evaluating workshops.* Austin, TX: Learning Concepts.

Freedman, A. M. (1978). Types of process inteventions. In J. W. Pfeiffer & J. E. Jones (Eds.), *The 1978 annual handbook for group facilitators.* La Jolla, CA: University Associates.

Gibb, J. R. (1961). Climate for trust formation. In L. P. Bradford, J. R. Gibb, & K. D. Benne (Eds.), *T-Group theory and laboratory method.* Boston: Houghton Mifflin.

Golembiewski, R. T. (1970). *Approaches to planned change: Part II microlevel interventions and change-agent strategies.* New York: Marcel Dekker.

Gustafson, J. P., & Cooper, L. (1978). Collaboration in small groups: Theory and technique for the study of small group processes. *Human Relations, 31,* 155-171.

Hanson, P. G. (1972). What to look for in groups. In J. W. Pfeiffer & J. E. Jones (Eds.), *The 1972 annual handbook for group facilitators.* La Jolla, CA: University Associates.

Lippitt, R. O., & Schindler-Rainman, E. (1975). Designing for participative learning and changing. In K. D. Benne, L. P. Bradford, J. R. Gibb, & R. O. Lippitt (Eds.), *The laboratory method of changing and learning: Theory and applications.* Palo Alto, CA: Science and Behavior Books.

Middleman, R. R., & Goldberg, G. (1972). The concept of structure in experiential learning. In J. W. Pfeiffer & J. E. Jones (Eds.), *The 1972 annual handbook for group facilitators.* La Jolla, CA: University Associates.

Miles, M. B. (1981). *Learning to work in groups: A practical guide for members and trainers.* New York: Teachers College Press.

Mill, C. R. (1980). *Activities for trainers: 50 useful designs.* San Diego, CA: University Associates.

Miller, S., Nunnally, E. W., & Wackman, D. B. (1976). The awareness wheel. In J. E. Jones & J. W. Pfeiffer (Eds.), *The 1976 annual handbook for group facilitators.* La Jolla, CA: University Associates.

Pfeiffer, J. W., & Jones, J. E. (1973). Design considerations in laboratory education. In J. E. Jones & J. W. Pfeiffer (Eds.), *The 1973 annual handbook for group facilitators.* La Jolla, CA: University Associates.

Pfeiffer, J. W., & Jones, J. E. (1975). Co-facilitating. In J. E. Jones & J. W. Pfeiffer (Eds.), *The 1975 annual handbook for group facilitators.* La Jolla, CA: University Associates.

Pfeiffer, J. W., & Pfeiffer, J. A. (1975). A Gestalt primer. In J. E. Jones & J. W. Pfeiffer (Eds.), *The 1975 annual handbook for group facilitators.* La Jolla, CA: University Associates.

Rice, A. K. (1965). *Learning for leadership: Interpersonal and intergroup relations.* London: Tavistock Publications.

Rossell, R. D. (1981). Wordplay: Metaphor and humor in the small group. *Small Group Behavior, 12,* 116-136.

Section V.
Multicultural Training

The Cultural Awareness Hierarchy: A Model for Promoting Understanding

Peter Muniz
Robert Chasnoff

Frequently, trainers are called upon to conduct training sessions that help participants increase their understanding of another culture. We trainers are tempted to rush in with what has been asked for—instant information and understanding. We bring films, speakers, reading materials (often fancy brochures), foods, entertainment, and case studies about the culture under discussion.

This kind of information is valuable in learning about another culture. However, several preliminary sets of understanding are required before understanding of another culture can be achieved.

This article presents the Cultural Awareness Hierarchy, a conceptual model that outlines six levels necessary for a full understanding of another culture. A training approach used to introduce the hierarchy is presented as well.

The agree-disagree questionnaire

To help participants become involved in the topic and the training session, a questionnaire similar to that shown in Table 1 is distributed. Before continuing to read this article, take a moment now to complete the questionnaire. Read each statement quickly, and decide whether you strongly agree (SA), agree (A), disagree (D), or strongly disagree (SD).

In training sessions, the questionnaire is used in the following manner:

- Each participant completes the questionnaire individually.
- The participants form subgroups to determine a group answer for each item. The subgroups are instructed to address each statement, to make

©1983 *Training and Development Journal,* American Society for Training and Development. Reprinted with permission. All rights reserved.

their decisions unanimous (or, at the very least, to arrive at them by consensus) and to avoid voting or merely giving in.

- The subgroups post their answers on large easel sheets, identifying which
were "trouble" items.
- The entire group looks at the data. Participants are instructed to examine
those items where responses of the subgroups are distributed over both
"agree" and "disagree," and those items with which the subgroups had
the most difficulty reaching a decision.

Table 1
Agree/Disagree Items

1. Hostile relations between countries often cancel any benefits that may be gained through cultural awareness training programs.	SA	A	D	SD
2. Many people cannot understand **other** cultures because they don't know or understand their **own** culture.	SA	A	D	SD
3. Highly skilled technicians who have very little self-awareness (or self-understanding), and who cannot communicate with people in their **own** country, will **not** be able to understand or accept another country's culture.	SA	A	D	SD
4. The words we use to describe our own behavior, in contrast with words we use to describe the behavior of people from other countries, often serve as greater intercultural barriers than our lack of cultural understanding. (Example: **"We** are patriotic. **They** are nationalistic.")	SA	A	D	SD
5. "Cultural differences" are merely different ways of coping with universal human feelings and situations.	SA	A	D	SD
6. An excellent technician who has no intercultural knowledge will succeed in another country more easily than the technician who has a lot of intercultural knowledge but very little technical skill.	SA	A	D	SD
7. When selecting people to go to another country, the best candidates are those individuals who have a subcultural (minority group) background that is the same as the culture of the country to which the individual will be assigned.	SA	A	D	SD

Following discussion of the questionnaire data, the Cultural Awareness Hierarchy is introduced.

The Cultural Awareness Hierarchy

The Cultural Awareness Hierarchy consists of six levels (Figure 1). To achieve
knowledge and understanding at level VI, one must first gain knowledge and
understanding at levels I through V. Cultural awareness training programs that
concentrate only on level VI risk failure.

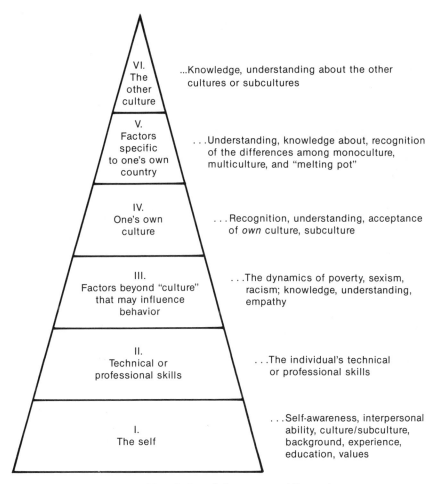

Figure 1. The Cultural Awareness Hierarchy

Copyright © 1979, Peter Muniz & Company, 41 Gifford Road, Somerset, NJ 08873 (this version slightly modified). (Reprinted with permission.)

The model is universal. It is applicable in a highly heterogeneous country or one with an apparently homogeneous cultural base. The hierarchy also may be used to deal with subcultures within one nation. The model may refer to specialized groups within a culture, such as a group of professionals as one population and their clients as another.

Level I—The self. The concept of self-understanding is the foundation of the hierarchy. It is based on personal factors, such as the individual's health, culture and subculture, education, work and other experiences, values, and interpersonal ability. Understanding at this step is fulfilled when an individual can describe how he or she relates to others and how others relate to him or her.

Why is understanding at this level so crucial before engaging in training about another culture? Take, for example, the case of a hostile individual with very little self-understanding, who alienates many people in his or her own culture. Very likely, such a person also will alienate people when working in another culture. Large doses of knowledge of the other culture will be rendered useless because of the general negative behavior and lack of self-awareness.

Level II—Technical or professional skills. Level II goes beyond personal traits and focuses on a person's technical or professional skills. An incompetent technician or professional working in another country will fail regardless of his or her knowledge about that country's culture.

Trainers and managers may be tempted to infuse large amounts of "cultural understanding" as a substitute for either confronting an individual's lack of technical/professional skills or implementing the necessary technical competency criteria in selecting individuals for assignment to other cultures.

People in host countries may have little patience with incompetent individuals who are supposed to be helping or working with them. They may view the incompetent individual as officially representing the sending country. They may believe they are held in low regard and thus receive the discards of the sending organization or country.

Level III—Factors beyond "culture" which may influence behavior. In the August 1980 *Training and Development Journal,* Luke L. Batdorf wrote, ". . . what is called a cultural problem is frequently not a cultural problem, but a problem of a different sort." When relationships between cultural groups are strained, there is a tendency to place the blame on lack of cultural understanding or, more politely, to refer to "the differences between the cultures." Frequently, this type of explanation deftly avoids the real issue—the "problem of a different sort." Level III focuses on factors **other** than obvious cultural differences as a way to confront the real issues that influence relationships and productivity.

At this level the emphasis is on identifying and understanding organizational and individual behavior in specific events, and distinguishing that behavior from what is often referred to as "cultural." Suppose, for example, people from one group are rich and people from another group are poor. The behaviors between the two groups may greatly depend upon such factors as their degree of hunger, self-interests, satisfaction of aspirations, skills and capability to function successfully. When the two groups represent different cultures or subcultures, there is a tendency to blame negative behaviors on cultural differences rather than on the real motivating forces.

Level IV—One's own culture. Most of us take our own culture for granted. We have seen it, heard it, felt it and tasted it all our lives. It is reality, and it feels right. If we were never to deal with another culture, perhaps we would never have to stop to understand our own.

However, once we need to relate to another culture, we must come to grips with our culture. After we have examined some of our basic cultural experiences, we are better able to see how people of other cultures deal with the same experiences. This examination is particularly important in the United States, where people who prepare to work in other countries generally know only one language and have had few contacts with people from other countries.

Participants' reactions to this approach are predictable. At first, they resist openly or question politely: "I came here to learn about other cultures, not my own." But after the initial difficulties, participants describe the activities as revealing, important, and satisfying.

In the U.S., a frequent cultural issue relates to the fact that one generation (or more) buried cultural aspects of their original, "native" country or culture as a price for assimilation into the dominant culture. Participants describe experiences and family stories they thought they had forgotten—about children being told not to speak their "native" tongue outside the home or to dress or behave in certain ways. These remembered events frequently are touched by rage, a sense of inferiority, or shame related to one's own cultural ties.

Level V—Factors specific to one's country. After dealing with one's culture, the next question is: What should one know about one's country? There are many topics and issues that must be understood. One issue that always emerges is diversity.

Again, using the U.S. as an example, diversity is the rule. But what kind of diversity? For generations, the U.S. was described as a "melting pot." The cultural ingredients were believed to lose their original identities and blend into a common product. More recently, however, the multicultural quality of the nation has been described as a "salad bowl." The latter image indicates a uniting of the ingredients, with each maintaining its own identity. The civil rights movement of Blacks, Hispanics, Native Americans, women, and other groups have underscored the multicultural "salad bowl" quality of the U.S.

Level VI—The other culture. Once levels I through V have been covered, level VI finally can be addressed. Trainers and consultants should apply levels I to V to themselves before attempting to train others in another country's culture. Self-awareness is extremely important for intercultural trainers.

We live by our perspectives. In her seminal study *Patterns of Culture,* Ruth Benedict warns about our temptation to view other cultures with our own as the standard. To do so leads to biased analyses and presentations of other cultures. We are in. They are out. We use such judgmental terms as **those** people, uncultured, barbaric, backwards, uncivilized, nationalistic, politically inexperienced, primitive, living in the dark ages. We accept terminology without thinking. For example, the whole world accepted a certain perspective for centuries in using the terms Far East and Mid East without realizing that they referred to distance from London.

Oversimplification that denies the modern, overlooks diversity or distorts the past may lead to misrepresentation. There are universals, alternatives, and specialties in every culture of every country. Oversimplification can give trainees a neat set of notes and a few catch phrases. Oversimplification can also lead to distortions that insult, reduce intercultural understanding, create conflict, and diminish productivity.

Flexibility in the hierarchy

The questionnaire that introduces the hierarchy should be adapted and developed according to a diagnosis of organizational and training needs. A good questionnaire contains about 18 items and touches on material at all levels of the hierarchy. Of course, the questionnaire is merely a vehicle. It rapidly moves into the background, and the major focus is on the hierarchy.

Some trainers familiar with the hierarchy have suggested that levels III, IV and V be interchanged; that levels III and V be interchanged; or that levels III and IV be interchanged. Another variation is to deal with these three intertwining levels starting with IV, then V, then III. Regardless of the position the three levels take in relation to one another, they must appear above levels I and II, and below level VI.

Traditional approaches to learning about another culture ensure a familiarity with superficial aspects of the culture. The kind of approach offered by the Cultural Awareness Hierarchy— involving, introspective, building progressively on the know—delivers a far deeper, lasting understanding of the culture, and the individual's unique response to it. In addition, the hierarchy offers a practical, methodical training system that can be adapted easily for a variety of circumstances.

REFERENCES

Batdorf, L. L. (1980, August). Culturally sensitive training. *Training and Development Journal,* pp. 28-41.

Benedict, R. (1959). *Patterns of culture.* Boston: Houghton Mifflin.

Cross-Cultural Training: A Multicultural, Pluralistic Approach

Edwin B. Fernández Bauzó

The concept of culture has been defined from different viewpoints. In this article, I present several definitions of culture and construct a composite definition to use with cross-cultural training.

- "Culture comprises inherited artifacts, goods, technical processes, ideas, habits and values" (Malinowski, 1931, p. 621).

- "Culture is the man-made part of the environment, man's symbols, ideas, values, traditions, institutions, pots and pans, and technology" (Montagu, 1961, p. 15).

- "Culture in the abstract consists of socially transmitted or learned ideas, attitudes, traits of overt behavior and suprapersonal institutions" (Steward, 1972, p. 5).

- "Culture is the way a certain society lives, the totality of manners, customs, values of a given society, inclusive of its socioeconomic system, political structure, science, religion, education, art and entertainment" (Wolman, 1973, p. 85).

- "Culture denotes a historically transmitted pattern of meanings embodied in symbols, a system of inherited conceptions expressed in symbolic forms by means of which men communicate, perpetuate, and develop their knowledge about and attitudes toward life" (Geertz, 1973, p. 89).

- "A culture can be thought of as a social system that possesses identifiable and interdependent structures or institutions. A culture is associated with a common set of shared beliefs, attitudes and values among its members, these orientations being reflected not only in the behavior of individuals but also in societal organization and functioning" (Feather, 1975, p. 195).

©1987 NTL Institute. All rights reserved.

- "Culture is fundamentally a group problem-solving tool for daily coping in a particular environment. It enables a unique group of people to grow in self-actualization and to create a distinctive world around them" (Harris & Moran, 1979, p. 10).

From these concepts, I select aspects that create a composite definition. This all-encompassing definition of culture holds that culture refers to the human-made part of our environment, that culture is an inherited and socially transmitted social system serving as a group problem-solving tool for daily coping in a particular environment, and that culture—in its most general manifestation—is the way a particular society lives, including its socioeconomic system, political structure, science, religion, education, art, and entertainment.

Cross-cultural training

The traditional conception of cross-cultural training is that of an approach to developing cultural awareness and transcultural competency in participants so that they may overcome national prejudices, habits, and actions. This is considered to allow participants to learn how to cope more adequately abroad and to work effectively in international settings. Cross-cultural training is thus based on the scientific investigation and comparison of behaviors among members of different cultural groups. This traditional conception accepts the national-geographical boundaries of a culture as the limits across which training is being offered.

This article develops the idea that cross-cultural training can also be carried out within the national-geographical boundaries of a country, and describes a program for conducting cross-cultural training. From this perspective, cross-cultural training is considered to give participants a better sense of the cultural basis of the self and helps them develop further their skills for intercultural interactions within the United States. This new way of looking at cross-cultural training is referred to as the **multicultural, pluralistic approach**.

The multicultural, pluralistic approach is based on recognizing cultural heritage and values as essential factors in understanding individuals, groups, organizations, and communities. This approach is a direct response to the special needs of pluralistic communities. The Human Interaction in a Multicultural Context Laboratory (HIMC Lab) offered by NTL Institute is the prototype workshop of the multicultural, pluralistic approach.

The HIMC Lab is an experiential program intended to promote learning about issues related to gender, race, age, ethnicity, and culture. Participants and staff are representative of the people involved in these issues, and those staffing the lab are committed to eliminating sexism, "agism," racism, and other forms of social oppression. The HIMC Lab enhances the individual's attempts to understand and reduce the effects of social oppression on the individual, both personal and professional.

The HIMC Lab is a five-day residential workshop. Sessions presenting theory address the concept of culture, the cultural basis of the self, cross-cultural communication, social oppression, and cultural pluralism. Participants can experience being part of the same cultural groups, multicultural learning groups, cross-cultural task groups (in "quintets"), and a multicultural, pluralistic community in which the majority of staff and participants are "persons of color"—that is, nonwhite. An exploratory, experiential activity is presented in the appendix to this article, and is an example of the work carried out in a multicultural lab.

Richard Arima, an Asian-American (Japanese) staff member of a multicultural lab, has said the following about the influence of culture on individuals:

> People that are born and grow into a culture and have always been in it are likely not to be very much aware of the cultural environment in which they dwell. It is only when we bump up against a different culture that we start to realize our own cultural heritage.... Our awareness of the culture within which we grew up is enhanced by contacting the anti-environment.... When we enter into another culture we experience a kind of culture shock and deal with the issue of what it means to be in a culture different from the one we have inherited. (Arima, personal communication, 1983)

One must note that within the theory and structure of the HIMC Lab cultural differences are seen as tied to different types of group membership, not limited to ethnic group membership. Both cultural differences and the socioeconomic environments of people are relevant to any type of cross-cultural training. Factors such as values, beliefs, traditions, customs, habits, and language must be specially considered when designing and implementing cross- cultural training programs, for people are sharply bound by race, gender, class, and generational and cultural values. This is the crux of the multicultural, pluralistic approach to cross-cultural training.

Prejudice, discrimination, and oppression

Prejudice is usually considered a learned prejudgment and a negative attitude (although prejudice may also be positive). When prejudice is institutionalized and backed by the existing social power structure, it is referred to as racism, sexism, agism, or some other term related to the group being discriminated against. Clark (1965), specifically addressing racial prejudice, emphasized that it debases all human beings: its victims, those who victimize, and—in quite subtle ways—those who are merely accessories to it. One can generalize this statement to all types of prejudice.

In the U.S., prejudice and discrimination are ingrained in all major institutions. Shulman (1974) found that during an experiment liberal white male college students were more willing to administer electric shocks to a black victim than to a white victim. Heussenstam (1981) conducted a study in which 15 college students, of whom none had received any traffic citations during the previous year, received a total of 33 traffic citations during the first 17 days after they had attached Black Panther bumper stickers to their cars.

A sophisticated method of **discrimination** against ethnic minorities is the measurement of intelligence. Terman (1916), one of the most influential persons in the intelligence testing movement, was convinced that black, Native American, and Mexican American children were inferior intellectually. Currently, Jensen (1969, 1973) has asserted that black people in the U.S. have an inferior intellectual potential that is not very susceptible to change under the influence of the environment.

A look at the history of the U.S. shows that violence has been an essential part of the physical and psychic domination of blacks, Native Americans, Hispanics, and Asian Americans. Harris (1974), a Native American, stated poignantly that in the U.S. Native Americans rank highest and lowest in important social matters: They have the highest rate of infant mortality and the lowest life expectancy, the highest rate of suicide and the lowest level of income, the highest rate of academic failure and the lowest level of education. Native Americans have the poorest homes and the poorest health; a high percentage of them are in prison and have been condemned to serving the harshest sentences (Harris, 1974). This clearly shows that Native Americans are an exploited, oppressed group.

Oppression is a situation in which social and economic privileges are denied to a particular class or group of people. Goldenberg (1978) asserts that to be oppressed is to be made obsolete almost from the moment of birth, making one's experience of oneself always contingent on an awareness of just how poorly one approximates the images that currently dominate a society. He affirms that oppression is a pattern of hopelessness and helplessness, in which one who is oppressed sees oneself as static, limited, and expendable.

Undoubtedly, the well-being of oppressed people in general, and of people of color in particular, is poor. Native Americans, blacks, Hispanics, and Asian Americans are an oppressed, aggrieved group of people who share a common experience of political, social, and economic exploitation. To improve the well-being of people of color and move toward the achievement of equality, an attack on all forms of social oppression is necessary.

The melting pot: The reality and the myth

The multicultural, pluralistic approach counters the idea of the U.S. as a melting pot of different people, viewing this as a sophisticated sociopolitical mechanism by which the ethnic and cultural aspects of individuals are undermined by the prevailing social order.

The melting pot notion holds that through the process of acculturation and assimilation, differences among people of diverse ethnic and cultural origins dissolve as they blend in with one another. The notion demands that different people and traditions fuse so that the U.S. can become a monocultural, monolingual society. In its essence, the concept of the melting pot seeks to force people to deny their cultural and ethnic identity and to incorporate an alien identity prescribed by the dominant group—which is white.

The melting pot notion is part of a body of ideas on which the economic, political, and social systems of the U.S. are based. It is a cultural myth rooted in the belief that national identity and strength are best achieved by demanding and imposing homogeneity on the people of the U.S. Its mythical nature is revealed when one finds that, after four centuries of history, the cultural and ethnic minorities of this nation have not melted into a homogeneous U.S. culture.

Ryan (1976), assuming a critical outlook, notes that "if there is one place in America where the melting pot is a reality, it is on the kitchen stove; in the course of one month, half the readers of this sentence have probably eaten pizza, hot pastrami, and chow mein" (p. 125).

Steinfield (1970) succinctly points out that, although white immigrants from Northern and Western Europe were "melting," blacks were enslaved, sold, denied voting rights, and lynched; Native Americans were shoved off the paths of westward expansion and massacred; Chinese and Japanese Americans were excluded; and Hispanics were conquered and oppressed.

One of the most common explanations for the "unmelting" of people of color and for the existence of inequality in the U.S. amounts to blaming the victims (Ryan, 1976). Goldenberg (1978, pp. 11-12) explains this scheme of personal culpability.

> Stated in its simplest form, the doctrine of personal culpability is a socially conditioned psychological set. Its purpose is to both encourage and predispose individuals to interpret their shortcomings or failures, their essential incompleteness, as evidence of some basically uncontrollable and, perhaps, unchangeable personal deficit. The doctrine of personal culpability serves to detract and distract one from focusing attention on the systemic constraints to growth. It encourages the internalization of blame and the heaping of abuse upon oneself. . . . The result is the transformation of social injustice into a perverted form of poetic justice: the myth is maintained by making the victim believe himself to be the principal author of his own victimization.
>
> The ultimate test of the efficiency of the doctrine of personal culpability is the degree to which the exploited individual or group incorporates the message he is asked to accept about himself and his group. . . . Indeed, oppression would be incomplete were it not for the acceptance of the notion of personal culpability by those so entreated.

Multicultural pluralism and an approach to cross-cultural training

Human life is bound and shaped by culture. Culture gives us lenses that are constructs for organizing our complex realities in meaningful ways. Cultural dimensions, such as the historical continuity of people and their psychosocial identity, are so powerful that they mold our world views and establish limits to our thoughts, feelings, and actions.

Therstrom (1980) states that ethnicity is particularly concerned with cultural content in which behaviors, thoughts, and feelings occur in a cultural context. Ethnicity exerts a ubiquitous influence on individual, family, and community life;

it influences one's attitude about life and death, and permeates all of one's life choices.

According to E. T. Hall (1977), the study and consideration of cultures and ethnicity is particularly important because people in the United States are generally intolerant of differences and tend to consider something different to be inferior. The idea of "mainstream America" reflects this stance. It legitimizes the requirement imposed on certain individuals and groups that they must abandon their sociocultural heritage when they move into mainstream cultural settings, and thus lose part of their personal identity.

Cultural pluralism offers an alternative for dealing with differences. It calls for us to understand and accept that all cultures function as models of different systems for individual, group, organizational, and community life. It asserts that the cultures of oppressed people have genuine, authentic reasons for being. Within cultural pluralism one has no choice but to move beyond one's own cultural heritage into the world of the other.

The multicultural, pluralistic approach is committed to addressing issues related to promoting multicultural social structures. It recognizes that social oppression runs deep in the U.S., with pervasive, destructive effects on individuals and groups of people. The multicultural, pluralistic approach in cross-cultural training fosters the creation of truly multicultural systems and provides participants with the knowledge and skills required to fight social oppression in specific work and social settings.

In brief, cultural pluralism first requires persons to become familiar with divergent cultures so that they can understand one another better and understand the rich diversity of human nature. Second, it requires persons to appreciate traditions of other cultures as different interpretations of life's purposes and values. Third, it requires persons to recognize the importance of other cultures' value systems. Cultural pluralism holds that a people's sense of identity is increased by diverse personal, family, group, racial, cultural, and ethnic factors—and that no culture is better than any other. Cultural pluralism takes for granted that the world is a spaceship on which human beings live. Therefore, all groups living together must relate to one another on the basis of equality, respect, tolerance, collaboration, and justice so that we can improve the quality of human life.

Cultural pluralism makes demands, both of people of color and of white people. It demands that people of color first perceive their cultures as being as valuable as the culture of white people, because all cultures are equal. It demands that we be familiar with different cultural groups and aware of the rich diversity of human nature; variety is the spice of life, and gives color and interest to society. Cultural pluralism demands that we appreciate other cultures' traditions and ways of being as different interpretations of the purpose of life. We must recognize the importance of other cultural groups' value systems.

Cultural pluralism demands that white people first appreciate different people, groups, and cultures. It demands that white people accept oppressed people's cultures as they are and not require that oppressed people become like themselves. It demands that white people endure ambiguity and be willing to live in conflict so that they can celebrate the many diverse capabilities within themselves. Finally, it demands that white people be able and willing to defend others' right to "be," and that white people confront other whites when necessary and otherwise act to fight oppression.

The impact of the multicultural, pluralistic approach in cross-cultural training is exemplified by the following statement from Michael Brazzel (quoted with his permission), a white male participant of the HIMC Lab:

> The multicultural lab provides whites with the rare chance to look at what it means to be white in a white-dominated society and to participate in a pluralistic learning community. . . . The multicultural lab gave me an opportunity to reflect on what it means to be a white man in a white-dominated society. I renewed my understanding that I am linked with people, that actions or support I give for oppression of others is fundamentally damaging to me in my life and death. (Brazzel, personal communication, 1983)

Given the current sociopolitical status of the world today, its increasingly "smaller size," and the skills leaders require to function adequately in this smaller world, creating and promoting a multicultural, pluralistic social system is a reasonable, worthwhile goal worth fighting for.

REFERENCES

Clark, K. B. (1965). *Dark ghetto.* New York: Harper & Row.

Feather, N. T. (1975). *Values in education and society.* New York: The Free Press.

Geertz, C. (1973). *The interpretation of cultures.* New York: Basic Books.

Goldenberg, I. (1978). *Oppression and social intervention.* Chicago: Nelson-Hall.

Hall, E. T. (1973). *The silent language.* New York: Anchor-Doubleday.

Harris, L. (1974). Preface. In K. Irvine (Ed.), *Encyclopedia of Indians of the Americas.* Ann Arbor, MI: Scholarly Press.

Harris, P. R., & Moran, R. T. (1979). *Managing cultural differences.* Houston: Gulf Publishing Co.

Heussenstamm, F. K. (1971). Bumper stickers and the cops. *Transaction, 8,* 32-33.

Jensen, A. R. (1969). How much can we boost IQ and scholastic achievement? *Harvard Educational Review, 39,* 1-123.

Jensen, A. R. (1973). *Educability and group differences.* New York: Basic Books.

Malinowski, B. (1931). Culture. *Encyclopedia of the social sciences* (Vol. 4, p. 621). New York: Macmillan.

Montagu, A. (1961). Culture and mental illness. *American Journal of Psychiatry, 118,* 15-23.

Ryan, W. *(1976). Blaming the victim.* New York: Random House.

Shulman, G. I. (1974). *Race, sex and violence. American Journal of Sociology, 79,* 1260-1277.

Steinfield, M. (1970). *Cracks in the melting pot: Racism and discrimination in American history.* Beverly Hills: Glencoe Press.

Steward, J. H. (Ed.)(1972). *The people of Puerto Rico: A study in social anthropology.* Urbana, IL: University of Illinois Press.

Terman, L. M. (1916). *The measurement of intelligence.* Boston: Houghton Mifflin.

Therstrom, S., Orlov, A., & Handlin, O. (1980). *Harvard encyclopedia of American ethnic groups.* Cambridge, MA: Harvard University Press.

Wolman, B. B. (Ed.) (1973). *Dictionary of behavioral science.* New York: Van Nostrand.

APPENDIX

Cultural pluralism: An exploratory activity

The following structured exercise was designed by Joan Bordman and me to be used with multicultural populations and with groups of diverse cultures and ethnic origins. The goals are the following:

- to help persons from diverse cultures develop lists of cultural values so that they may look at differences in a pluralistic manner;
- to help persons from diverse cultures develop and share values of their own cultures or ethnic groups;
- to help persons from diverse cultural and ethnic groups behave according to values not typical of their own cultures or ethnic groups (these should be values to which they are attracted); and
- to encourage pluralistic behavior.

Group size. This exercise is designed for 8-10 participants. Several groups may be directed simultaneously.

Time. Part I requires two hours, as does Part II.

Materials. The exercise requires newsprint pads, felt-tip marking pens, and masking tape.

Physical setting. The exercise requires enough space to allow participants to talk freely and move around without interrupting the work of others.

Part I

The facilitator should begin by spending approximately five minutes defining cultural pluralism and its related behavioral components.

Definition. The idea of cultural pluralism has been viewed by many as an alternative for dealing with differences among people, especially those related to social, religious, language, ethnic, and cultural differences. Cultural pluralism demands that people accept, understand, and value the idea that all cultures serve as significant models for human life for different groups of people. Cultural pluralism finds that all cultures are genuine and offer legitimate reasons for being and feeling. It also finds that no culture is better than any other. Finally, cultural pluralism finds that people's healthy sense of identity is enriched by diverse family, ethnic, cultural, and national factors. All existing human groups with different combinations of these factors should live together on a basis of equality, collaboration, respect, tolerance, sympathy, and justice so as to improve the quality of human life.

Values. The facilitator should next ask participants to spend about 10 minutes developing their own lists of values, giving them the following examples that have come from past use of this exercise:

- black: adaptability, loving life, nurturing;

- Hispanic: family life, competence, friendship;
- Native American: giving, patience, mystical;
- Asian: respect of age, family, perseverance; and
- white: theoretical, emphasis on the individual, competition.

Dyads. The facilitator should ask participants to form dyads (pairs), with each dyad consisting of two persons from the same ethnic and/or cultural background. The dyads should then discuss which values they agree represent their cultural backgrounds (this should take 20 minutes).

Cultural/ethnic group values. The dyads should be asked to gather with all the other pairs from their own cultural and/or ethnic groups so that they may select the values common to all the dyads within one's group or that appear most frequently. Each group should write on newsprint five values that meet these criteria (this should take 20 minutes).

Discussion. The values representing the various cultures and/or ethnic backgrounds should then be reported to all participants and discussed in detail (this should take 35 minutes).

Part II

Part II has two purposes. First, it seeks to help persons from diverse cultural and ethnic groups behave according to values not typical of their own cultural and/or ethnic groups but to which they are attracted. Second, it encourages pluralistic behavior.

Definition. The facilitator should spend 10 minutes presenting the definition of cultural pluralism and its behavioral components.

Value examination. Each participant should look at the lists of values for those groups to which one does not belong. The facilitator should ask each participant to choose the value from those lists that one is most attracted to so that one may experiment behaving according to this value (this should take 15 minutes).

Pairs. Each participant should select a person from the group whose value has been chosen and ask that person to teach one how to behave according to that value (this should take 10 minutes).

Trios. Participants should form trios (groups of three) with persons of the same cultural and/or ethnic background. They should behave according to the values they have chosen, with each person spending 15 minutes behaving experimentally while the other two interact to make the experience enriching to the group (this should take a total of 45 minutes).

Reflection. After each trio has allowed each member to experiment, the facilitator should give the participants five minutes to spend time alone thinking about their experiences in their trios.

Discussion. The trios should then be asked to reunite so that they may share their realizations gained during reflection on their new experiences, and talk about what they consider most significant. Each trio should then develop a statement to give to all the participants about the exercise (this should take 30 minutes).

Group statements. All the participants should meet to listen to the reports of the trios (this should take 30 minutes).

Structure. The facilitator may give more structure to the group statements by asking the trios to answer the following or similar questions:

- How easy or difficult was it for you to behave according to your chosen value?

- What factors helped you to behave according to your chosen value? What factors inhibited you?

- In what ways were you able to accept and encourage others to be "different" from you? In what ways were you unable to do this?

- If you were to repeat this exercise, what would you find not helpful to you?

Actualizing Synergistic Multicultural Training Programs

Patricia Bidol

What is the impact of actualizing a synergistic multicultural training (MCT) program? In an MCT program, participants celebrate their differences and enjoy the richness of their diversity as they equitably interact with one another (NTL Institute, 1980). They create a training group with a cultural climate that fulfills their joint needs without violating their individual identities (Moran & Harris, 1982). After completing this training, participants can more effectively interact with groups from the same and different cultures. They thus create an innovative group culture—which is synergistic—rather than only cooperatively sharing knowledge about their own cultures.

This article is designed to increase trainers' capacitites to facilitate MCT programs. It focuses on the milieu of laboratory education, but the principles and approaches discussed are applicable to most training approaches used within organizations or external learning workshops. This article presents an overview of the current theory, concepts, and interventions used by multicultural practitioners, discussing the following:

- the goals of laboratory education,
- assumptions regarding multicultural T Group training,
- a model for synergistic multicultural training,
- factors present in MCT programs,
- the functioning of trainers in MCT programs, and
- the directions for research assessing trainers, processes, participant learnings, and the impacts of MCT programs.

In their review of the history of T Groups, Bradford, Gibb, and Benne stated that the laboratory education approach was developed because of the following:

©1987 NTL Institute. All rights reserved.

> The founders of the first laboratory saw the group as the link between the individual person and the larger social structure... [with] the group serving two sets of interrelated functions: the re-education of the individual toward greater integrity, greater understanding of himself and of the social conditions of his life, greater behavioral effectiveness in planning and achieving changes in his social environment, and the facilitation of changes in the larger social structures upon which individual lives depend. (Bradford, Gibb, & Benne, 1964, p. 5)

MCT programs are designed to enable participants to function more effectively in settings in which individuals from diverse cultural heritages interact with one another. An MCT program such as the Human Interaction in a Multicultural Context Laboratory offered by NTL Institute is based on recognition of the participants' cultural heritages and values as essential to understanding themselves and relating positively to others. MCT programs typically seek to do the following:

- enable participants to increase their awareness of their own personal and cultural traditions,
- increase participants' abilities to recognize the strengths and limitations of monocultural strategies in a multicultural work setting,
- increase participants' awareness of their own behavior and their behavior's effects on others,
- increase participants' awareness of cultural behavior options, and
- increase participants' skills in working effectively with monocultural and multicultural groups.

If an MCT program has these goals, the expected outcomes are that participants will be able to assess their behaviors from a cultural perspective, to plan and implement support groups of persons from the same and other cultures in their back-home settings, to diagnose organizational barriers to pluralistic behavior, to assess the impact of social oppression such as racism and sexism on themselves and others, and to create more effective multicultural work groups.

Assumptions regarding multicultural training

MCT prepares adults to live positively in a culturally diverse society, to respect cultural differences and similarities, and to resist dehumanizing others because of their race, ethnicity, sex, class, age, or other differences. MCT strives to provide participants with the values, skills, and knowledge to make maximum use of the inherent capabilities of all members of society. The following assumptions underlie MCT.

1. The sociopolitical climate of the United States forces persons to conform to the white culture of the majority and does not provide mainstream society support for maintaining the country's multiple cultural heritages (Padilla, 1981).
2. In a multicultural society, many individuals possess bicultural membership, with accompanying pressures to remain loyal to the subculture while

maintaining the capacity to function in mainstream society (Padilla, 1981).

3. Most training, including MCT, is often conceptualized and implemented in mainstream Western, individualistic terms, which may not meet the learning needs of individuals from different cultural heritages (Ivey, 1981; Schein, 1981).

4. Process features such as training norms, decision making, leadership styles, and dimensions of incongruity are usually based on mainstream, monocultural norms (Ivey, 1981).

5. MCT programs recognize that all cultural groups have both similarities to and differences from mainstream culture, and that both should be supported (AACTE Commission on Multicultural Education, 1980).

6. MCT programs recgonize that equitable distribution of resources requires fully democratic and multicultural decision making, leadership functions, and communication styles (Ramirez & Castaneda, 1974).

7. MCT programs enable participants to identify the intrapersonal and interpersonal impacts of social oppression both on members of traditionally powerful cultural groups and of culturally oppressed groups. This process includes such dimensions as moral confusion, social ambivalence, internalized oppression, and double social psychological consciousness (Avakian, 1982; Memmi, 1968).

8. The most effective MCT programs are designed by multicultural teams of trainers, or at least based on the norms of the cultures with an impact on the training (Bidol, 1981).

A synergistic multicultural training model

The implementation of synergistic multicultural training, according to my conception, is based on the following premises.

- As a result of the discussions among individuals from diverse cultures on "affectively loaded" topics, this training occurs in a dynamic, fluid, turbulent environment.

- Most participants are bicultural (e.g., Armenian-American individuals or black Americans) and face concomitant stress regarding one's identity.

- Because the dominant culture has such ubiquitous effects, the trainers and participants find it difficult to avoid being unduly influenced by its norms as they strive to create a synergistic multicultural training climate.

- Effective MCT programs are implemented with a blend of traditional and nontraditional processes.

This model is based on the open systems theory approach used by organization development consultants to change the formal and informal tasks and processes of an organizational system. The model's "input" sources are transformed to produce multiple "outputs." Figure 1 illustrates that these input, transforma-

tion, and output features are not independent, but interactive. This interacton—
or "interface"—among components causes the MCT program dynamics to be in
a constant state of flux. The model indicates that **the probability of two-way interaction among the components is always present.** For example, the communication style of each person is influenced by that person's cultural identity, and the
interaction among those with different communication styles influences the trust
levels of group members.

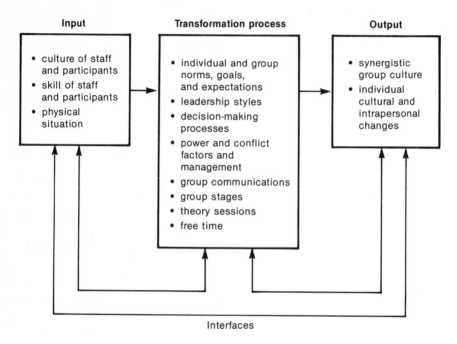

Figure 1. Synergistic multicultural training model

The multicultural aspects of the model's compnents are discussed in greater
detail below.

The **inputs** of the model include the following:

- the cultures of the staff and participants, including all aspects of each
  individual's cultural identity;

- the staff and participants' skills in group processes involving such matters as communication, leadership, decision making, and conflict
  resolution;

- the physical situation, including the geographic location of the laboratory,
  the nature of the rooms and food, and reactions of "locals" to laboratory
  staff and participants (e.g., reactions of locals in a rural Southern setting to multicultural laboratory members, or reactions of urban participants to walking at night to sleeping quarters in an unlighted, isolated
  rural area).

The **transformation processes** are the interactions of the following individual, group, and community-level components:

- individual and group norms, goals, and expectations for the outcomes for each individual and for the group;
- the leadership styles of the staff and participants and the cultural implications of these;
- the decision-making processes of the staff and group members, the cultural implications for the cultures they reflect, and their impact on all members;
- power and conflict factors, their management by the group, and their cultural dimensions;
- group communications, including styles, first and second language dimensions, oral and nonverbal means, and intercultural aspects;
- group stages of development, from entry to closure, including the impacts of cultural aspects on individuals and the group;
- theory sessions on generic training and multicultural topics;
- free time and its impact on the intrapersonal internalization of learnings and on the interactions among individuals (including the presence or absence of multicultural interactions.)

The **outputs** occur at several levels for each of the individual, group, and community dimensions, having at least minimal interdependence with the other levels. These outputs include the following:

- synergistic group culture formation—or the lack of it—and the impact of this on each individual's belief in and capacity to create synergistic group cultures in the back-home environment;
- changes in the cultural and intrapersonal identities of individual group members. Some practitioners believe that some aspects of each individual's personality are generic to all humans, but that many are shaped by cultural influences. As discussed below, changes in cultural identities can make participants more accommodating to the existing culture of the majority, or can create viable and equitable synergistic multicultural identities, or can deepen one's existing monocultural identity.

The **interfaces** of the model represent the interdependence of the components. The degree to which mutual benefits occur is a byproduct of the nature of the interactions among units. During the transformation processes, dysfunctional outcomes from the interactions usually result from a lack of desire for in-depth multicultural interactions or from a lack of ability to use in a positive way various cultural approaches in such areas as communications, decision making, leadership, or conflict management.

Factors affecting multicultural training groups

In MCT programs, many factors are present that result from the mix of cultural patterns and assumptions of the group. In this section I review the impact of

"metagoals," multiple world views, racial identity development, multicultural communications, assumed similarities, and assumed differences on the life of MCT
programs.

The metagoals of different MCT programs can be diverse. These can range
from fostering accommodation to the status quo, to deepening the basic cultural
identity of an individual, to expanding participants' capacities both to value their
heritages and to function positively in the mainstream culture (Draguns, 1981).
Multicultural group goals could also be evaluated along two axes: the "emic-etic"
axis and the "autoplastic-alloplastic" axis (Draguns, 1981). At the emic end, one
assumes that all training is embedded in its cultural context, and at the etic extreme one assumes that Western training is universally applicable (with minor
modifications). Autoplastic training changes are changes in the individual participants, and alloplastic changes are those in the external environment of the participants. Synergistic MCT programs face the challenge of enabling participants
to balance the degree of individual and system change so that their learning needs
are met without violating their basic values. A synergistic MCT program empowers all participants and provides them with new insights into the creation of
equitable multicultural groups, organizaitons, and systems (Bidol, 1981).

The multiple world views of a multicultural laboratory's participants also affect the laboratory's interactions and the training outcomes. As a multicultural
group interacts to produce a positive synergistic cultural climate, it must surface
the various world views of its members. These are used to create a climate in which
all the viewponts can be accepted and used as the foundation for perspectives that
reflect the needs of this group. These perspectives include the following:

- fact finding should be objective and use the scientific method, versus
  the view that it should be subjective, holistic, and intuitive;
- individual growth occurs when the individual functions at a self-contained
  and individual level, versus the view that it occurs when the individual
  functions better with respect to her or his reference group;
- leadership should be based on ideological contribution, versus the view
  that it should be based on power and skill;
- leaders are extremely assertive, versus the view that they help all become
  "leaders";
- equity is more important than accommodation to mainstream culture;
- group-level interactions are more important than individual-level
  interactions;
- all individuals control their own fates, versus the view that social oppression contributes to the degree of control an ethnic group member
  possesses.

Individuals in race-conscious societies are consciously or unconsciously resolv-
ing the implications of their racial identities (Jackson & Hardiman, 1982). Societies
that are gender conscious or class conscrious, or conscious of other cultural differences, also cause individuals to resolve the implications of these differences.

As a result, all members of these societies consciously or unconsciously resolve aspects of their personalities, such as race, sex, or ethnicity. The stages individuals undergo as they perform these developmental tasks are similar, whether they address racial identity development or gender development. In MCT programs, as evident from the following description of typical development behaviors, group members must be able to identify the stages their groups are currently undergoing. This awareness of the stage of an MCT program should enable group members to design appropriate ways of interacting with one another.

Jackson and Hardiman (1982) developed a model for racial identity development in which they identified five major developmental stages that individuals experience as they grow toward a positive racial identity.

1. The **naive stage** is present during childhood and not likely to appear during an MCT program.

2. At the **acceptance stage**, a member of a minority or majority culture in the U.S. perceives that "white is always right." White standards, beliefs, practices, and world views must be implemented everywhere (including all aspects of an MCT program). Racism is not considered relevant, because minorities who work hard enough should succeed. Minority group members at this stage want to be acceptable to whites and probably try to look as "white" as possible in their dress, speech, and interactions. Whites at this stage are either openly bigoted or "color blind," and believe that minority groups are not ready for true leadership positions. MCT program members at this stage do not want a synergistically pluralistic group, but rather one that operates from white cultural assumptions.

3. At the **resistance stage**, the member of a minority group values her or his racial heritage and identifies the presence of racism in all Western organizations. Individuals are outraged at the racial injustices perpetuated by the white culture on minority cultures, and whites are thus viewed with suspicion by minority group members. The minority group member becomes distanced from members of the majority culture and their practices. Whites at the resistance stage recognize that racism pervades the entire culture and that whites in this society benefit from racist practices. They become active in activities designed to eradicate racism.

4. At the **redefinition stage**, individual minority group members redefine their cultural identities in terms that are not reactive to white culture but that actively identify aspects of their own cultural heritages. This usually requires that the individual psychologically and socially limit her or his interactions with whites. Whites at this stage focus their identities on defining "whiteness" so that this acknowledges both racism and the positive aspects of white culture. In MCT programs, minority group members at this stage are not interested in forming synergistic multicultural groups. White MCT program members actively explore the strengths and limitations of their culture and cannot plan synergistic multicultural groups.

5. At the **internationalization stage**, minority group members and whites actively integrate their new consciousness into all aspects of their identities and role functions. They work to eradicate racism and to work in interracial networks to create viable multiracial organizations. In MCT programs, group members

at this stage work to interact authentically with all members and desire to create an authentically, mutually empowering multicultural group.

Communication in cross-cultural groups is complex because of the various cultural communication patterns present. In addition, in multicultural groups many individuals are speaking in a second language, rather than their native languages. The use of first and second languages in a group increases the probability of group members' losing fleeting allusions, nuances of intonations, and subtleties of gestures present in the group's communications or their own. They will have the illusion that full meaning is shared unless they or the trainer initiate multicultural feedback processes to ascertain the degree to which communications are being received. Intercultural communications are shaped by interactions that are both verbal and nonverbal, implicit and explicit, preconscious and conscious, intentional and unintentional (Wright, 1984). Without violating cultures that value the implicit, indirect expression of one's thoughts and feelings, the effectiveness of multicultural groups is increased when the members understand all the ways they shape their communications.

In multicultural groups, the phenonmena of "assumed shared similarities" and "assumed differences" are probably present. If someone from a different cultural background dresses, speaks, and walks in the fashion of another's culture, one often assumes that few cultural differences exist between these two interacting individuals (assumed similarity). If someone walks, dreses, or talks in a manner different from that of another's culture, one assumes many cultural differences exist between the two interacting individuals (assumed differences).

The phenomenon of assumed differences increases in intensity when persons who appear culturally different are vastly outnumbered in a group. The cultural group processes of the culture of the majority of the group members is usually considered normative for the group. These assumptions cause misinterpretations among the group members. Effective multicultural interactions require group processes to be shaped by the members and the trainer if they are to respond to different cultural, intersubjective needs of group members. The capacity to respond to the cultural, intersubjective needs of participants requires that stereotypes operating in an MCT program be identified and replaced with positive images. In effective multicultural groups, each member accurately understands one's self, one's cross-cultural interactions, and others.

The role of the trainer
in multicultural training sitations

As presented in the synergistic multicultural training model, interdependence exists between inputs and the transformation process (the outputs). That is, the cultures of the staff and participants (inputs) affect the interactions of the training group (transformation process). If the participants and trainer do not explicitly describe their different cultural reactions to the group's decision-making process, leadership styles, conflict management styles, and the like, then they will likely perpetuate their stereotypes of one another or impose the culture of the majority on all the members (outcomes). The following research findings and recommendations for trainers have enabled multicultural groups to produce training situations supportive of all the members' goals and growth.

During my research on NTL T Groups, I found that several mutlicultural issues emerge during the development of both the individual and the group. Although multiculrual issues are not the only dimensions of the group's life, they do affect the growth of the group in areas such as leadership style, decision making, and communication patterns (Bidol, 1980). This research on 40 multicultural participants of the Human Interaction Laboratory identified their perceptions that the following multicultural factors were significant for their T Groups.

1. They felt safer exploring their racial/ethnic "mind sets" and preferred cultural interaction styles if the trainers established an explicit norm at the first session regarding the inclusion of multicultural issues in a "generic" laboratory (this was not advertised as a multicultural training program).

2. Trainers who shared their multicultural identities and problems were positive role models for group members to do the same.

3. Sessions on theories of multicultural communications and racism (and other forms of social oppression) were extremely helpful.

4. When trainers and group members surfaced multicultural aspects of the group's communications, the groups could consciously include multicultural awareness into their generic group processes.

5. The inclusion of racial development issues for minority group members and whites enabled all group members to become engaged in discussing racial development concerns.

6. Whenever trainers or group members did not process key multicultural aspects of the group's life, this reinforced the participants' feelings that these issues were too volatile to examine consistently.

7. When trainers or group members denied their own dysfunctional multicultural group behaviors, this perpetuated the tendency to fail to "own" these behaviors, thus making them difficult to modify.

8. When group members could process both subtle and obvious aspects of multicultural interactions, their learnings were enriched. Readers should note that the most effective multicultural comments were presented along with generic process comments on given group interactions. Merely commenting on multicultural issues during a time period devoted to multicultural issues was not helpful, nor was it considered helpful for trainers and group members to make multicultural observations without including generic training observations.

9. The inclusion of a few formally scheduled "same-culture" sessions during the total community sessions was considered helpful.

10. Using various cultural communication modes, leadership styles, and

decision-making processes deepened a group's capacity to create a synergistic multicultural group.

Research on multicultural groups and the experience of successful multicultural practitioners have identified the following as key concepts for multicultural trainers.

1. Trainers must use a variety of intervention styles so that they can facilitate the growth of group members from diverse cultural backgrounds (Sue, 1981).

2. Racial development theory and theory of world views should be correlated with process variables in multicultural groups (Sue, 1981).

3. Trainers must avoid any tendencies to assess participants' motivation by unconsciously judging the congruence of their learning goals with those of the trainer or the majority of the group (Lambert, 1981).

4. Trainers must realize that the risk of joining a T Group is often higher for a participant from a minority group (Block, 1981).

5. Many researchers perceive that participants will be more trusting and disclose more if the trainer and most group members are of the same cultural background as the participant (Block, 1981).

6. The denial of racial differences in a group denies the salience of being a minority group member in a white racist society and ignores the impact of group members' and trainers' being white (Block, 1981).

7. Using silence, story telling, and guided imagery facilitates the sharing of cultural traditions of many minority cultures (Moss & Goldstein, 1973; Nujoweket of the Micmacs, 1978).

Within the multicultural group, the effective MCT trainer exhibits the following behaviors:

1. The trainer enables the group to increase its awareness and appreciation of members' own and one another's cultures.

2. The trainer is well versed in various cultural mind sets and communication patterns and uses this knowledge appropriately in commenting on process and discussing theory.

3. The trainer facilitates the group's capacity to make decisions that are individually acceptable and compatible with all of the members' cultures.

4. The trainer enables the group to positively accept the ambiguity accompanying the formation of a synergistic, multicultural group.

5. The trainer is knowledgeable about the individual, group, organizational, and societal manifestations of prejudices and social oppression—such as racism or sexism—and enables group members to see how prejudice and social oppression are overtly and covertly present in the interactions of the MCT program.

6. The trainer understands the theory of racial development and facilitates

the positive growth of minority and majority group members in MCT programs.

Summary and conclusions

The increasing formation of multicultural training programs and the inclusion of multicultural concerns in generic training programs are promising trends that support the actualization of a democratic society that is equitable and pluralistic. At this time, action research is needed to build upon existing perceptions of effective multicultural training. The research model proposed by NTL Institute (1980) is a systems model focusing on the following variables:

1. situational variables such as the cultural composition of staff and participants, laboratory climate, and the impact of multicultural research on the laboratory;

2. dynamics of multiculturalism, racism, and sexism in formal and informal laboratory settings;

3. staff behavior with respect to multicultural issues, including racism and sexism;

4. outcomes as perceived by staff and participants.

The use of macrolevel research models such as NTL's and research on the microlevel behavior of staff and partricipants should contribute to the theoretical and practical bases used by mutlicultural trainers.

REFERENCES

AACTE Commission on Multicultural Education. (1980). *Multicultural teacher education: Guidelines for implementation* (Vol. 4). Washington, DC: American Association of Colleges of Teacher Education.

Avakian, A. V. (1982). Myth of the melting pot: The relationship of non-dominant cultures to American culture. *New England Women's Studies Association Seminar, Salem, MA.*

Bidol, P. (1980). *Research on racism and sexism in an NTL Human Interaction Laboratory in summer of 1980.* Unpublished findings.

Bidol, P. (1981). A preservice model for multicultural education. In M. Dawson, E. F. Provenzo, R. L. Collins, C. Nieto, C., & P. Bidol (Eds.), *Educational equity: The integration of equity into preservice teacher education programs.* Washington, DC: ERIC Clearinghouse on Teacher Education.

Block, C. P. (1981). Black Americans and the cross-counseling and psychotherapy experience. In A. J. Marsella & P. B. Pedersen (Eds.), *Cross-cultural counseling and psychotherapy.* New York: Pergamon Press.

Bradford, L. P., Gibb, J.R., & Benne, K. D. (1964). Two educational innovations. In L. P. Bradford, J. R. Gibb, & K. D. Benne (Eds.), *T-Group theory and laboratory method.* New York: John Wiley & Sons.

Dennis, R. M. (1981). Socialization and racism: The white experience. In B. P. Bowser & R. G. Hunt (Eds.), *Impacts of racism on white Americans.* Beverly Hills: Sage.

Draguns, J. C. (1981). Cross-cultural counseling and psychotherapy: History, issues, current status. In A. J. Marsella & P. B. Pedersen (Eds.), *Cross-cultural counseling and psychotherapy.* New York: Pergamon Press.

Ivey, A. E. (1981). Counseling and psychotherapy: Toward a new perspective. In A. J. Marsella & P. B. Pedersen (Eds.), *Cross-cultural counseling and psychotherapy.* New York: Pergamon Press.

Jackson, B. W., & Hardiman, R. (1982). *Racial identity development: Implications for managing the multi-racial workforce.* Unpublished manuscript.

Lambert, M. J. (1981). Evaluating outcome varaiables in cross-cultural counseling and psychotherapy. In A. J. Marsella & P. B. Pedersen (Eds.) *Cross-cultural counseling and psychotherapy.* New York: Pergamon Press.

Memmi, A. (1968). *Dominated man.* Boston: Beacon Press.

Moran, R. T., & Harris, P. R. (1982). *Managing cultural synergy.* Houston: Gulf Publishing Press.

Moss, R. N., & Goldstein, G. S. (1973). An encounter experience among the Navajo. *Social Change, 3,* 3-6.

NTL Institute. (1980). *Issues on racism for NTL trainers.* Paper prepared during Workshop for Professional Development in Racism, Cincinnati.

Nujoweket of the Micmacs. (1978). *Indian plan for research on whites.* Unpublished data.

Padilla, A. M. (1981). Pluralistic counseling and psychotherapy for Hispanic Americans. In A. J. Marsalla & P. B. Pederson (Eds.), *Cross-cultural counseling and psychotherapy.* New York: Pergamon Press.

Ramirez, M. & Castaneda, A. (1974). *Cultural democracy, bicognitive development, and education.* New York: Academic Press.

Schein, E. H. (1981). Does Japanese management style have a message for American managers? *Sloan Management Review, 23,* 55-68.

Sue, D. W. (1981). Evaluating process variables in cross-cultural counseling and psychotherapy. In A. J. Marsella & P. B. Pederson, (Eds.), *Cross-cultural counseling and psychotherapy.* New York: Pergamon Press.

Wright, J. E. (1984). The implications of cognitive science. In W. G. Gudykunst & Y. Y. Kim (Eds.), *Methods for intercultural communication research* (pp. 31-46). Beverly Hills: Sage.

Doing Training, Doing Us

Dick Vittitow
Marion Vittitow

Those in the Sri Lankan Sarvodaya Shramadana Movement hold the view that whatever a person does in service to the community also affects that person. This is best expressed through the example of the individual who volunteers to build a road for the community: As that person builds the road, the road builds that person (Macy, 1983). This idea that the "doing" affects the internal self as the external world is changed connects strongly with how we have come to feel about— and conceive of—training. If we allow it, the more we work with training, the more training works with us.

This article outlines some of the guidelines that have emerged for us as a result of this process in which training affects views and attitudes toward training, as well as the underlying assumptions that influence and determine them. We relate how our views of training changed and expanded because of doing a specific workshop, Leadership for Development: A Program in Effective Application of Development Theories and Skills at the Community Level (referred to hereafter as "L/Dev"), offered by NTL Institute.

We are not talking about the significant learnings gained during training, but look at a different level—a deeper or higher level of learnings. We are focusing on how our "world view"—or philosophy, or paradigm—of training was affected. We are describing how a level of previously existing principles, emotional awareness, and beliefs was stirred up and resettled in a new contextual/conceptual framework from which we now view training.

What emerged from this experience was a strengthening of values already held, a revealing of firmer directions in our life and work, an offering of new guidelines for how we ought to work and what we ought to act upon. As a result of the workshop, how we saw reality changed and caused us to act differently. This shift in our work as trainers is what we wish to describe.

Paulo Freire identifies a process of the individual in reflection and action that is similar to what we attempt to describe in this article. For Freire, as an individual reflects on reality, this reflection process stirs in one a requirement for action.

©1987 NTL Institute. All rights reserved.

Action changes reality. As a result, the individual must then reflect on this new reality, which may again demand action (Freire, 1970). We especially are concerned with the part of Freire's work that addresses how doing our work not only affects the external world, but also begins to affect the internal world—is, us.

For us, then, training is much more than a process through which adults learn new skills, information, values, and attitudes. Training can be an active engagement and a deliberate strategy in which persons work on issues of personal development that affect not only themselves but the external world.

We feel strongly that personal development is a thread to global development. Training, as life work and not just a job, not only involves being of service to others, but also the ways being of service supports one's own development.

We hope this article is supportive, especially to those actively reviewing the meaning of their work. Too often, we believe, such review is conceived of and based solely on the work of training as a business or profession. In reviewing one's work during the year, trainers may choose criteria based on how well they are doing compared to others, on the number of days they work during the year, on the number of corporate clients they have, or on the amount of money they make. Instead, we seek to identify a personal set of criteria based on such questions as the following: Am I doing in my work what my life requires? How am I being affected by the work I am doing? Am I growing, changing, developing in the ways I want?

Building a road can be drudgery; so can training. According to the Sri Lankan Buddhists, however, both the road and training can be seen as paths to spiritual development. We are just beginning to know this.

Leadership for Development Workshop

Before describing the emerging guidelines coming from our work with the L/Dev workshop, we briefly describe its purposes and design. Within this context, the "road" we were working to build may become clearer, and we hope the guidelines that evolved as the road refocused us will become meaningful.

As we worked in Nepal with a new Integrated Rural Development Program, we became aware—as we had in earlier work in Indonesia, Bangladesh, and other developing countries—that persons dedicated to development were hungry for skills, concepts, and methods to make their important work with the poor and disenfranchised more effective and satisfying for all concerned.

We felt the need for a workshop specifically addressed to the needs of these "leaders" of development programs and activities, because so little is known about the leadership elements that can be successfully learned and applied, especially to Third World development efforts. We also recognized that not only would the design of such a program be demanding, but that to promote and gain participants from throughout the Third World and then administer the program would be extremely difficult.

We responded to these complex issues in February 1981 by proposing to NTL Institute that we work together with this organization to develop the L/Dev workshop. After a slow process of piecing together a network through which to promote the workshop, and exploring and finally creating a design, the first workshop was held in August 1983 and the second a year later, both in Bethel, Maine. The program directly responds to NTL's mission statement and commitment to social action, and was its first to focus on Third World development.

The program is designed for men and women from Third World countries involved in planning, implementing, and coordinating programs to develop community resources in service to the poor. It has been attended by persons from countries in Africa, Asia, and Central and South America. The participants are asked to come in teams if this is possible. They work in large government organizations, small agencies, and private voluntary organizations. During these two years, for example, we have had host country staff from the Peace Corps, Foster Parents Plan, housing programs in Panama, the Permanent Secretary of Cooperatives and Marketing—and his staff—from Uganda, and National Training Institute staff from Zaire.

For our definition of development, we accept that of President Nyerere of Tanzania:

> The expansion of one's own consciousness, and therefore of one's power over one's self, one's environment, and one's society, must ultimately be what we mean by development.

We make a number of assumptions about development based on major research and experience, and we explore and test these assumptions throughout the workshop.

- Development is basically a learning issue (not just an economic or technical issue).
- Leadership is the major factor in developing systems appropriate to the disenfranchised.
- Effective team efforts are essential to successful development programs.
- Organizational structures, programs, and resources should be shaped by the unique needs of the problems and people to whom they are addressed.
- Organizational, community, and national development has as its base self/personal development.

The approach used is highly participative and experiential, in contrast to the educational methods used in most of the countries represented. The participants live during the workshop in a common area with equal, shared living arrangements that enable a support and learning community to develop. Some of the workshop sessions are held in the living area so as to strengthen this community.

Each of the program's 14 days is designed using a specific theme, with the morning devoted to theories, concepts, and back-home applications and the afternoons to practicing pertinent skills (i.e., specific skills of participation, coordination, "bottom-up" planning, dissemination, action research, taking initiative, and creative adaptation) and clarifying values and attitudes. The evenings are set aside for personal development group work, with participants deciding how to focus best on their own learnings, back-home needs, work in a small groups, and professional and personal growth. In these small groups each participant presents a dilemma that person confronts back home, and the group responds with analysis and consultation.

Many of the activities involved small groups. This is not only done to complete tasks, but also to increase the participants' skills in managing and developing task-team effectiveness. The workshop uses films, case studies, readings, and discussions to give participants ample opportunities to clarify and articulate values and attitudes about development work, development programs, and their own involvement.

Many of the workshop experiences are designed so that throughout the workshop persons explore and live what they wish to learn. All of us have found our learnings gained during the program to be rich and satisfying.

Emerging guidelines

From these experiences, guidelines have emerged that strongly influence and affect our training work and life. The following materials set in bold type emphasize these guidelines.

1. Criteria for our decision. Trainers use numerous different criteria in determining what training they are going to provide and with whom they are going to work. For us, practical considerations became increasingly less important, and **the fervor we felt for our work, its significance for us, and importance to others became much stronger influences in moving us to action.**

As we initially explored whether or not to do the L/Dev workshop, we were impressed by the number of questions related to "business" we were asking ourselves, and by the dominance of the business model for selecting criteria for determining whether or not to do the workshop. Some of these questions included the following: Can we afford to do this? How much money will it take, and how much money will we make? What is the market? What is the product? In seeking answers, we were trying to be realistic. We were trying to deal with our hesitancy and uncertainties objectively, and trying to identify clear indicators that would push us toward a decision. As we reviewed all the "business" criteria we could think of—all the "tough" questions—the answers all told us not to go ahead with workshop. Seemingly, we were trying to develop a workshop for clients who would not be able to pay for it, which donor agencies that might pay for it would not understand; however we proceeded, it appeared we would not be able to cover the cost of developing the workshop.

Against these "practical" and financial considerations were the needs and persons the L/Dev workshop was intended to serve. The idea for the workshop came to fruition in February 1981. We were completing training and consulting work with the staff of the Integrated Rural Development Team in Nepal. The work demands they were trying to meet were overwhelming. The director was especially besieged: He was under tremendous pressure from the staff for support and direction, from the local and national politicians who wanted achievement, and from the recipient population, which was rather vocal in claiming that it saw nothing happening as a result of the program. As we thought of L/Dev, we thought it should serve a person such as the director—someone under pressure, committed to trying to be effective, seldom finding time for reflection. Thinking of this, we decided to do the workshop.

In many countries in which we had worked, we had seen that with new skills in such areas as problem solving, group effectiveness, and communications, the development worker could significantly increase her or his influence in working with others. Supporting this experience, research increasingly indicates the importance of training to development efforts. David Korten's article (1980) on community organizations had an enormous impact on us, for his study of five successful community organizations found that "leadership and teamwork, rather than blueprints, were the key elements."

In weighing the "pros and cons" as we decided whether or not to develop the workshop, we finally crossed the threshold leading to action because of the increasing fervor we felt. We thought that applied behavioral science skills were crucial to development work, that we could make them available to development leaders through training, and that it was important for us to exercise the initiative to do so. We considered this a low-risk, high-gain situation. If we did not succeed with the workshop, we would lose only time and money; if we succeeded, we could provide important support for significant development efforts. As we began working on developing the workshop, our internal sense of commitment increased and strengthened enough to sustain us whenever we felt the task impossible or overwhelming.

As our internal fervor grew, the initial criteria of a "sound business decision" increasingly faded in importance. What could have been construed as a decision that did not make much "business sense"—and still does not—has, through experience, increasingly seemed wise to us.

Our no longer looking at the work we do from a business point of view is not the result of some conversion. We have never strongly sought commercial benefits from our work. Instead, what we felt was that our internal core of values that influence our stepping over the "threshold to action" as trainers would increasingly be triggered by criteria that require our work to be socially significant and personally important to us. We felt extraordinarily enriched by the benefits we received in support of our own development from the L/Dev workshop.

2. Desired outcomes. Clear goals and objectives are important, but the significance of the L/Dev workshop lies in the **tone, rhythms, and patterns of the relationship each of us create and respond to. Our increasing interest in these qualities involved us more in the art of training than the science.**

Desired outcomes for the L/Dev workshop were important to us. We considered the work of our participants to be so important that the workshop had to increase their skills and abilities so that they could make a real difference in their back-home work. Therefore, we considered it essential to have a planned but flexible design and structure, and to be clear about goals and objectives. We negotiated these, kept them open to influence, and tried to increase "ownership" of what we did in the workshop.

Simultaneously, from the beginning we paid much attention to the mood, feeling, tone, rhythms, and patterns of our relationship during the workshop. We cared as much about the context (why and how we were doing things) as the content (what we were doing.)

It has been said that in the early days of NTL Institute, trainers were so anxious and excited about arriving participants that they met them at their cars and helped them carry their bags to their rooms. We literally did this. We were excited about participants who had come from around the world to be with us and one another, and we wanted them to feel welcome and valued.

Strange as this may seem to those who have visited the NTL conference site in Bethel, Maine, and know its relaxed, informal atmosphere, we had an opening ceremony for the L/Dev workshop. We invited a Third World country ambassador to officiate—and lend prestige to—the opening. NTL officials made opening statements to set the context for the program, and participants briefly introduced themselves and shared some of their reasons for coming and their hopes for the workshop. We were moved by this experience, and it reminded us of how much we in the West tend to play down the importance of opening and closing rituals.

During the workshop we tried to pace ourselves so that we were listening to and being aware of the differences we all represented. We tried our best to respect our differences and not lose them in the rush to find cohesion and commonalities. Listening became one of the most important skills we worked with, and was a strong norm for the program.

Time was provided for singing, dancing, and storytelling, and all of us found healing in this. Symbolically and practically, we in the L/Dev workshop were a new world coming together, an event that in the outside world seemed impossible.

Throughout the L/Dev workshop we broke many current training taboos. We got deeply involved with the participants and their work, and we tried different ways of staying in touch with them after the workshop. We wanted to stay involved emotionally with their successes and failures. We made plans to visit them whenever our travels allowed.

Desired outcomes cannot be achieved by clear goals and objectives alone. Training is partly a science, but mainly an art. Learning comes about through caring and trying to reduce some of the current boundaries that promote distance between trainers and participants and discourage connections and closeness. In doing the L/Dev workshop, we were increasingly clear about how awkward all we humans are in relating to one another, especially across national boundaries. We tried to acknowledge our awkwardness and to act to reduce it, and were less embarrassed by both our awkwardness and our actions as we continued our work.

3. Learning and discovering. The more our work addresses significant issues of leadership and development, the more clearly we see that answers are at best temporary and that the questions we seek to answer continually need rephrasing. This promotes in all of us, both trainers and participants, a sense of being in a state of **beginning and exploration.**

As we worked on the twin themes of development and leadership, we felt somewhat like mountain climbers. Climbing one mountain did not guarantee you could climb another, but more often meant only that you might be less frightened by recurring difficulties or more challenged or excited by the continually unique world being encountered. As L/Dev trainers, we found it more important to understand the qualities of sustaining our commitment, to constantly refocus energy, and to manage ourselves rather than be subject-matter specialists.

The L/Dev workshop has not moved us to an anti-intellectual position; far from it. Our curiosity and interests have expanded through our involvement. Our readings, our research and study, our discussions have become even more important. From this intense activity, however, we did not set the expectation that we would become experts in either leadership or development. Knowing more seemed, ironically, to make us aware of more that we knew less about. Hence we found ourselves continually beginning anew the more we experienced.

In this work we focused on many insights. One is that successful development work must begin with self-development. This means that the task of the development worker is to work continually on her or his own development and be aware of what is happening internally that must be brought out through action. A leader cannot lead someone to a place where the leader has not been, but can only accompany or follow that person. Therefore, self-development was a major area for exploration in the L/Dev workshop, and is an ongoing discipline for us all.

Another insight is that development is primarily a learning process. Maintenance learning largely involves formal learning and addresses how we maintain the known world. Language, history, mathematics, and science largely support our understanding of how the world works. Innovative learning deals with how we prepare to deal with new situations and effect a desired world (Botkin, Elmandjra, & Malitza, 1979). Maintenance learning contributes little to how we effectively live with increasingly complex problems and situations. Innovative learning, however, has us acquire new skills, approaches, and insights that might provide solutions not presently available.

In the L/Dev workshop, we refocused on increasing skills in innovative or anticipatory learning through testing solutions for consequences, lateral thinking exercises, intuitive forecasting, expressive activities, and examining and testing assumptions we had made during development work. We examined the dominant paradigm that influenced how development programs were designed and challenged the way paradigms may or should be changing and what the consequences would be for our development work.

We recognized that, more than anything else, development work is based on ambiguity and uncertainty, and that although we may not be able to change that, we can improve our skills of living and working with ambiguous and uncertain situations. These are skills that, like the edge of a good knife, must continually be sharpened.

If one looks directly at development needs—especially in the Third World— one is overwhelmed by the depressing, pessimistic forces working against responding to these needs. Implicit in training and L/Dev is the optimism that if we continue to refocus, to relearn, and to gain new skills, we might discover something important not only to ourselves, but the world.

4. Interest and support. The L/Dev workshop, which gathered persons from all over the world, could not have been held without the active support of hundreds of other persons. This act of **people making something important happen for others, even though they themselves may have gained no direct or immediate benefit, for us epitomizes development work and training.** It combines elements of naivete, vision, trust, and action.

About 10 years ago, an article published in *Psychology Today* tried to explain successful entrepreneurship. According to that article, one of the major factors is that the creative entrepreneur works out of a strong sense of naivete. If the person knew how difficult, perhaps impossible, it is to do what the entrepreneur seeks to do, he or she would never attempt it.

As we look back, it appears as if everyone involved in the L/Dev workshop were heavily influenced by naivete. Everything seemed to indicate that presenting the workshop was impossible: We had no means of communicating about it, did not know to whom we should send communications, and were not sure that those interested could make it to Bethel, Maine, the workshop site. We were confident, however, that if we persisted, something positive would result.

For example, NTL Institute had never sponsored or marketed an international workshop, and had no clear sense of where to begin. A feeling of eagerness and a sense of purpose, however, helped make the L/Dev workshop happen. Together, we invented or borrowed everything we needed, including the feeling that at least part of the time we knew what were were doing. This approach of learning through doing seemed satisfying to those involved, and sufficient to move us forward.

Perhaps, though, more than naivete kept us going. Perhaps we allowed ourselves to be influenced by things we really cared about, but were afraid or reluctant to admit it. In 1961, President Kennedy released tremendous interest and support for development work by founding the Peace Corps. That interest continued for a while, but development work in the United States—and its commitments abroad—have withered. Today, development work abroad on an official level is largely left to the military, bureaucrats, and rather dull diplomats. In 1982, the L/Dev workshop provided a small way for many different persons to contribute ideas, communication, support, and encouragement to a dream.

In a world that requires so much, and in which training especially has so much to contribute, one can only wonder why interests and commitments are so often parochial. One can imagine and hope that soon universities and other institutions that restrict and confine their interest and excitement to such things as computers and technology will awaken to development. The L/Dev workshop provided for us an exciting, important example of what it is like for people to work with people.

We hope that those with dreams, commitments, and concerns will move forward in both small and large ways to invite support and involvement from many who care but lack an immediate means of action. Perhaps, in order to act, trainers need less sophistication and professionalism and stronger and healthier doses of naivete. Even more important, trainers need to dream of the work they want—and act on that dream.

5. The internal versus external world. The boundaries between that which is internal (within oneself) and external (outside oneself) are unclear, and the work of training addresses the difficulty of accepting that we are neither autonomous in the universe nor able to sustain a sense of wholeness and union within it. **Our struggle deals with trying to find some resolution of this conflict by working toward the paradox of a "holistic autonomy."**

Despite our distinct differences, coming from so many parts of the world, we in the L/Dev workshop found striking similarities among what we cared about, the problems we were working on, and the world we dreamed of. We were startled to find that no matter how difficult and unique the situation and problem on which an individual was working, someone else had an even more complex problem and even fewer resources to depend on. Problems common to all included bureaucracy (which seems epidemic and encompassing); discrimination against women, the young, and the rural poor; the detachment of the educated toward the disenfranchised; the increased reliance on violence to protect against inertia; and the use of the military to support the status quo. All of us were saddened that the wealthiest country in the world, the United States, seems increasingly to diminish both its understanding and its commitments to a more independent world. Its vision seems more geriatric, concerned with security and safety, and maintained by more bombs and new electronic watchdogs.

Despite these depressing realities, each participant felt firmly optimistic that we can each make a difference. We find it difficult to explain what in these different cultures, and among people with such divergent realities, would generate this shared creed and vision that a better world is possible, even likely.

Perhaps in life a force exists that demands to express itself and work against those toxins that would destroy it. Freud (1961) called this force Eros, and believed it was at work in each of us in the service of humanity. We remember seeing this life force at work in Bangladesh. At the time we were training extension agents, young men working at the village level who faced what seemed to us impossible tasks. We were never surprised at the numbers who quit through a resignation of spirit; what amazed us were the numbers who persisted in their belief that they could and were making a difference in their country's development and with the people with whom they worked. We believed them and took encouragement from them.

So much in the world supports the notion that, perhaps because of some genetic mutation, humans are set on a course of destroying ourselves and our world. For us, however, our involvement allowed us to know of some exceedingly wise and resourceful persons, working largely on their own, who are gaining skills and strengths and maintaining their faith in development. We found ourselves separate yet connected. Knowing this, we found it a challenge to continue.

Summary

Our experiences thus far have moved us to refocus on five guidelines for our lives and work.

1. Fervor is what impels us over the threshold leading to action.

2. The qualities of tone, rhythm, and patterns of relationships have the most significant impact on training and living.

3. A sense of being in a state of beginning and exploration refocuses energies in training and living.

4. The act of people making something important happen for others exemplifies development in general and supports specific activities connected with development, such as training.

5. The struggle with the paradox of holistic autonomy and the attempt to reach resolution is central to training and living.

We have observed the importance of training as a deliberate strategy in which persons work on issues of personal development that affect the external world. We see more clearly that training can be an active engagement, much in the service of Eros (Freud, 1962), which supports the movement of individuals toward groups, groups toward communities, and communities toward humankind.

REFERENCES

Botkin, J. W., Elmandjra, M., & Malitza, M. (1979). *No limits to learning: Bridging the human gap.* Elmsford, NY: Pergamon.

Freire, P. (1970). *Pedagogy of the oppressed.* New York: Sudbury Press.

Freud, S. (1961). *Civilization and its discontents* (J. Strachey, Ed.). New York: W. Norton.

Korten, D. (1980). *Community organization and rural development: A learning process approach.* Detroit, MI: Ford Foundation (reprinted in *Public Administration Review*).

Macy, J. (1983). *Dharma and development: Religion as resource in the Sarvodaya self-help movement.* West Hartford, CT: Kumarian Press.

About the Authors

John D. Adams, Ph.D. is president of Resources for Human Systems Development, Inc., a consulting practice specializing in individual and organizational development and based in Arlington, Virginia. Prior to setting up this practice in 1975, Dr. Adams was director of professional development of NTL Institute and a visiting faculty member at the University of Leeds, England. He is a member of NTL Institute.

Tom Armor, Ph.D. is an organization development consultant living in Los Angeles. His recent work has been in adapting microcomputer applications to organization development and laboratory training.

William H. Barber, Ph.D. is professor of psychology, Eastern Washington University, and a consulting psychologist in Spokane, Washington. He is a member of both NTL Institute and the A.K. Rice Institute.

Edwin B. Fernández Bauzó, Ph.D. is an associate professor in the psychology department, College of Social Sciences, University of Puerto Rico, Rio Piedras Campus. He was a member of the original design group for NTL Institute's program entitled Human Interaction in a Multicultural Context Laboratory.

Debbie Bennett is a graduate student in the social/organizational psychology doctoral program at the State University of New York at Buffalo. In 1984 she received her B.A. degree in psychology and sociology from SUNY/Potsdam. Currently, she is enrolled in NTL Institute's Graduate Student Professional Development Program (GSPDP) and is codesigning a communications assessment workshop for a Buffalo manufacturer.

Patricia Bidol, Ph.D. is adjunct associate professor of behavior and environment at the University of Michigan. She is also an organizational consultant with government, education, trade union, business, and military organizations. The focus of her work is on racism, sexism, multicultural issues, affirmative action, and democratic management. She is a member of NTL Institute.

Ronald K. Boyer, Ph.D. is associate professor of psychology at the University of Cincinnati, where he teaches organizational behavior. As an organizational consultant he has worked with industrial, health care, educational, and public systems. He also manages a small public utility system. Dr. Boyer is a member of NTL Institute and Certified Consultants International, and a licensed psychologist in the state of Ohio.

Harold Bridger is a founding member and senior consultant of the Tavistock Institute of Human Relations, London, and president of the International Institute

of Human Relations, Zurich, Switzerland. Mr. Bridger has been, and is currently, a social science consultant to numerous organizations, including multinational,
public, and private bodies in many fields. He is particularly concerned with helping organizations build their own capability to deal more effectively with the continuing and increasing change, turbulence, and uncertainty occurring in the
business and social worlds of today and tomorrow. In recognition of his work, the
British Institute of Management awarded him the Bowie Medal for his "substantial contribution to the advancement of knowledge about management, and for
his innovative work and its influence on both institutions and companies alike in
bridging the gap between the academic researcher and the practicing manager."
Mr. Bridger is a qualified psychoanalyst and a member of the British Psychoanalytic
Society, of NTL Institute, and many other professional bodies.

Barbara Benedict Bunker, Ph.D. (Columbia University, social psychology)
is an organizational consultant, an associate professor of social psychology at the
State University of New York at Buffalo, a partner of the Portsmouth Consulting
Group, and a member of NTL Institute. Her writing and research include work
on organizational effectiveness, social change, conflict resolution, stress and support systems, small group processes, role relations of women and men at work,
and training in applied social psychology. Currently, she is conducting research
on commuting couples, executive women in Japan, and male/female styles of competitive behavior. Dr. Bunker was director of NTL Institute for seven years. From
1978 to 1981 she served as chairperson of the board of directors of NTL. She was
a Fulbright lecturer at Keio University and International Christian University
in Tokyo in 1984.

Robert Chasnoff, Ed.D. was the president of Laboratory for Applied
Behavioral Science, Inc. He provided consultation, training, and evaluation services to profit-making and nonprofit organizations and multicultural macrosystems.
He had also been an internal manager and an internal consultant. Dr. Chasnoff
earned a B.A. degree from the University of Connecticut and master's and doctoral degrees in supervision from Columbia University. A member of NTL Institute, he also held membership in the Organization Development Network, the
American Society for Training and Development, and the International Association for the Study of Cooperation in Education. He published widely. Dr. Chasnoff
was a professor at Kean College of New Jersey (Union) and served as a consultant to the Cooperative Learning Project at the University of Minnesota. He died
October 18, 1985.

Wilfred H. Drath is publications editor at the Center for Creative Leadership. He is the editor of the Center's newsletter, *Issues & Observations*, and has 13
years' experience as a writer and editor, including six years as a free-lance writer.
Bill holds an A.B. degree in English from the University of Georgia and has completed graduate work in English at the University of North Carolina at Chapel
Hill, where he was an instructor in English composition in the adult education
curriculum.

William B. Eddy, Ph.D. is Helen Kemper Professor of administration and
associate dean of the School of Business and Public Administration at the University

of Missouri-Kansas City. Dr. Eddy has published extensively in the area of behavioral science applied to management. He is the editor or author of several books, including *Public Organizational Behavior and Development* (Little, Brown) and *Handbook of Organization Management* (Marcel Dekker), and numerous articles, and has been coeditor of the journal *Administration and Society*. His latest book, *The Manager and the Working Group*, was published in April 1985 by the Praeger division of CBS. Dr. Eddy holds B.S. and M.S. degrees from Kansas State University and a Ph.D. in industrial psychology from Michigan State University. He is a fellow of the American Psychological Association, a licensed organizational psychologist, and a member of NTL Institute.

Katharine Cole Esty, Ph.D. is a social psychologist, a consultant with Goodmeasure, Inc. (a Boston-based management consulting firm), and an NTL member. Her consulting work focuses on organizational effectiveness and work group productivity. Her current interests include women in senior management and the "downsized" organization.

Philip G. Hanson, Ph.D. is currently chief of the Psychology Service at the VA Medical Center, Houston, Texas, and associate professor of psychology at Baylor College of Medicine and the University of Houston. He has been associated with NTL Institute since 1964.

Clenard C. "Chip" Henderson, Jr. is founder and president of the Henderson Company, a firm offering consulting and training services in organizational and human resource development to for-profit and not-for-profit companies and institutions. Mr. Henderson has more than 16 years' experience in management, consulting, and training in organization effectiveness. Much of his experience was obtained during his tenure in the R&D and product development divisions of the Procter & Gamble Company. Mr. Henderson maintains professional affiliation with NTL Institute, the American Society for Training and Development, the Organization Development Network, and the Association for Black Psychologists. In addition, Mr. Henderson has taught in the department of Afro-American studies and the Institute of Consultation and Training at the University of Cincinnati. He has also been a visiting professor in the National Urban League's Black Executive Exchange Program for predominantly black colleges and universities.

Michael Ichiyama is a doctoral candidate in psychology at the University of Cincinnati. In addition to clinical work, his interest include research on self-concept and interpersonal behavior in small groups. Mr. Ichiyama was recently an NTL Institute summer research fellow. His dissertation focuses on the application of the SYMLOG framework to the study of reflected appraisals.

Kaleel Jamison was president of Kaleel Jamison Associates and The Living School. As a consultant to business organizations and a human relations trainer for more than 18 years, she developed a methodology that addresses human development concerns on a system-wide basis. Her specialty areas included competition, communication, conflict management, career planning, personal growth, management development, and improving work relationships among persons of different colors, genders, and cultures. She was accredited by Certified Consultants International and staffed professional and managerial seminars for NTL Institute.

Her articles appeared in *The Executive Female, Personnel Journal, Fair Employment Practices*, and other professional journals. Her book about leadership, self-empowerment, and personal growth, *The Nibble Theory and the Kernel of Power*, was published by Paulist Press in 1984. Ms. Jamison died in September 1985.

Robert Kaplan, Ph.D. is a behavioral scientist and director of new program development at the Center for Creative Leadership in Greensboro, North Carolina, as well as the chief developer of the Workshop in Organization Action. He has conducted research on managerial work, group effectiveness, and organizational diagnosis and change, and has published numerous papers in these areas. Before joining the Center in 1979, Dr. Kaplan was associate professor of organizational behavior at Case Western Reserve University. A certified group facilitator and organizational consultant and member of NTL Institute, Dr. Kaplan holds a doctorate in organizational behavior from Yale University.

Judith Katz, Ed.D. is an associate with Kaleel Jamison Associates, a Cincinnati-based consulting firm specializing in developing a multicultural work place. She has worked in the field of human relations and training for the past 13 years. Dr. Katz has held academic positions at San Diego State University and the University of Oklahoma in Norman. She has served as vice chair of the board of directors of NTL Institute, is a member of NTL, is accredited by Certified Consultants International as a group trainer, and is a certified neurolinguistic programming practitioner. She is the author of *White Awareness: Handbook for Anti-Racism Training* and *No Fairy Godmothers, No Magic Wands: The Healing Process After Rape*, and more than a dozen articles related to human resource issues and training. Dr. Katz conducts training for NTL Institute and Western Behavioral Sciences Institute in the areas of communication, improving relationships between women and men, and valuing differences.

Otto Kroeger is a management consultant specializing in the use of the Myers-Briggs Type Indicator (MBTI). He is a partner of Otto Kroeger Associates, a multifaceted organization that also conducts training seminars in the use and application the MBTI. Mr. Kroeger is a member of the OD Network, ASTD, and ACC, and has been a member of NTL Institute for 20 years. He has trained trainers of the MBTI program for NTL. In MBTI language, Mr. Kroeger is an ENFJ.

Ronald Lippitt, Ph.D. was professor emeritus of the University of Michigan and a cofounder of NTL Institute (with Kurt Lewin, Leland Bradford, and Ken Benne) in 1947. He had a doctorate in social psychology—having studied under Lewin—and a child development diplome from work with Jean Piaget. He was codeveloper of the concept of group dynamics with Lewin in 1940, and wrote the basic book entitled *Dynamics of Planned Change* in 1957. Dr. Lippitt most recently worked with communities, school and health systems, industries, and colleges on long-range planning, team building, and participative management. He died October 28, 1986.

Bernard Lubin, Ph.D. is professor of psychology, medicine, and administration, former chairperson of the department of psychology, and director of the doctoral program in community psychology at the University of Missouri at Kansas

City. He received his doctoral degree in clinical psychology from Pennsylvania State University, is a diplomate in clinical psychology (ABPP), a fellow of the American Psychological Association, the American Group Psychotherapy Association, and the Association for the Advancement of Science. He has written more than 180 publication, including six books, and is listed in *Who's Who in the World, Who's Who in America,* and *American Men and Women of Science.* Dr. Lubin is a member of NTL Institute.

Neil McGillicuddy received his B.A degree from the University of Buffalo in 1982. He is presently a doctoral student in the University of Buffalo's social psychology program. During his graduate career, he has become a mediator at the Buffalo Dispute Settlement Center, conducted research on mediation and social conflict, and worked on program evaluations. The clients for these evaluations included a town youth board, a city hospital, and a large corporation.

Jane Moosbruker, Ph.D. is an organization development consultant from Bolton, Massachusetts. In private practice for 15 years, Dr. Moosbruker consults primarily to "high-tech" and medical systems. Her areas of focus include the management of change, organizational structure, open-systems planning, team building, and conflict utilization. Dr. Moosbruker has a doctorate in social psychology from Harvard University. She has taught in the psychology department of Boston College and in the School of Dental Medicine at Harvard. She has published numerous articles in books and professional journals, and is a member of NTL Institute, the Academy of Management, the Massachusetts Public Health Association, the Society for the Psychological Study of Social Issues, and the Organization Development Network.

Peter Muniz is the president of Peter Muniz & Company. With B.S. and M.B.A. degrees from the City University of New York, his educational background includes both technical and human resource training. Mr. Muniz is a member of the American Society for Training and Development, the American Society for Personnel Administration, and the International Society for Intercultural Education, Training, and Research. His organizational experience includes line and staff positions at managerial and nonmanagerial levels. His consulting and training activities are conducted in both English and Spanish in the United States (including Puerto Rico) and other countries. Mr. Muniz has also spent one year in Panama training Panamanian trainers and consultants. He has published writings on a wide range of training and consulting topics.

Thomas Nochajski is currently enrolled in the doctoral program in social psychology at the State University of New York at Buffalo. He received his B.A. degree in psychology from SUNY/Buffalo and recently completed the Graduate Student Professional Development Program (GSPDP) with NTL Institute. He has been trained as a mediator for community disputes in both adult and juvenile programs of the Buffalo Dispute Settlement Center and is currently codesigning a communications workshop for a Buffalo manufacturing company.

Chuck Phillips is a independent consultant and trainer based in Wilton, New Hampshire. He combines more than 20 years' of diverse experience in business and industry into an integrated training and consulting perspective for organizational improvement, growth, and evolutionary change. Mr. Phillips worked for General Electric Company for 18 years (9 of those as manager of organization development) and brings that internal/external experience to his practice. He is particularly interested in the development of consultants and trainers. Mr. Phillips is a member of NTL Institute.

Larry Porter, Ed.D. is a senior consultant with University Associates, Inc. He has been a member of NTL Institute since 1969, was a member of the NTL office staff from 1970 to 1975, served on the NTL board from 1977-1980, and has edited or coedited the last five editions of NTL's *Reading Book for Human Relations Training.* Dr. Porter has been a free-lance consultant and member of the OD group at Lawrence Livermore National Laboratory (1976-1980). He has been a member of the Organization Development Network board of trustees since 1973, and edited the ODN's publication, *The OD Practitioner,* from 1973-1981. He lives in a small coastal town just north of San Diego, Cardiff-by-the-Sea.

W. Brendan Reddy, Ph.D. earned his doctoral degree from the University of Cincinnati. He is presently the director of the Institute for Consultation and Training, and professor of psychology at the University of Cincinnati, Cincinnati, Ohio. He is a member of the American Psychological Association and a professional member of NTL Institute. Dr. Reddy's primary interests are in organization development, training, team building, and third-party intervention. He has consulted, taught, researched, and published in these areas.

Birge D. "Ric" Reichard, Jr., Ph.D. is a psychologist, organization consultant, and president of Berkeley Developmental Resources, Inc. He is a former vice president and professional director of NTL Institute, and currently a member of the organization.

Eva Schindler-Rainman, DSW is an internationally known consultant based in Los Angeles, California. She is a member of NTL Institute.

Crescencio Torres, Ph.D. is a consultant specializing in the communication process through neurolinguistic programming (NLP). He is a member of NTL Institute and certified in group development and training through Certified Consultants International. Dr. Torres is certified as an NLP trainer and practitioner and conducts training events focusing on the application of NLP to systems. He is the author of several articles addressing NLP and human resource issues and was the first to develop a diagnostic instrument that identifies a key components of NLP technology.

Dick Vittitow and Marion Vittitow, Ph.D. are human resource and systems development consultants. Much of their work in the past 10 years has been in Third World countries, with an emphasis on leadership, management, and organizational skills. In 1986-1987, the Vittitows began conducting a series of Leadership for Development workshops around the world and continued studying with and visiting people involved in development activities. They are NTL members.